LOBBYING
RECONSIDERED

REAL POLITICS IN AMERICA

Series Editor: Paul S. Herrnson, *University of Maryland*

The books in this series bridge the gap between academic scholarship and the popular demand for knowledge about politics. They illustrate empirically supported generalization from original research and the academic literature using examples taken from the legislative process, executive branch decision making, court rulings, lobbying efforts, election campaigns, political movements, and other areas of American politics. The goal of the series is to convey the best contemporary political science research has to offer in ways that will engage individuals who want to know about real politics in America.

LOBBYING RECONSIDERED

UNDER THE INFLUENCE

Gary J. Andres

Vice Chairman, Research and Policy,
Dutko Worldwide

Research Fellow, Center for
Congressional and Presidential Studies
American University

PEARSON
Longman

New York   San Francisco   Boston
London   Toronto   Sydney   Tokyo   Singapore   Madrid
Mexico City   Munich   Paris   Cape Town   Hong Kong   Montreal

Editor-in-Chief: Eric Stano
Executive Marketing Manager: Ann Stypuloski
Production Manager: Denise Phillip
Project Coordination, Text Design, and Electronic
    Page Makeup: Integra Software Services Pvt. Ltd.
Cover Design Manager: Wendy Ann Fredericks
Cover Art: Jacek Stachowski/Images.com/Corbis
Photo Researcher: Integra Software Services Pvt. Ltd.
Senior Manufacturing Buyer: Roy Pickering
Printer and Binder: R. R. Donnelley & Sons/Harrisonburg
Cover Printer: R. R. Donnelley & Sons/Harrisonburg

Library of Congress Cataloging-in-Publication Data

Andres, Gary J.
    Lobbying reconsidered : under the influence / Gary J. Andres.—1st ed.
        p. cm.
    Includes bibliographical references and index.
    ISBN 0-13-603265-6 (alk. paper)
    1. Lobbying—United States.   2. United States—Politics and government—2001–   I. Title.
JK1118.A66 2009
328.73'078—dc22

                                                                    2008019452

Please visit us at www.pearsonhighered.com

ISBN 13: 978-0-13-603265-6
ISBN 10:   0-13-603265-6

1 2 3 4 5 6 7 8 9 10—DOH—11 10 09 08

CONTENTS

CHAPTER 5

PARTISANSHIP AND THE ADVOCACY INDUSTRY   90

CHAPTER 6

LOBBYING IN A HYPER MEDIA AGE   120

CHAPTER 7

THE NEW LOBBYING TOOLBOX   137

CHAPTER 8

LOBBYING AND STRATEGIC CHOICES   169

PREFACE

After the election in 2000, the transition team of then President-elect George W. Bush assembled a small group of veteran lobbyists to help map out Senate confirmation strategies for the new cabinet. Experienced former legislative liaison personnel from the Nixon, Ford, Reagan, and George H.W. Bush White House staffs populated this team of knowledgeable advocates. Internally, they were known as the "Sherpas," each one guiding the nomination of a soon-to-be cabinet member through the often-treacherous Himalayas of approval by the U.S. Senate.

I was part of that cadre of confirmation guides, and the experience taught me a lot about the process of advocacy in Washington. It revealed that lobbying involves a lot more than just relationships, friends, access, favors, and influence—the dialect most speak when describing interest-group power. Instead, the process was much more complex. As one former White House aide once said, the real world of advocacy is like the difference between checkers and three-dimensional chess. My other jobs all taught me similar lessons, while serving on the White House staff, as a congressional staffer, as a lobbyist with a corporation, and in my current role overseeing research and policy at a global public affairs firm.

These experiences convinced me that extant writing about the world of interest groups and their advocates is not necessarily wrong; it's just too narrow. The common notion of "lobbyist as influence peddler" struck me both as cynical and incomplete.

Lobbying Reconsidered: Under the Influence offers a broader perspective on this important dimension of American public policymaking. In the preface of his book, an undergraduate professor of mine, Leland Ryken of Wheaton College in Illinois, describes himself as a "travel guide," helping students navigate the unfamiliar world of verse. In a similar vein, and invoking my background as a "Sherpa," I hope to use my experience and insights in the lobbying world to help you navigate beyond the conventional wisdom, and guide you to a deeper, broader understanding.

"Lobbying" is now a big business in Washington, with many more dimensions than during the 1960s and 1970s. It is larger, more structurally complex, and tactically varied than suggested by the soft stereotype of Gucci loafers. It's also a dynamic enterprise, very different today than even a few short years ago.

Working in and around the lobbying industry for the past quarter of a century, I've seen a lot of how this world works—the good, the bad, and the ugly. I've also read a lot of journalist and academic musings about lobbyists – some of it good, but also, frankly, much of it bad and ugly. After reading this book, students and scholars alike should have a much better understanding of the role of lobbyists and interest groups in the American system, including the tools that produce successful influence and those that don't. It will also demonstrate the limits of lobbying and why money or other resources don't always translate to political power or influence. And finally, that much of what lobbyists do, and how and why they do it, is not "lobbying" at all. Probing a little deeper into the real behaviors, motivations, and tactics of the new advocacy world will help debunk many myths and improve public understanding.

I owe a debt of gratitude to many who helped inspire and shape this volume. Five political scientists read the entire manuscript and provided keen insights, perspective, and constructive criticism. For their time, thoughtful critiques, and feedback I thank Barry Rundquist, Bird Loomis, Paul Herrnson, James Gimpel, and Jim Thurber.

My friends in the lobbying business also shaped this volume. I want to thank Pat Griffin, Bert Carp, Bob Russbuldt, and Nick Franklin, who also read and commented on the entire book. Others like Bruce Gates, Tim McKone, Greg Crist, Steve Perry, Ron Kaufman, Marybeth Kerrigan, Kim Bayliss, and Sarah Levin read individual chapters and/or agreed to let me attribute their observations and insights by name. I also am indebted to the entire family at Dutko Worldwide—too many to mention by name—for their support, friendship, and lessons they have taught me over the years. And a special thanks to my other "partners" at the firm not mentioned above, Mark Irion, Arthur Silverman, Craig Pattee, Darren Willcox, Brad Card, David Beightol, Bill Simmons, Sally Painter, and Karen Tramontano for their friendship and support.

Two of my Dutko colleagues deserve special credit. First, I want to thank Brandon Smith, who helped compile charts, conducted some of the research, and generally organized the manuscript development. Second, I owe a very special debt of gratitude to Lauren Lawson, who literally read the entire manuscript at least three times. Her careful eye and disciplined editing greatly improved this book. Any remaining errors or omissions are, of course, my own.

Finally, I could not have completed this project without the love and encouragement of my family—what we affectionately call "Team Andres" in our household. The "unit" consists of my children Peter, Betsy, Doug, Tatum, and Joe. They all played a role, generously giving me the time, the energy, and the editorial commentary derived from their bottomless well of affection to write and complete this book. Then there were those two canine creatures, Nellie and Libby, who kept me company in the study early in the morning and late at night as I wrote and they slept. And finally to my wife and best friend, Sue, whose love, laughter, and spontaneity make every day a joy to live. Thank you for walking with me hand-in-hand on this exciting journey. And thank you for giving me the freedom to pursue this project. It is truly a part of me, and I dedicate it to you.

Gary J. Andres

INTRODUCTION

Potential Client: *All I need is someone to make one call to Karl Rove at the White House. He can fix my problem.*
Lobbyist: *That's not what you need; it's not what we do; and, it won't fix your problem.*
Potential Client: *I thought that's what lobbyists did?*
Lobbyist: *Only on TV.*

The lobbying industry suffered a black eye in 2005 and 2006 after prosecutors punched so-called influence peddler Jack Abramoff with a flurry of felony charges ranging from fraud to tax evasion. In the months leading up to his conviction, the press overflowed with sordid stories about lavish dinners and exotic trips hosted by the former lobbyist. Accounts dripped with quid pro quo innuendo, painting a disquieting picture of how private interests play the so-called influence-peddling game in Washington. Insider access gleaned through personal connections, campaign contributions given in luxury skyboxes, and feting lawmakers with lavish meals, expensive gifts, and five-star travel were the tools of choice. Congressmen and staff allegedly responded by providing special favors, inside information, and earmarked pork barrel spending. Hollywood central casting could not have chosen a more prurient depiction of the K Street influence peddler. A screenplay must be next.

But these broad brushstrokes paint a false picture. This book draws a different portrait. By "getting under the influence," I demonstrate that both academics' and the media's view of lobbying are far too narrow. *What* lobbyists do, as well as *how* and *why* they do it, deserves reconsideration. Moreover, many of the best-intentioned "reforms" of lobbying or other attempts to "open up the system," often empower, rather than tame, the interest-group beast.

The media's focus on the Abramoff affair masks the true face of the advocacy world. Lobbying is changing, and its transformation represents a major—and misunderstood—current in the American public policy process. Like the difference between the Soap Box Derby and the NASCAR, the advocacy industry has grown steadily bigger, increasingly complex, and more prevalent, serving as a significant engine in both policymaking and electoral politics. This book examines the evolution of advocacy and develops a more complete storyline of how and why it has changed. It also investigates the lobbying industry's often overlooked structural and tactical complexities, offering a more realistic assessment of interest-group impact on public policy and some predictions about where the advocacy enterprise may move next. Finally, this book highlights some of the unintended consequences of the changing rules of the interest-group universe.

The lobbying industry is now big business. In 2006 there were over 30,000 registered lobbyists in Washington, twice as many as six years earlier. This doesn't even count the legions of media consultants, Internet advocacy advisors, pollsters, grassroots specialists, and political action committee managers who support the enterprise but do not register to lobby.[1] Monthly spending on lobbying more than doubled between 1999 and 2005.[2] But that is only the tip of iceberg. If we look "under the influence," an even bigger, dynamic industry exists. Some argue the total number of individuals involved in the advocacy business tops 100,000, with combined spending on all these activities of $8 billion annually.[3] A bigger lobbying industry neither guarantees better public understanding nor the political omnipotence of interest groups. Despite its burgeoning size and growing presence in the public policy process, lobbying is still a mysterious and enigmatic practice, often wrapped in the soft stereotypes of Gucci loafers rather than hard facts.

A BROADER PERSPECTIVE ON LOBBYING

In order to better understand lobbying, we need to place it in a broader context – focusing on what these advocates do, as well as how and why they do it. This book draws upon several earlier strands of scholarly work that place lobbying in a broader context. These new lenses will help readers develop a clearer and more realistic view of why the advocacy world looks the way it does today, the motivations underlying the behavior of lobbyists, and the role they play in policymaking.

Studies of interest groups—their structure, behavior, organizational challenges, and power—have a long and venerable history in political science. But much of this older perspective is narrow and incorrectly shapes our views of the real world of lobbying. Scholarly interest in this research agenda ran hot and cold during the twentieth century. Much of the impetus behind it sought to prove political power was not concentrated in a power elite.[4] What emerged was a school of thought called "pluralism," which argued policymaking was fragmented, or *plural*, and neither subjugated nor controlled by a dominant few.[5]

But pluralism also had its detractors. And while researchers rejected the notion of a single power elite, critics argued that the pluralist model—while good in *principle*—was undemocratic in *practice* because of challenges related to organizing citizens to act on their interests, imbalances in what moved on to the political agenda, and policy control by narrow, unrepresentative interests in certain policy areas.[6]

Most media accounts, and as a result many ordinary citizens, seem stuck in a view of lobbying heavily influenced by pluralist critics such as E.E. Schattschneider (*The Semi-Sovereign People*), Grant McConnell (*Private Power and American Democracy*), or Theodore Lowi (*The End of Liberalism*). All argued forcefully that private interests dominate the American public policymaking process. These groups, and their lobbyists, demand particularized benefits such as tax breaks, pork barrel spending, or favorable regulations. And, because of their expertise at exploiting the levers of power, or setting the agenda, they usually "win." In this zero sum, closed game, the "public interest" suffers. As another scholar noted, "In a nutshell, what they (critics of pluralism) argued was that private interests, many of them rather narrow, dominated much of the American polity. Public policy had no authentic public-interest rationale and instead was the handmaiden of private power."[7]

Pluralism also assumed that as long as all groups competed fairly and everyone was represented—much like classical economics—the "influence market" would reach some type of fair and optimal equilibrium.[8] But critics noted a series of "market failures," including barriers to entry, imperfect information, lack of competition, and even monopoly power by some advocacy organizations. One review of interest-group literature put it this way: "Rather than promoting democracy through conflict and competition, groups came to be seen as a drag on the democracy."[9]

But while the detractors of pluralism make some valid points, their critiques of interest groups suffer from limitations as well and don't fit very well with the modern world of lobbying. For example, there is an implicit tone in much of this writing that *lobbyists never fail and therefore have too much influence*. Critics of the pluralism model also take a rather static view of policymaking, assuming the players and issues in a closed government policymaking process (what they call "subgovernments") rarely change. Yet in the real world, the process is more dynamic. The critics of pluralism also cannot account for the rapid growth in the lobbying world and why interest groups continue to invest resources even in losing efforts. Finally, these theories are not very helpful in predicting why different level of resources and tactics are deployed in various policymaking circumstances.

This book also demonstrates that lobbying is less omnipotent than some of the older interest theorists and the press suggest—principally because of the many changes in the lobbying environment laid out in the next several chapters. Combining these two thoughts, I argue that even though the advocacy industry has *grown*, it is not necessarily more *effective*. The prowess of lobbyists and interest groups can vary a great deal over time and in different policy settings.

Moreover, it isn't necessarily always the case that the public interest and private interests represent a zero-sum game. Sometimes benefits for so-called private interests can benefit the public interest too.[10] And a corollary to this view is that more lobbyists or a bigger advocacy industry does not translate to more private power. A host of checks and balances mitigate the power of the advocacy industry, but these are limits not widely understood by conventional wisdom among scholars, the press, or the public at large. A bigger, more institutionalized, tactically varied advocacy industry does not imply more power for lobbyists or benefits for the interests they represent. Lobbying power is more nuanced, conditioned by circumstances such as the type of policy under consideration, the partisan nature of the issue, and its visibility as well as the level and skill of advocacy resources deployed.

John Kenneth Galbraith developed the term "countervailing power" during the 1950s. He argued that one way to control monopoly power of one part of a market was to develop monopoly power in another. You could offset the power of sellers by promoting a countervailing power among buyers.[11] Or as applied to lobbying, promoting increased union power could offset growing corporate dominance. And while Galbraith was heavily influenced by the post–World War II context of expanding cor-porate and union dominance in the U.S. economy, one part of his argument still rings true. Lobbyists often mobilize and try to create "countervailing power." But even Galbraith's useful concept has limitations in the real world of lobbying. In today's highly fractured, public, and indeterminate policy world, these moves are always undertaken with great uncertainty. As we shall see, attempts to build *countervailing power* under conditions of uncertainty often lead to major lobbying activity and investment, often with less influence and accomplishment than suggested by the media or critics of the pluralist model.

Surprisingly, despite decades of debate among scholars in this field, what lobbyists actually did remained largely a mystery. One expert noted that political scientists were startled to learn scholars paid very little atten-tion to lobbyists, despite volumes of research on interest groups. Until 2002, he wrote, "no one had ever followed lobbyists through their daily activities and simply charted who they talked to and what they talked about."[12]

So in many ways, these earlier strands of political science research were incomplete and often contributed to public misunderstanding about lobby-ing. Yet despite some of these omissions, there are several strands of schol-arly thought and research that do help organize our thinking about the advocacy world and provide perspectives that guide the remainder of this book.

First, interest groups' environments matter. Changes in interest groups' external challenges lead to shifts and adjustments in lobbying structures, strategies, and tactics. In other words, disruptions in the political equilibrium of organized interests—such as the growth, fragmentation and activism of government, new technology, and political polarization—have caused change and evolution over the past several decades in the institution of advocacy.[13] Others argue changes in the public policy environment over the past 40 years have provided many institutional lobbying interests with the incentive to increase their activism when it comes to advocacy.[14]

> In the latter twentieth century public policy is of such immense scope that issues continually arise which affect the assets of particular institutions. Environmental regulation, safety and health regulation, rules regarding employment practices, the host of grant and entitlement programs, tax policies—the list is long. Even an institution of the most modest size and aspiration will encounter both threats and opportunities in this policy array, and insofar as its resources permit may seek to increase its understanding of these possibilities and to influence them.[15]

Some more contemporary experts draw a similar conclusion: "Groups have mobilized in Washington in response to the growth of activities in government".[16]

And advocacy adjustments never occur in a vacuum—when one interest wins, its competitors usually respond. Smart victors know another battle always looms. The environments of interests are rarely placid, so their advocates are usually ready to pounce. This back-and-forth of strategic, tactical, and structural changes in the way organized interests operate results in the dynamic process outlined in later chapters.[17]

These changes in lobbying structures and tactics are part of a dynamic process. Interest groups are always adapting based on changes in their environment. They add staff, create new structures such as political action committees (PACs), hire specialized lobbyists, pollsters, and media specialists. These transformations in the lobbying world continue. Even descriptions of how and why interest groups lobbied as recently as five or ten years ago are now seriously outdated.[18]

Second, focusing too much attention on how lobbyists persuade also provides an incomplete and inaccurate view of the advocacy world. Some of their work involves pressure tactics, but the bulk of interest-group work and lobbying is focused on issues such as education, agenda setting, information gathering, interpretation, prediction, and managing uncertainty. Another flaw with many academic and journalistic accounts of lobbying is that they focus too much on the end of the process and not enough on why policy-makers consider particular issues in the first place. Often, getting an item on the legislative or regulatory agenda is a more important indicator of influence than the final roll call vote. Recognizing this oversight in many of the academic and journalistic accounts of lobbying, two interest-group scholars recently observed, " . . . efforts at agenda setting, issue definition, and framing do more to determine winners and losers in politics than any arm-twisting before the final roll-call vote."[19]

Third, while structural changes (e.g. creating a Washington office, hiring outside lobbyists, forming a PAC) are usually made to reduce uncertainty for organized interests, they normally don't *guarantee* the desired result.[20] Unlike other examples in the business world, where organizations make structural changes to address problems or reduce uncertainty, the public policy environment is fundamentally different— certainly less rational and predictable. Whereas investments in new personnel systems or payroll systems may have the predicted impact for a business, effects of creating new structures for influencing public policy are not quite as foreseeable. Forming a Washington office or hiring an outside lobbying firm, for example, may help an organization gather information and reduce uncertainty about government actions, but it does not *guarantee* a public policy outcome. Many of the new structures adopted by organized interests are best understood as methods to gain information, reduce uncertainty, define issues, and get measures on the agenda. Political "influence" is either not the goal or better evaluated in some way other than just looking at a final vote.

Fourth, policy context affects lobbying. How broad the "scope of conflict" is on an issue and where that controversy occurs are all critical to the structures, styles, and methods of lobbying.[21] Advocating for an appropriations earmark is a fundamentally different exercise than trying to change the Social Security or Medicare system. Trying to realize a major change in the tax code requires a different type of lobbying than avoiding a tax increase. Lobbying the White House might be done more effectively using different tools than used when trying to influence a congressional committee. The examples could go on and are illustrated throughout this book. Students of lobbying need to understand that effective advocacy varies across different policy, political, and institutional contexts.

In sum, what lobbyists do, why they do it, and the impact of their advocacy are both misunderstood and changing. While American public policy is neither controlled by a power elite nor operates as a perfectly competitive pluralist model, much of the way some of the critics of pluralism described interest groups during the 1960s just doesn't seem to fit with the more open, dynamic, fractured world of advocacy today.

CAUSES AND CONSEQUENCES OF LOBBYING CHANGE

We begin our reconsideration of lobbying by looking at the causes and consequences of change in the advocacy world over the past 40 years. As mentioned above, external environments matter. Several transformations in the external environment of organized interests have shaken up the lobbying world. I explore these causes of change in more detail later in this chapter and throughout the book, and they include

1. Growing complexity, decentralization, "sunshine laws," and the size and activism of government over the past 40 years.
2. Modifications in the legal and regulatory treatment of money in elections and public policy.
3. Increased partisan polarization—particularly in the last two decades.
4. Expansion and fragmentation of media and technology, including the development of the 24-hour news cycle and the Internet.

But just as there are *multiple causes* of change in the lobbying business, there are also *multiple consequences*. Taking a more comprehensive view of these numerous consequences for the lobbying world itself is critical to developing a better understanding of advocacy by interest groups. I argue throughout this book that these multiple changes in the environment of organized interests have altered the *structure, style, and substantive methods* of lobbying.

Changing *structures* include the trend away from representation by "peak associations," such as the American Medical Association, Pharmaceutical Manufacturers of America, or the Chamber of Commerce, to more companies and organized interests participating individually by forming Washington offices and PACs or hiring their own outside lobbyists.[22]

A different *style* of lobbying refers to the blurring lines between the politics of public policymaking and the politics of elections.[23] Lobbying now imports many of the tactics of modern day political campaigns, and interest groups have integrated these new tactics into their advocacy methodology. An example of this is the growing trend toward campaign consultants becoming lobbyists and vice versa.[24] Also, a pandemic of partisanship has infected the style of the lobbying business, deepening ties between legislative leaders and partisan lobbyists, and leading to the rise of more specialized, partisan advocates whom many organized interests incorporate into their lobbying teams. While the virus of polarization has been explored in other contexts, such as among voters and in Congress, its impact on lobbying is less understood.[25] But partisanship is also both a cause and an effect of change in the lobbying business. Growing partisanship produced a different style of lobbying, but an increasing number of partisan lobbyists are also changing public policymaking and elections.

The shifting structures and styles also have led to new *substantive methods*, which move well beyond the traditional "access-based" lobbying model to a more robust set of tactics and strategies. These new conditions have created an "electoral/advocacy complex," in which campaign-based tools such as research, message development, grassroots (mobilizing voters to contact elected officials with an advocacy message), earned media, and paid media are employed in winning advocacy campaigns. Media and conventional wisdom focus an inordinate amount of attention on direct lobbying by individual advocates. The real lobbying world is far more complicated, drawing on both direct and indirect methods, changing over time and in different contexts.

But one size does not fit all, and *not* every organized interest deploys all these new advocacy weapons. Organized interests face important strategic decisions in this new world of lobbying. Factors such as the scope of the issue (broad Medicare reform versus a narrow legislative earmark), the level of economic resources of the organized interest, the perceived risk/reward, and the actions of competitors will all shape the strategic decisions concerning which weapons in the arsenal to deploy.

Despite the confusion that engulfs our understanding of the lobbying world advocacy in America will continue to grow and change—which could further the misunderstanding. But before investigating why and how lobbying has changed, it's important to note some elements that stayed the same.

The perceptions of advocates and their tactics include some static elements, such as lobbyists' public reputation and certain core tactics. One American academic expert on lobbying captures this notion well: "It is curious that lobbying, which is protected by the constitutional right to petition, should be so thoroughly distrusted by the press and the public. Many lobbyists are sensitive to the stigma attached to their profession and try to avoid being labeled as a lobbyist."[26] The quote itself is unremarkable, particularly in light of the Abramoff affair. It is startling, however, that the comment was not made four months ago or even four years ago. Lester Milbrath wrote it over four decades ago in his 1963 book *The Washington Lobbyists*.[27] Some myths die hard.

Even lobbying methods considered relatively new, such as grassroots advocacy, have a long history in American government. There are numerous examples of groups using grassroots contacts with Congress in the late nineteenth century and early twentieth century.[28] The Anti-Saloon League developed a list of over 500,000 activists and was a driving force behind prohibition.[29] Others document similar activities by industry and trade association groups to lobby on trade policy 50 years ago.[30] And access-based lobbying, the form of advocacy premised on personal relationships, while not the focus of this book, will always play a role in how interest groups attempt to shape public policy. Chapter 2 outlines how and why these old views of lobbying endure.

Yet change is the real focus here, particularly transformations witnessed since the 1960s, the period many scholars point to as the advent of advocacy growth.[31] And the structures, style, and substantive methods of the lobbying industry have evolved, not by accident, but in response to a continually changing environment of political, policy, technological, and competitive adjustments. These changes in the lobbying industry, as well as their causes and consequences, are the primary thrust of this book.

THE CAUSES OF CHANGE—A CLOSER LOOK

GROWING GOVERNMENT COMPLEXITY, DECENTRALIZATION, SUNSHINE LAWS, AND ACTIVISM

This book focuses on four major causes underlying the changing world of lobbying. First, a bigger, more complicated and activist government over the past 40 years has substantially altered the challenges and opportunities for organized interests. Nowhere has this trend manifested more than in the proliferation of congressional staff and the explosion of the Washington bureaucracy, both significantly impacting the lobbying business. Fresh and unpredictable demands by multiple government actors, all pursuing individual goals and objectives, have created new laws, hearings, investigations, regulations, and other proposals requiring some type of response from those affected. As some interest-group experts argued recently, "Groups do not automatically form and come to Washington; there must be a demand for them. Government creates that demand."[32]

The increasing complexity of policy in general over the past four decades also produced a new era of hyper-regulation. But it's important to note that increased lobbying occurs in response to both new regulations *and* deregulation. Either can destabilize those all-important external environments and affect the supply and demand for lobbying. The impact of new regulations on interests is obvious. They often raise costs, uncertainty, litigation risks, and require new investments. However, deregulation—and its new rules and requirements—can often advantage some and harm others. While some believe deregulation of, say, trucking, airlines, energy and telecommunications means fewer regulations—in reality it produces new and different rules leading rent-seeking interest groups to look for advantage over competitors through public policy. Most important, however, it means more instability.

More complexity leads to intra-interest group conflicts and who fights who in the policy process is also often misunderstood in conventional wisdom. Advocacy battles don't always pit business versus labor, or corporations versus consumers, but rather pit business versus business—a nuance often missed in the popular press. Telephone companies versus cable companies, energy producers versus utility firms, railroads versus truckers are just some of the intra-business lobbying battles occurring daily in Washington. These fights often unfold in the context of new regulations or deregulation as one side of the business community tries to get a competitive advantage over another. As two noted interest-group scholars write, " . . . the greatest restraint on business may not be its critics but, rather, the divisions within and between industries."[33] Such skirmishes are among the most common in Washington today, yet they receive little attention. These battles—and especially the concept of one side of a business responding to its competitors—have also fueled the growth of lobbying because these actors possess substantial economic resources, risk, and considerable financial stakes. Jeffrey H. Birnbaum, a long-time observer of the changing advocacy world who writes about lobbying for *The Washington Post*, understands these nuances well. In an article covering the fight between the National Association of Broadcasters and two satellite radio companies seeking to merge he observes, "The reason [for the lobbying fight] is an object lesson for the nation's capital: Government has grown pivotal to the business world and in some cases, its decisions are make-or-break for individual companies or industries."[34]

The combatants frequently shift allies as well. Lobbying friends on one issue might be foes on another. Advocacy collaborators this month might be enemies down the road. Chapters 7 and 8 outline in more detail how intra-business competition often provides a significant stimulant of new lobbying methods and shifting tactics.

Increased complexity in the Washington public policymaking process also stimulates the demand for lobbying. Understanding the structures, rules, and processes requires more professionalized representation. Moreover, as the number of advocacy tools and channels of influence increases, so does the need for help in sorting through the various tactical options. Bert Carp, a well-respected Washington lobbyist, who also used to run a major corporate Washington office and worked in the Carter White House, explains these intricacies: "The system has now become so complex, how can anyone deal with it without professional assistance? It's like sending someone to federal district court without an attorney. Sooner or later they're going to go to jail."[35]

The growing size of government and its complexity continue to reshape the lobbying world. And while it is unclear that the lobbying industry will contract anytime soon, the lesson for those who seek to reduce its size and influence is clear—cutting the scope and complexity of government is a sure way to contract the magnitude of the advocacy business.

Congressional decentralization, fragmentation, and government sunshine laws are other factors that have stimulated the growth of the lobbying industry. As the number of congressional subcommittees and sunshine laws all expanded during the 1970s, the number of individuals involved in the policymaking process and their level of accountability to more stakeholders grew. The impact on lobbying and interest groups was clear: the more lawmakers involved in the process, the greater the number of people that required advocacy. Pat Griffin, a former senior White House aide and Washington strategist put it well, "Accountability (through sunshine laws) and the number of decision-makers both increased during this time period, which required a change in the way people lobbied. The more people involved in the process, the more targets of opportunity for lobbyists. Accountability, transparency and more people involved all conspired to reshape the lobbying world."

Fragmentation and more players engaged in the process created another new phenomenon in the lobbying world, "venue shopping."[36] In today's public policymaking environment, change can occur in a variety of places. Congress can modify laws, but the executive branch might be able to issue an executive order to accomplish the same end. Legislators might write new policies, but the president can veto bills. And Congress, of course, can always pass legislation again notwithstanding the objections of the president (veto override). These are just a few examples of how policy can occur in a variety of venues. Part of the strategic choices involved in lobbying today involves deciding when to pursue advocacy in Congress versus the Administration or both. When and why interest groups might pursue strategies and tactics aimed at, say, the White House instead of a congressional committee are discussed in more detail in Chapters 7, 8, and 9.

REGULATING MONEY IN ELECTIONS AND PUBLIC POLICY

Modifications in the legal and regulatory treatment of money in politics and public policymaking also impact lobbying. Money—"the mother's milk of politics," as some have called it – also pervades the interest-group world and because of that, it's a topic that recurs throughout this book. It helps elect friends of advocacy groups or tries to defeat their opponents. It provides access to lawmakers for lobbyists. It funds grassroots campaigns and issue advocacy advertising, to name of few of its uses. When government gets bigger or more fragmented, money in the public policy system becomes more important. As partisan polarization increases, so does the role of money. Finally, as the media fragments and the Internet grows in importance as an advocacy tool, the role of money shifts as well.

Several important changes in laws and policy governing campaign finance have also affected the advocacy world over the past 40 years. Instead of dealing with these modifications in a separate chapter, I discuss and integrate them at various points in the book, demonstrating how they have altered the lobbying world. For example, I explore the impact of changing laws and regulations on the growth of political action committees and their role in lobbying in Chapter 3. Chapter 4 demonstrates how as the number of policy and political actors in Washington expands, so does the role and need for additional financial resources. In Chapter 5, the burgeoning number of congressional "leadership PACs" is discussed in the context of the blurring lines between the politics of elections and the public policymaking process in a hyper-partisan age. Chapters 6 and 7 also outline how changes in the legal interpretation of so-called "soft money" have led to the rise of issue ads as a growing tool in the arsenal of interest groups. And, finally these chapters also explore how passage of the Bipartisan Campaign Reform Act (McCain-Feingold) led to the growing prominence of so-called

527 organizations as more important players in the advocacy game. In other words, it's hard to separate political money from any aspect of the new advocacy world.

Changes in campaign finance rules also have contributed to a host of unintended consequences in lobbying. For example, laws passed during the 1970s that limited the size of personal contributions also significantly increased the amount of time lawmakers had to spend raising money. Investing more time raising money meant even more interactions with lobbyists and reliance on interest groups to meet personal campaign reelection goals. It also meant lobbyists spent more of their time in the money-raising business. These unintended consequences are discussed in more detail in Chapter 5.

PARTISAN POLARIZATION

Increased partisan polarization in Washington is a third dominant change in the environment of organized interests. And while its impact on elections, Congress, the President, and the public policy process has been a dominant research topic among some political scientists, the consequences of partisan polarization on the lobbying world remain largely unexamined.[37] Advocacy now takes place in a more polarized, hyper-partisan environment. Electioneering and fundraising now operate nonstop, creating what has been described as "the permanent campaign."[38] It is not unusual, for example, for lobbyists to specialize in courting just one party or branch of government (like lobbyists specializing in representing clients with the White House). And as the power of congressional leadership has reasserted itself over the past decade, partisan ties between lobbyists and legislative leaders have also become more important. The so-called "K Street Project"—while largely misunderstood and misrepresented in the press—is one example of this growing link between leaders and lobbyists.[39] Recognizing the expanding connection between leaders on both sides of the aisle and lobbyists is an important piece of the new advocacy puzzle. Yet the Washington media's depiction of the "K Street Project" misses the larger significance of these connections.

An increasing number of campaign consultants are also moving from partisan politics into the public policy lobbying world.[40] This shift raises both ethical and substantive questions. I explore these issues in more detail in Chapter 5.

Finally, I argue partisan polarization has had another major impact on the advocacy world—strengthening the hand of lobbyists and interest groups. As partisanship and bickering increased, lobbyists often became an even more important channel for the exchange of information, strategy, vote counts, and tactics across the aisle. A Democratic lobbyist reinforces this point: "Members don't really talk to each other any more across the aisle, but lobbyists do. In many ways, polarization empowers lobbyists." This unintended consequence of polarization and its impact on lobbying is explored in more detail in Chapter 5.

OLD MEDIA FRAGMENTATION, THE INTERNET, AND NEW MEDIA

Fourth, the growth and expansion of media and technology, including the fragmentation of the media world, the development of the 24-hour news cycle, and the Internet are reshaping the advocacy industry. News outlets, blogs, and online portals, with their voracious appetite for content, now shape public policy debates in Washington. Again, sorting out how to respond to or leverage these new opportunities has spawned a cottage industry in Washington of new media/Internet strategists and consultants. It also has led to the evolution of the "lobbying toolbox," discussed in more detail in Chapter 7. Taken together, these changes in the external environment of organized interests have changed the *demands* on lobbyists and induced a new *supply* of lobbying activities.

THE CONSEQUENCES OF CHANGE—A CLOSER LOOK

But changes in the lobbying world not only included multiple causes – they also produced multiple effects. One such consequence is what political scientists call "hyper-pluralism." It is manifested most dramatically in the fragmentation of interest groups, from a culture where trade associations were the central source of lobbying in the 1960s and 1970s to a more individualized system where corporations, unions, and specific advocates employ their own staffs and hire their own lobbyists. Some have labeled this trend a shift from "peak associations" to "direct participation" by organized interests.[41] The health care industry, for example, used to rely on broad-based associations of doctors, hospitals, and pharmaceutical companies. Now representation is much more company-specific, and the number of health care lobbyists has ballooned. Instead of relying exclusively on associations, many individual drug companies, biotech firms, and individual hospitals have created their own Washington offices, formed their own PACs, and hired outside lobbying firms. Every year, an increasing number of interest organizations try to influence the public policy process through direct participation. This shift from peak associations representing the dominant force in advocacy to more individualized, direct participation has had a profound effect on lobbying. This book focuses on the causes and consequences of this "Lobbying Alone" strategy.

In an ironic twist, while many organized interests shifted from association-based lobbying to individualized participation, they also now participate in and create more coalitions. But this trend is less paradoxical than it appears. Many interests, while seeing the benefits and need for individualized participation, also recognize the loss of lobbying clout by going at it alone. So as a result, individual credit card companies such as Visa and MasterCard formed an ad hoc coalition lobbying for bankruptcy reform. Baby Bells, progeny of AT&T, set up individual Washington offices and PACs during the 1980s but also formed a coalition to lift the restrictions imposed on them by a district court as part of the breakup of the Bell system. Thus organized interests act in two seemingly contradictory ways: taking steps to institutionalize their individual participation by "Lobbying Alone" but also seeking the benefits of broader association. They try to get the best of both worlds. These developments in the lobbying world, adapting some new tactics and structures while maintaining some of the old, parallel the theory of "disjointed pluralism."[42] Writing about congressional change, one scholar notes, "Congressional development is disjointed in that members incrementally add new institutional mechanisms, without dismantling preexisting institutions and without rationalizing the structure as a whole."[43] Others have described the process of change in public policy as one of "punctuated-equilibrium."[44] This theory argues that most policy in the United States is relatively static, but it is "punctuated" by periods of change. Lobbyists must always be prepared to respond to these potential transformations— or, in some cases, devise strategies to begin the *punctuation* process. As a result, the advocacy industry is never stable either; it's dynamic, shifting, and open-ended. Understanding the strategic choices that produce *punctuated-equilibrium* conditions are explored in more detail later in this volume.

Shifting styles in lobbying is another consequence of change. One example of this new style is that lobbying has begun to emulate political campaigns. I call this the "electoral-to-public policy progression." Certain tactics first get applied in campaigns and then adopted by lobbyists and interest groups. Research, message development, earned media, paid media, and grassroots are just a few examples of the way electoral politics has infused the tactics of organized interests. This trend underscores one of the major conclusions of two scholars of lobbying, who argue the blurring lines between the politics of policymaking and the politics of elections, as well as the decreasing distinction between "inside" and "outside" lobbying, are two major changes in modern advocacy.[45]

Finally, adopting new substantive methods is another consequence of the evolving world of lobbying. If changes in the public policy process, partisan polarization, technology, and the media have created new *demands* on lobbyists, the advocacy industry has responded with a new *supply* of influence tools.[46] This book demonstrates how the new "demands" in the public policy environment have created an enhanced supply of not only lobbyists, but a whole new set of advocacy tools. These new methods of advocacy have transformed organized interests beyond relying only on "access-based" lobbying to the utilization of a more robust set of tactics and strategies— methods that also reflect the new era of partisan polarization and emulate political campaigns. Again, the "new toolbox" reflects increased levels of partisanship, blurring lines between inside and outside lobbying, collapsing differences between the politics of campaigns and the politics of public policy, new technology, evolving strategies of competitors and growing activism, fragmentation, and specialization by the government.

Using this *supply-side influence* (focusing on the lobbyists as opposed to the effect these advocates have on policy) framework to analyze the new structures, styles, and substantive methods of advocacy will help in reconsidering the new world of lobbying. This approach will demonstrate the advocacy world is bigger, more complex, and dynamic than suggested by conventional wisdom. These new insights will also help clear up many misconceptions about the true nature of lobbying in the American public policymaking process.

A DIFFERENT DEPENDENT VARIABLE—HOW THE POLITICAL ENVIRONMENT SHAPES LOBBYING

Little is written about how change in the political milieu confronting organized interests reshapes their lobbying structures and strategies. Chapter 7 includes a more thorough discussion of the limited research in this area. One scholarly paper emphasizes this point: "Political scientists have thoroughly studied how organized interests influence the political system and legislative outcomes but much less attention is paid to how the political system and legislative outcomes shape organized interests."[47] Another argues further, " . . . lobbying cannot usefully be studied in isolation from the factors which influence it. Lobbying is a part of the political, electoral and governmental processes, but only a part, rather than the whole, of them."[48]

But while making a useful point, these arguments only scratch the surface. The constellation of influences shaping the lobbying industry is even more complex. Some scholars focus needed attention on how varying cultural, legal, and political factors in different parts of the world—such as Washington, London, and Brussels—affect lobbying.[49] This comparative perspective is necessary and critical. Yet other factors, like changes in media, technology, partisanship, size and fragmentation of government, regulatory activism, and industry competition all affect the demand *for* and the supply *of* lobbying too. That is the thrust of this book.

RECIPROCAL IMPACTS—LOBBYIST FACILITATION OF GOVERNMENT GROWTH?

Another piece of the reconsideration puzzle means recognizing modifications in the advocacy world are reciprocal—interest-group growth also stimulates bigger government. As the supply of lobbyists and their services grows, it stimulates demand for even more government action. One group of interest group scholars puts it this way: "The growth and proliferation of interest groups in the United States has long been considered a major cause of growth in the size and scope of the U.S. government."[50] Over four decades earlier, others made a similar point arguing the behavior of "rent seeking" actors increased government spending.[51]

These arguments make common sense. All these advocates and interest groups must do something to justify their existence. And sometimes they encourage action in the public policy arena that might not have occurred but for the supply of lobbyists creating new demands. The impact of lobbyists on the growth of earmarks is one recent example. Advocates encouraging lawmakers to hold hearings or investigations beneficial to a lobbyist or harmful to a policy competitor is another. Hence the cycle of government expansion and fragmentation leads to more advocacy growth, in turn resulting in further frenetic legislative and bureaucratic activity, and creates the bottomless political whirlpool we see in Washington today. It is the new iron law of advocacy: *more lobbyists beget more government and more government begets more lobbyists.*

RESEARCH APPROACH

This book is the byproduct of over 20 years of serving as a participant and observer in the fields of lobbying and public policy. For the past two decades, I have done a lot of my own "soaking and poking" and "hanging around" the edges, as well as deep inside the belly of the lobbying industry. During that time, I have kept journals, made observations, and always looked at the world of advocacy through the twin prisms of practitioner and scholar. I served as a congressional aide, where I was the target of lobbyists' entreaties. I was a corporate lobbyist for one of America's largest telecommunications firms. I served on the senior staff of the White House, as Deputy Assistant to the President for Legislative Affairs, and most recently as the managing partner in charge of research and strategic communications for one of Washington's premier lobbying/public affairs firms.

In addition to the scholarly literature and my personal experiences and observations, I draw on information and anecdotes collected from interviews and discussions with congressional staff, White House aides, Washington lobbyists, and communications consultants. Some of the anecdotes are 20 years old, but others are quite recent. The more recent interviews were done "on the record" in most cases, and the persons are quoted by name. Some sources preferred to provide only informational quotes, and they are attributed by their background and affiliation only. Other remarks, quotes, and observations are from meetings I attended or conversations I had over the years. They are included to illustrate a point, and they add richness and color to the narrative—but the person saying them did not know they would be included in a book, so only their background and affiliation is listed. Collectively, these sources enable me to give an insider's account of changes in the strategies, tactics, and structures of so many different aspects of the advocacy industry. The lobbying world has changed a great deal in those two decades. And it will continue to evolve. The chapters that follow are intended to add to the body of knowledge about the lobbying world, eliminate many of the misconceptions around it, and provide readers with a fuller, more sober understanding of the roles advocacy groups play in the American public policymaking process.

A NOTE ON DEFINITION

Several points on definitions are critical to grasping the nuances and better understanding the new advocacy world. Throughout this book, the terms *lobbyist, interest-group representative*, and *advocate* are used interchangeably. For example, in discussing lobbying Congress or the executive branch, it's done by lobbyists, interest groups (and their representatives), or their advocates. When referring to "interest-group lobbying," an individual or a group of individual lobbyists or advocates do it. Some may think interest groups, like a trade association such as the American Medical Association or a labor union such as the AFL-CIO, are different than paid individual lobbyists. They obviously are at one level. Yet when describing the practice of advocacy and its strategies and tactics throughout this book, "lobbying" by a group or an individual is considered the same thing. In other words, when describing how General Motors "lobbies," terms like lobbyists for General Motors, advocates for General Motors or an auto industry interest group are synonymous.

Lobbying is also most accurately defined broadly. It includes *direct contacts* about specific public policy matters as individuals communicate with lawmakers or other government officials. But lobbying also includes *indirect contacts* such as grassroots and issue advertising campaigns. Some refer to this distinction as the difference between "inside" and "outside" lobbying.[52] Nevertheless, for the purposes of this volume, it's all lobbying—and part of the increasingly tactically varied "toolkit," beyond just direct contact with policymakers.

So when discussing the growth of the "advocacy industry" or "advocacy establishment" throughout this book, that includes individual lobbyists, and

the personnel in the government affairs/public affairs departments of interest groups (such as trade associations, corporations, labor unions, and public
or single issue groups). It also includes a cadre of others, such as communications specialists, pollsters, grassroots organizers, and more. Anyone involved
in trying to impact public policy, directly or indirectly—or attempting to
reduce uncertainty and gather information about the government and political external environment—is part of the burgeoning lobbying industry. The
specific tactical tools used by lobbyists and a discussion of how, when, and
where interest-group representatives deploy them is discussed in more detail
in Chapters 7 and 8 of this book.

But even these broader definitions do not explain all the public scorn
heaped on lobbyists. These views are deeply rooted in the American political
psyche. Reconsidering lobbying means understanding the origins of these
negative public attitudes—and that these views are not new. Students of
lobbying need to begin with this important conclusion: the Jack Abramoff
scandal was not the apex of paid advocates or interest-group representatives
behaving badly—he was just another chapter in a much longer volume. But
as we shall see later, there are many books in the library of lobbying. Shed-
ding new light on the subject will help relieve the persistent public illiteracy
about the advocacy world.

ORGANIZATION OF THIS BOOK

Chapter 2 discusses the congressional, cultural, and historical foundations of
lobbying. What is lobbying, who are lobbyists, and why is there a need for
these advocates in our constitutional framework? Definitions of lobbying,
advocacy, and inside versus outside lobbying are offered. Public perceptions
of lobbyists are discussed. Are these views new or old? How was lobbying
conducted earlier in American history? How did the U.S. model of government pave the way for the changes we've seen in the last three decades? Has
everything changed in the lobbying world or have some things remained the
same? Patching together a more ornate mosaic about the past brings today's
new world of lobbying—its size, complexities, and misunderstandings—
into sharper focus.

The third chapter creates a framework to understand the growth in the
"advocacy industry" by looking at change from a variety of levels, including
the growth in corporate Washington offices, increasing numbers of trade
associations, the proliferation of PACs, the rise of consultants and lobbying
firms, and the new world of coalition advocacy. It also investigates how and
why the lobbying industry has changed from an enterprise dominated by
peak associations like the Chamber of Commerce or the American Medical
Association to increased participation by individual corporations and

specialized organizations. The old trade association structures still remain, but new forms of individualized lobbying participation have emerged as well. These and other illustrations of how interests groups develop and evolve are evidence of an advocacy version of "disjointed pluralism."[53]

Chapter 4 probes even more deeply into the causes of change, particularly the emergence of hyper-regulation and government activism. It examines how the increase in the size of the federal bureaucracy and regulatory agencies, the growth of legislative staff, and the proliferation of congressional subcommittees all have affected the lobbying business. It also investigates how a more complex, fragmented, activist, and open (through sunshine laws) public policymaking process has reshaped the lobbying world. This chapter catalogues these changes and fits them into a broader theoretical understanding of why organizations change their structure, style, and substantive methods as well.

Chapter 5 focuses on how lobbying has changed due to the pandemic of partisanship. Topics include the emergence of "partisan" lobbying firms, the "K Street Project," the new role of money in politics under the Bipartisan Campaign Reform Act (McCain-Feingold), and the blurring lines between electoral politics and public policy development. It also explores the increasing connection between some lobbyists, organized interests, and political parties. It also points out some of the unintended consequences of political and congressional reforms. Another part of lobbying reconsidered means understanding that many changes intended to remove money, power, and influence out of the system often—ironically—strengthen the hands of lobbyists.

Chapter 6 probes why new media, the Internet and the 24-hour news cycle, and advances in technology have also contributed to changes in lobbying. Everything from monitoring blogs as part of lobbying campaigns to highly targeted advertising using new media is now a growing part of the lobbying world. In a hyper-competitive environment, an increasing number of organized interests are looking for ways to impact the media—old and new—and adopt these new technologies for advocacy. Hyper-media has also fundamentally altered the structure, style, and methods of lobbying.

Chapter 7 investigates the modern lobbying toolbox, comparing and contrasting today's tactics and strategies to those of the 1970s and 1980s. The primary research method uses personal interviews with lobbyists, senior congressional staff, and executive branch personnel, which highlight the contours of modern lobbying, how it has changed and how it has stayed the same. Each of the tactics described in this chapter could serve as the subject of a separate monograph. Yet instead of exploring a laundry list of changing tactics in exhaustive detail, this chapter demonstrates how each fits into the framework described as the "electoral/advocacy complex." These tactics—based on the interviews and observations—have emerged as a result of three forces predicted by the theoretical framework.

First, as we shall see, forces in the external environment—public policy-makers, competitors, or changing technology—demand these new tools. Second, where used, they are all highly *integrated* into the overall advocacy campaign. And third, all of these tactics adopted in the public policy arena are carried over from successful political campaigns. The new utensils that fit this campaign-infected model of advocacy include tactics such as research, message development, paid media, earned media, grassroots, managing consultants, PACs, and utilization of new media resources, such as blogs and the Internet. Taken together, these new tools all build a *narrative*, a storyline that helps advocates break through the many competing voices in the ultra-competitive world of public policy.[54]

But not every interest organization uses "the new toolbox"—or at least all of its utensils. Why? This question is explored in Chapter 8. What are the strategic choices that lead some lobbying organizations to use more than others? Why do some choose to "expand the scope of conflict," while others stick to a more private inside game? Examples include how broader issues such as Medicare reform used more of the toolbox, while narrower lobbying such as an appropriations earmark do not. The chapter also investigates the "venue shopping" in advocacy. Why do some interest groups, under certain circumstances, choose to lobby only Congress, while others may choose to lobby the White House or executive branch? And when is lobbying multiple branches of government (or none) a better tactical advocacy approach? The different tactical and strategic goals in lobbying the White House versus lobbying Congress are not well understood—nor are the value and methods involved in pursuing a filibuster or anti-filibuster strategy in the Senate. The nuances of lobbying in different contexts are explored in more detail in Chapter 8. This chapter also includes a more in-depth case study showing how all the tools fit together in a modern day lobbying campaign.

Explaining the strategic choices underlying lobbying decisions is an important missing link in much of the literature on lobbying. We don't know a lot about the factors causing lobbyists and interest groups to choose different tactics at different times and why. This chapter begins to develop such a typology, laying out in a more systematic way how strategic decisions get made and conditions that drive lobbying actions. Interviews with lobbyists serve as the basis for this chapter as well.

Chapter 9 concludes our reconsideration of lobbying, developing a series of generalizations that will help students of the advocacy world understand it better. It summarizes why lobbying is so misunderstood, focusing on its constantly changing nature, its problems with definition, the public's willingness to stereotype it, and Americans' lack of appreciation for the public policymaking process. This chapter also investigates the "limits" of lobbying. It supports and extends Salisbury's conjecture, demonstrating that organized interests do their best to reduce uncertainty, but they are far from consistently influential or politically omnipotent as often portrayed in the media. As we shall see, when organized interests seek predictability, it doesn't always translate to political power. Or to update an older conclusion using the Abramoff vernacular, lobbyists sometimes engage more in *information gathering* than *influence peddling*.[55] This chapter shows why—contrary to conventional wisdom—a bigger lobbying industry doesn't necessarily mean a more powerful lobbying industry. Despite the growth and change in the advocacy world, there are clear reasons why interest groups and lobbyists are not politically omnipotent. I revisit Galbraith's theory of countervailing power as a way to understand lobbying growth, investment, change, and its mixed record of success.

SUMMARY

The 2005–2006 lobbying scandals generated lots of media heat yet very little light about the new world of Washington advocacy. These sensationalized stories reinforce false stereotypes. Caricatures of lobbying were perpetuated by critics of pluralism during the 1960s who argued policy was often made in a closed, static system, controlled by a small number of lawmakers, bureaucrats, and lobbyists. This highly negative view of interest groups underlies much of the media reporting we see today about lobbying. But neither the press nor the older interest-group theorists accurately explain the advocacy world as it looks and behaves today.

While groups do attempt to develop countervailing power as suggested by Galbraith, in today's more open, fragmented, public process, gauging the impact of advocacy initiatives is difficult. This often leads to an overinvestment of lobbying resources in some cases, and underinvestment in others. It also means powerful, well-funded interest groups "lose" more often than suggested by conventional wisdom. By not focusing enough on lobbying failures, the uncertainties or limitations of advocacy, the dynamic nature of lobbying, and the variation in advocacy contexts (i.e. different policy areas), many are left with the inaccurate conclusion that lobbying is *always* too influential.

Advocacy needs to be viewed as an integrated, ongoing competition between interest, rather than a single "play" in an isolated game.[56] The central questions of what lobbyists do, why they do it, and how they deserve reconsideration. Answering these questions will smash many of the myths that swirl around the interest-group world.

Political, technological, competitive, and public policy trends have transformed the structure, style, strategies, and substantive methods of the influence business over the past 40 years. And in turn, the advocacy industry is changing the public policymaking process and electoral politics in America as well. Yet too much of what most Americans know about lobbying is like shallow topsoil. It is truly more structurally diverse, tactically varied, and politically limited than suggested by conventional wisdom. As we shall see, the lobbying industry is large because the government Leviathan is big, powerful, complex and regularly creates uncertainties for interest groups. Yet efforts to reign in the advocacy industry—without reducing the scope of government—often create unintended consequences and are more likely to shift lobbyists into different activities rather than reduce their numbers. These are all reasons why reconsidering lobbying means digging below the surface of its historical, cultural, and legal precursors, which is our next stop in *getting under the influence.*

NOTES

1. Jeffrey H. Birnbaum, "Washington's Once and Future Lobby," *Washington Post*, September 10, 2006, B01.
2. Ibid.
3. Testimony before the U.S. House of Representatives, Committee on Rules, "Lobbying Reform: Accountability Through Transparency," *Hearing*, 109th Congress, 2nd Sess., March 2, 2006.
4. For a good review of the development of pluralist thought in political science, see Andrew S. McFarland, *Neopluralism: The Evolution of Political Process Theory* (Lawrence, KS: The University of Kansas Press, 2004).
5. Ibid. 15.
6. Ibid. 31.
7. Gary Mucciaroni, *Reversals of Fortune: Public Policy and Private Interests* (Washington, D.C.: The Brookings Institution, 1995), vii
8. Theorists like Arthur F. Bentley, *The Process of Government* (Chicago: The University of Chicago Press, 1908) and David B. Truman, *The Governmental Process: Political Interests and Public Opinion* (New York: Alfred Knopf, 1951) are two of the most prominent examples of scholars promoting the idea that citizens could all be represented, actually or "potentially," through their involvement in groups.
9. Frank R. Baumgartner and Beth L. Leech, *Basic Interests: The Importance of Groups in Politics and in Political Science* (Princeton, NJ: Princeton University Press, 1998), 57–58.
10. My thinking on this point about lobbying power varying across time and in different sectors, as well as not being a zero-sum game, was influenced to a great deal by and is consistent with Gary Mucciaroni's book referenced above. I also believe many of the assumptions in scholarly literature he refers to have been adopted by the mainstream media and most reporters who cover lobbying.
11. John Kenneth Galbraith, *American Capitalism: The Concept of Countervailing Power* (Boston: Houghton Mifflin, 1952).
12. McFarland, *Neopluralism*, 14.
13. David Truman, *The Governmental Process* (New York, NY: Alfred Knopf, 1951); Robert H. Salisbury, "An Exchange Theory of Interest Group," *Midwest Journal of Political Science* 13 (1969): 64–78; Robert H. Salisbury, "Interest Representation: The Dominance of Institution," *American Political Science Review* 78 (1984): 64–76; Robert H. Salisbury, *Interests and Institutions: Substance and Structure in American Politics* (Pittsburgh, PA: The University of Pittsburgh Press, 1992), 340; and Heinz, John P., Edward O. Laumann, Robert L. Nelson, and Robert H. Salisbury, *The Hollow Core* (Cambridge, MA: Harvard Univeristy Press, 1993).
14. Salisbury, "Interest Representation: The Dominance of Institutions"; Salisbury, *Interests and Institutions.*
15. Salisbury, "Interest Representation: The Dominance of Institutions," 68.

16. Beth L. Leech, Frank R. Baumgartner, Timothy M. Lapira, and Nicholas A. Semanko "Drawing Lobbyists to Washington: Government Activity and the Demand for Advocacy," *Political Research Quarterly* 58(1) (March 2005): 19–30.

17. Interest group adaptation perspectives are drawn from Salisbury, "The Paradox of Interest Groups in Washington," *Interests and Institutions*, 339–361.

18. Salisbury, "The Paradox of Interest Groups in Washington," *Interests and Institutions*, 340–347.

19. Baumgartner and Leech, *Basic Interests*, 178.

20. Heinz, Laumann, Nelson, and Salisbury, *The Hollow Core*.

21. E.E. Schattschneider, *The Semi-Sovereign People* (New York: Hold, Rinehart and Winston, 1960).

22. Heinz, Laumann, Nelson, and Salisbury, *The Hollow Core*, describes this change as a move "from peak association to individual representation."

23. Allan J. Cigler and Burdett A. Loomis, *Interest Group Politics*, 6th ed. (Washington, D.C.: CQ Press, 2002), 382, raises this issue of the blurring lines between the politics of public policymaking and the politics of elections as one of their book's principal conclusions.

24. James A. Thurber, "From Campaigning to Lobbying," *Shades of Gray: Perspectives on Campaign Ethics* (Washington, D.C.: Brookings Institution Press, 2002), 151–170.

25. Jon R. Bond and Richard Fleisher, *Polarized Politics: Congress and the President in a Partisan Era* (Washington, D.C.: CQ Press, 2000), for example, discuss the impact of polarization on voters and Congress but not how it impacts lobbying.

26. Connor McGrath, *Lobbying in Washington, London, and Brussels: The Persuasive Communication of Political Communication* (Lewiston, NY: Edwin Mellen Press, 2005), 6.

27. Lester W. Milbrath, *The Washington Lobbyists* (Chicago, IL: Rand McNally, 1963).

28. Kenneth M. Goldstein, *Interest Groups, Lobbying and Participation in America* (Cambridge, UK: Cambridge University Press, 1999); and Pendleton Herring, *Group Representation before Congress* (Baltimore, MD: Johns Hopkins University Press, 1929) are two good examples.

29. Ibid. 22.

30. Raymond Bauer, Ithiel de Sola Pool, and Lewis Dexter, *American Business and Public Policy* (New York, NY: Atherton Press, 1964).

31. Jack Walker, "The Origins and Maintenance of Interest Groups in America," *American Political Science Review* 1983: 285–295; Mark J. Rozell, Clyde Wilcox, and David Madland, *Interest Groups in American Campaigns: The New Face of Electioneering*, 2nd ed. (Washington, D.C.: CQ Press, 2006).

32. Leech, Baumgartner, Lapira, and Semanko "Drawing Lobbyists to Washington: Government Activity and the Demand for Advocacy," *Political Research Quarterly* 58(1) (March 2005): 19–30.

33. Jeffrey M. Berry and Clyde Wilcox, *The Interest Group Society*, 4th ed. (New York, NY: Pearson Longman, 2007), 32.

34. Jeffrey H. Birnbaum, "Bit Players XM, Sirius Hold A High-Stakes Merger Game," *Washington Post*, July 25, 2007, D1.

35. This quote is based on an interview I did with Mr. Carp for this book. See my sections on methods later in this chapter for a more complete description of the methodology.

36. I am indebted to Burdett Loomis of the University of Kansas for suggesting this concept to me.

37. Bond and Fleisher, *Polarized Politics: Congress and the President in a Partisan Era*.

38. Sidney Blumenthal, *The Permanent Campaign* (New York, NY: Touchstone, 1982); and Thomas Mann and Norman Ornstein, *The Permanent Campaign and Its Future* (Washington, D.C.: Brookings Institution, 2000).

39. The "K Street Project" was a loosely organized initiative to help Republicans who wanted to leave government jobs find employment as Washington lobbyists. I discuss its origins, structure, and mission in more detail in Chapter 5, which is a discussion of the impact of partisanship on the advocacy world.

40. Thurber, *Shades of Gray*.

41. Heinz, Laumann, Nelson, and Salisbury, *The Hollow Core*.

42. Eric Schickler, *Disjointed Pluralism: Institutional Innovation and the Development of the U.S. Congress* (Princeton, NJ: Princeton University Press, 2001).

43. Ibid. 17–18.

44. Frank R. Baumgartner and Bryan D. Jones, *Agendas and Instability in American Politics* (Chicago: University of Chicago Press, 1993).
45. Cigler and Loomis, *Interest Group Politics.*
46. Burdett Loomis first developed this concept of the "supply side" of lobbying. See Burdett A. Loomis, "Doing Good, Doing Well and (Shhhh!) Having Fun: A Supply-Side Approach to Lobbying," paper presented at the 2003 meetings of the American Political Science Association, Philadelphia, PA. August 28–31.
47. T. Roof, "The More Things Change, the More They Stay the Same: American Political Institutions and Organized Labor's Legislative Influence since World War II," paper delivered at the annual conference of the *American Political Science Association*, 2002.
48. McGrath, *Lobbying in Washington, London, and Brussels*, 2.
49. Ibid.
50. Leech, Baumgartner, Lapira, and Semanko, "Drawing Lobbyists to Washington," 19.
51. James Buchanan and Gordon Tullock, *The Calculus of Consent* (Ann Arbor: University of Michigan Press, 1962).
52. See Goldstein, *Interest Groups, Lobbying and Participation in America*, 3, for a discussion about how political scientists distinguish between inside and outside strategies.
53. Schickler, *Disjointed Pluralism.*
54. Darrell M. West and Burdett A. Loomis, *The Sound of Money: How Political Interests Get What they Want* (New York, NY: Norton, 1999), persuasively make the case that interest groups with high levels of resources can more effectively build and communicate narratives to break through and more effectively make their case. My research extends and further specifies their findings.
55. Salisbury, *Interests and Institutions.*
56. Robert H. Salisbury, "Interest Structures and Policy Domains: A Focus for Research," In William Crotty, Mildred A. Schwartz, and John C. Green, eds. *Representing Interests and Interest Group Representation* (Washington, D.C.: University Press of America, 1994), 17–18.

FOUNDATIONS OF LOBBYING

It always startles people when you say you're a lobbyist. They stare at you with a sort of embarrassed horror as if you'd just made a shocking confession, as if you'd said, 'I'm really illegitimate' or 'I've just eaten five children.'[1]

Lobbyist

My dad is definitely not a 'lobbyist.' All he does is work at the Environmental Defense Fund and talk to Congressmen about how to protect the environment.[2]

Third Grader

Our story opens with this important plot background: lobbying is both a dynamic big business and a grossly misunderstood practice in American culture today. It also plays an increasingly important role in public policymaking and electoral politics in the United States, yet it remains a mysterious and murky enterprise in the minds of most citizens.

This chapter investigates the foundations of lobbying in America. It begins by exploring lobbyists' "image malaise" and argues interest advocates' bad reputation results from poor definitions of the practice and a variety of flawed assumptions concerning their impact on public policy. The chapter then turns to a brief discussion about the institutional and constitutional bases of lobbying. Next, it outlines how interest groups conducted advocacy in an earlier era, including how the press and scholars wrote about these activities, and public perceptions of lobbying in the late nineteenth and twentieth centuries. It then focuses on two elements of lobbying rarely discussed in the press or in academic studies: the positive contributions of lobbyists and those of interest groups. These are some of the "upsides of influence." The chapter also reconsiders the practice of advocacy through a broader and less conventional lens, moving beyond the traditional focus on one-way pressure group tactics or corrupt behavior. This expanded perspective on interest groups and lobbyists will help us better appreciate the dramatic changes described later in this book. It will also continue the process of getting "under the influence," fostering better understanding of lobbying and removing many gross misconceptions and myths.

AN ENDURING PUBLIC SCORN

Pinpointing a "golden age" of lobbying, an epoch when advocacy was viewed as a noble undertaking, will always present a challenge to political historians—principally because it is an era that never existed. At best, lobbyists have always been the Rodney Dangerfield of American public policy—they just don't get any respect. At worst, they rank just above Islamist terrorists in terms of public scorn. Yet this "image malaise" has endured since the earliest days of the republic. Lobbyists' lousy reputation is a durable component of interest-group history.

One of the classic texts on lobbying written nearly 60 years ago is filled with illustrations going back to the nineteenth century. Quoting an article from *The Nation*, in 1869, E. Pendleton Herring notes, "The professional lobbyist is a man who everybody suspects; who is generally during one half of the year without honest means of livelihood; and whose employment by those who have bills before the legislature is only resorted to as a disagreeable necessity."[3] Or as Herring himself concludes after reviewing attitudes of writers going back to the founding: "The general attitude toward the lobbyist in those days was one of contempt. The word lobbyists was a term of opprobrium, and very justly so."[4]

Students of lobbying should begin with a simple conclusion. Despite the public and media outrage about a lobbying scandal like the Jack Abramoff affair, his actions were not unique in American history. This enduring narrative of corruption weaves through the annals of advocacy like a serpentine stream. But the often narrow focus on sordid and scandalous influence peddling clouds the full landscape, distorting public understanding.

So even as the lobbying industry has changed dramatically in structure, style, and substantive methods since the 1970s, its public perceptions have not. One account of lobbying perhaps sums up the enduring public scorn best, " . . . being a lobbyist has long been synonymous in the minds of many Americans with being a glorified pimp."[5] No wonder one prominent DC lobbyist said he is embarrassed to tell his own mother he is a lobbyist.[6] Washington strategist and former Clinton White House official Patrick Griffin agrees, "It's funny, if you refer to them as 'stakeholders' everybody says, 'Sure, they need to be part of the process.' But the minute you call a stakeholder a 'lobbyist' it's as if they grow horns."

Before examining some of the historical roots of lobbying, it's important to examine why these negative perceptions endure. Three major reasons underlie the advocacy industry's image malaise. First, some blame the public. Most citizens know little about the role interest groups and lobbyists play in the process. And as a result, public perceptions are usually incomplete and open to misleading characterizations.[7] One scholar wrote, "As a job, lobbying is highly subject to stereotyping and misunderstanding."[8] Secondly, the press also contributes to prurient conclusions. One observer notes, "Journalists as a rule have not been much interested in the stuff of lobbying unless it gives off a foul aroma."[9] Finally, others suggest politicians gain benefit by criticizing lobbyists in order to strike a populist tone. One veteran Washington lobbyist said, "Often during election times, politicians have a tendency to beat up on lobbyists because that seems to be something that resonates with the public."[10] Other observers of life on Capitol Hill have an even more cynical view:

> The lobbyists are more the tools of Congressional Clans than the manipulators of Congress. They are the means by which Congressional Chiefs control the junior politicians and sometimes each other. The exercise of power is frequently a painful act, and the truly powerful often exercise it from behind a façade of intermediaries who deflect the heat and hatred arising from it.
> ... Today's circle of retainers is made up of congressional staff, bureaucrats, and lobbyists, who absorb the public derision and criticism while the public continues to elect and reelect their political masters.[11]

These views are interesting for several reasons. First, they all seem to work together in giving lobbying and interest groups a bad name. The public, the press, and politicians all reinforce each other. Citizens believe Washington is dominated by special interests, stories in the press reaffirm this conclusion, and then politicians rail against special interests as a way to make themselves look good. But this kind of finger pointing only reinforces the public's cynical view. Second, these perceptions have been around throughout American history and have changed very little. Finally, it's a little ironic that in a dramatically changing lobbying world, one of the constants is a horrific public reputation. It's even more ironic that a practice that some citizens believe should be banned (some say special interest groups should not be allowed to lobby Congress) is protected in the same section of the Constitution (The First Amendment's right to petition the government for redress of grievances) that protects speech and religion.

Yet to grasp how the industry has changed—and why attitudes toward lobbyists have endured—it's important to take a brief historical detour, a look back at an earlier period, to understand better the foundations of lobbying in the U.S. public policymaking process. This short historical review makes clear that while advocacy in America has evolved, it has also been viewed through a narrow and jaded lens, leading to limited understanding and certainly more confusion than clarity. Looking back at the history of lobbying and then taking a broader perspective on interest-group behavior are the next steps in "getting under the influence."

THE INSTITUTIONAL FRAMEWORK OF LOBBYING IN AMERICA

Understanding changes in American lobbying and its role in the public policy process requires analyzing the institutional framework of advocacy. What are the unique features of American government that resulted in the emergence of lobbyists and interest groups? It may surprise some to learn that interest groups were contemplated from the beginning of the American republic. The Founders considered them both part of the potential *problem* facing the new republic *and* a path toward the *solution*.

Of course, in the earliest days of American politics, interest groups and lobbyists, at least as we know them today, did not formally exist. But their emergence was clearly anticipated by James Madison, in Federalist No. 10.[12] The Founders thought interest groups (what Madison called "factions") were inevitable in American politics because as people pursued their self-interest, and government impinged on their freedom, conflicts would inevitably arise. The biggest risk, according to the Framers, was that certain interests or factions would grow too dominant and begin to impose their views and preferences on other sectors of society. Political asymmetry among others could provoke serious illness in the body politic. But Madison had an elixir.

And he wrapped his cure into the very design of American government. Republicanism (elected representatives making decisions that reflected the "public interest" as opposed to narrower "private interests"), separation of powers among legislative, executive and judicial branches, and a bicameral legislature, representing individuals (the House) and geographic regions (the Senate), were among the principal institutional features aimed at limiting the power of individual interest groups.

As outlined in the previous chapter, the view that competition among groups limits the power and dominance of any particular faction is called "pluralism" in the lexicon of political science. From a normative perspective, it may work well according to Madisonian theory, but some believe it runs into serious problems in its real-world application. Here are a few examples of this point of view.

Theoretically, anyone can form a group and advocate for a particular position in the public policy process. All Americans are free to petition the government and promote a particular legislative or regulatory outcome. There are, in effect, no barriers to entry.

But here's the rub according to critics of lobbying and pluralism. Not all interests are created equal. Some have more money and other resources. Some are better organized. Others might have enhanced connections to more powerful individuals such as legislative majority party members or representatives in leadership positions. And some views are not represented at all. While there are well-organized groups like farmers who push for higher prices, those who bear the brunt of higher food costs often have no formal group representing them.[13]

Differences in resources, political skill, and level of organization all create conflicts between Madisonian theory and real-world practice—difficulties long analyzed and debated among political scientists.

Another problem for pluralism in practice is what political scientists call "subgovernments."[14] Many issues are so specialized and complex that only a small proportion of the population cares deeply about an outcome. Subgovernments or "iron triangles," as they are also sometimes called, refer to policymaking that emphasizes the collaboration of specialized congressional subcommittees, bureaucrats in the executive branch with issue expertise, and narrow groups of lobbyists acting on highly constricted sets of issues. Instead of laws and regulations getting made through the input of outside interest groups, subgovernments can easily exclude citizens from the process because of lack of transparency or other factors that shut out certain individuals. And while subgovernments may be impervious to ordinary citizens, they are not to lobbyists and interest groups with the issue expertise and political resources to penetrate. This view of how interest groups—especially narrow, highly specialized advocates—can shape policy in the direction of their narrow self-interest provides fodder for those critical of lobbyists to complain about problems with the pluralist school of thought.[15]

Focusing too much attention on the pluralist/anti-pluralist debate is not the purpose here. It is important to note, however, that the anti-pluralist school of thought has advanced the idea that private interests always trump the public interest, and that lobbyists usually win at the expense of ordinary citizens. And the public debate about lobbying and anti-interest group rhetoric—including press coverage, citizen perceptions, and the remarks of politicians—often trace many of the same normative and empirical concerns raised in the pluralism debate. Whether or not pluralism's critics are right is not the point. But many of the assumptions and conclusions in the academic debate have migrated into the more popular sphere of political discourse in America. Some of the long-standing questions about interest groups and lobbyists dating back to the founding of this country were reinforced during the 1960s by the critics of pluralism, who saw the policymaking process as closed and biased toward private, well-financed, largely corporate interests.

INTEREST GROUPS IN AN EARLIER ERA—THE RISE OF ASSOCIATION-BASED ADVOCACY

In order to set the stage for a discussion about how lobbying has changed in recent decades, let us next turn to how it was practiced in an earlier era. We don't know a lot about lobbying during the nineteenth century, but we can draw a few important generalizations from earlier descriptions of scholars and press accounts. Understanding the structure, style, and methods of lobbying in this earlier time period helps us discern how it's profoundly different today.

Given the political freedoms granted Americans, the many points of potential institutional influence outlined above, and the growing impact of the new government on their lives, it's no surprise citizens sought to shape government action in the earliest days of the republic. Evidence of interest-group activity in American politics exists as far back as the eighteenth century. For example, there are anecdotes about businesses banding together in 1757 and contributing liquor to induce citizens to vote for George Washington for the Virginia House of Burgesses.[16] Religious groups were also among the earliest organized lobbying forces, trying to shape public policy on issues related to the removal of Native Americans from their land and those related to slavery.[17]

But lobbyists and interest groups expanded their activities in American public policy more dramatically during the later part of the nineteenth century. The rise in organized advocacy paralleled the growth in industrial revolution, as railroads, steel companies, oil and gas concerns, and utility holdings—to name a few—expanded in size and economic power. And these interests joined together in a particular way to advocate and protect their interests. As the nation and government grew, so did the opportunities and need for more lobbyists and interest groups.

While there are some notable exceptions, such as the Standard Oil Company or U.S. Steel, that participated individually in the public policy process, trade associations heavily dominated lobbying in this earlier era. Few trade associations formed after the Civil War, but the movement gained momentum during the same period that saw the rise of the major corporation toward the end of the nineteenth century.[18]

Trade associations and individuals representing them were the principal agents in lobbying from the beginning of the industrial era until around the mid-1970s. It is striking when reading historical reviews of lobbying that nearly every account of interest-group activity focuses on trade associations as the advocacy medium. The Anti-Saloon League, for example, had a mailing list of a half million people it used to mobilize in favor of Prohibition, according to one scholar.[19] Activities of the American Cotton Manufacturers Institute, the National Beet Growers Association, the Association of American Railroads, the National Coal Association, the National Milk Producers Federation, and the National Petroleum Council are among the most prominent mentioned by scholars describing nineteenth- and early-twentieth century interest-group behavior.[20]

The growth of trade associations as a lobbying force expanded during the early-to-mid-nineteenth century and escalated during the Industrial Revolution and into the period of World War I. But if government was increasingly important in the affairs of businesses and other interest groups, why didn't individual firms get more involved politically as they are today? Why the emergence of trade associations as a lobbying force? Some scholars argue that trade association proliferation was encouraged by the government itself and business leaders for commercial and competitive purposes. As Truman (1951) notes, the government was one impetus behind the growth of labor organizations and trade associations, but not for obvious reasons. He argues that both received strong encouragement from government, especially during the period of World War I, as the federal government's responsibilities for economic planning increased. He says that forming these groups became a government objective during wartime.[21] Working with a group representing an entire industry made it much easier for government policymakers to reach a collection of companies in key industries such as raw materials, natural resources, or transportation. This is a familiar theme through the history of lobbying – government growth produces more interest group activity.

Commercial business advantage was another reason for the growth of trade associations. Some note, for example, that the same factors that caused businesses to form trusts and other combinations—pools, market sharing, and price agreements—were responsible for association growth in America.[22] During the nineteenth and early-twentieth-century, because of encouragement from government and business leaders, trade associations played this uncertainty-reducing role for many major interests during rapid industrial growth.

Heavy dependence on associations as the main lobbying vehicle continued until the mid-1970s. But for roughly the past 40 years, individual companies and more specialized groups have gradually replaced trade associations as the principal institutions for lobbying. Trade groups still exist and have even grown in number, but in most industries it's the individual companies—the Hospital Corporation of America, not just the American Hospital Association; Chevron, not just the American Petroleum Institute; Verizon, not just the United States Telephone Association—that now play the dominant role in the lobbying process. "We rely on the trade association for the little things or the issues we don't want to spend a lot of time on," according to the head of a Washington office for a major telecommunications company. "We can't afford to let the association do our work in Washington anymore on the big-ticket items. We need to do it ourselves. There is too much at stake now," he said.

There are, however, some major exceptions. In cases where the members of the trade association are either smaller organizations or even individuals, these trade groups remain dominant advocacy forces. "Associations such as the Independent Insurance Agents & Brokers and the National Association of Realtors are still the powerhouses for the insurance agent and Realtor worlds. The reason is their members do not have the resources to open their own offices, and they are completely dependent on their associations to promote their agendas," according to Bob Rusbuldt, President of the Independent Insurance Agents & Brokers.

During the early-twentieth-century, the lobbying firm—so prevalent on the public policy scene today—was non-existent. And except for the occasional mention of a very large corporation, trade association lobbying dominated the early history of interest groups' advocacy in America. The causes and consequences of structural change in lobbying—away from an association-only based model to a more individualized participation—is an important and often overlooked change in the advocacy world.

Depictions of advocacy by both media and scholars during this earlier period focus almost exclusively on the negative side of interest-group behavior. And the critiques of private interests are typically vague and general, demonstrating little rigor for terms like "public interest." Even Mark Twain weighed in with negative depictions of lobbyists in popular literature. Again, McConnell emphasizes this point. *Private Power in America* begins its discussion of interest groups and advocacy in the United States by focusing on four congressional investigations of lobbying spanning 50 years in the first part of the twentieth century. Lobbyists, according to the conventional wisdom during this period, could only do one thing: get caught in various influence schemes involving major associations and questionable campaign finance practices.[23] McConnell's view is that lobbying is only conducted by pressure groups pursuing their own private interests. His pejorative attitude toward lobbying assumes all interest groups are equally problematic and draws little distinction between typically undefined "private interests" and what impact their action might have on the equally nebulous "public interest." There is an implicit assumption in his argument that somehow groups pursuing their own interests always harm the "public."

The vagueness of terms "private interest" and "public interest" throughout many of the earlier descriptions of lobbying is another troubling weakness. There is little calibration between issues such as lobbying for an appropriations earmark, new environmental regulations, ending prohibition, more spending on defense, or outlawing the death penalty. Many of the analyses of advocacy during this earlier era view public policymaking as a binary exercise. There are only two sides of an issue: lobbyists representing "private interests," arrayed against an undefined "public interest." And guess which side most writers think should win? But this is a false choice. Most lobbying poses much more nuanced issues. If a pharmaceutical company argues for an expanded drug formulary so more of its products are included as choices for Medicaid recipients, and a managed care company opposes, lobbying for more restrictive choices of medicines to save the government money and lower the budget deficit, which interest group is pursuing the "public interest" and which a "private interest"? In this case is the "public interest" saving the government money and lowering the federal budget deficit or providing potentially life saving medicines to low income people? Real-world advocacy questions like this are complex. But earlier examinations of advocacy tended only to describe lobbying as pitting private interests against public interests, all usually wrapped in some prurient anecdotes about sleazy advocates. Some of the more recent accounts of lobbying reject the notion that private interests and public interests are always in a zero-sum game. But historically, the public interest/private interest dichotomy is a concept that leads to misperception and misunderstanding.[24]

Partisanship was also less of a factor in lobbying in the nineteenth century compared to today, but nonetheless, it still influenced interest groups. Some corporations and businessmen were heavily involved in financing political campaigns in the late nineteenth century. Keeping with the "lobbyist as a corrupt agent" theme, however, most of what we know about these activities swirls around characters such as industrialist Mark Hanna, who raised funds for the Republican Party and William McKinley's 1896 presidential campaign. Hanna allegedly approached businesses and told them the administration would only do business with companies that contributed to Republican campaigns.[25] The "pay to play" system so often associated with the way Washington works seems to have taken root and sprouted during this time. Lobbyists, according to this view, were less motivated by ideological or partisan connection than they are today. Instead, whoever contributed the most money garnered the best connections with lawmakers and politicians, irrespective of the lobbyists' political orientation.

If the structure of lobbying relied heavily on trade associations, and the style of interest groups was less influenced by partisan polarization, what were the methods of advocates in this earlier era? Casual observers of today's lobbying world, cynical about the process due to revelations of wrongdoing by influence peddlers like Jack Abramoff, would be aghast by the culture of interest-group advocacy in the nineteenth century. Mark Hanna—at least according to early accounts—was only the tip of the iceberg. You would never know it based on enduring negative public attitudes toward lobbyists, but lobbying has come a long way in terms of rules, disclosure, and regulation—and frankly, the types of acceptable behaviors by interest groups and lawmakers alike.

In fact, during the nineteenth century, many of the trade associations actually hired incumbent senators and congressmen to serve as their lobbying representatives. It seems "conflict of interest" rules were a little more relaxed in this earlier era. One scholar, for example, notes that many senators were on retainer to major business interests.[26] He writes that Senator Daniel Webster (Whig-MA) represented numerous clients before federal agencies and on the floor of the U.S. Senate while simultaneously serving as an elected official. Senator Webster was not reluctant to write letters to his constituents about his service in Washington and his clients reminding them to pay their bills.[27] The Massachusetts senator was so successful in mixing lobbying with legislation that John Quincy Adams reportedly remarked that Webster's political tactics were "interwoven with the exploration of a gold-mine for himself."[28]

Lobbying during this period is also typically described as "access-based." Ainsworth recounts the story of Sam Ward, a powerful post–Civil War interest group representative known as the "King of the Lobby," who amazed everyone with his grasp of foreign languages, colorful stories of worldwide travel, poetry, and warm personality.[29]

My friend and former colleague the late Dan Dutko used to tell a similar story about when he first started in the advocacy business. "It used to be all about who you knew. Some lobbyists could build an entire practice around knowing a subcommittee chairman. This one member would more or less take care of a lobbyist and do what he and his clients needed."

Former White House Office of Legislative Affairs Director Patrick Griffin, who has worked inside and outside government for nearly three decades, underscored this point, "It wasn't really necessary to have a grassroots program—or any other new tactics—when 15 white guys were running this town."

Commenting on why his lobbying firm recently acquired a grassroots company, one advocacy professional put it this way:

> It used to be that you could go hire one well-connected lobbyist and every-thing would be taken care of . . . . That world has changed . . . . We wanted to acquire a grassroots firm so we could have a dedicated presence at every level. (Sen.) Pete Domenici (R-N.M.) reads the *Albuquerque Journal* before he reads *The Wall Street Journal*.[30]

Today's lobbying world stands in sharp contrast. In a more open, accountable, fragmented, diffuse, complex and partisan environment, interest groups need more than personal connections in their lobbying toolbox. While it may upset the muckrakers, Mark Hanna's and Sam Ward's tools have dulled in this new world.

Trade association-based lobbying, focus on scandalous behavior of interest groups, and the assumption that if lobbyists were "for" some-thing, it was always the opposite of the public interest are some of the generalizations that capture the way advocacy was described and under-stood during the nineteenth and early-twentieth centuries. Lobbying was also less partisan and campaign-infused than it is today, although it certainly contained a partisan element. And the methods were focused more on personal relationships and access-based advocacy. Still, it is clear that the way academics and the media portrayed lobbying distorted how it really works. This dominant narrative contributed to a highly negative view of interest groups and lobbyists in the U.S. public policy process that persists today. But is there another way to look at those who petition the government for the redress of grievances? Again, getting under the influ-ence with a little more granularity, we find some unexpected positive elements of lobbying.

AN UPSIDE OF INFLUENCE?

Looking under the influence, we see positive aspects of interest-group behavior often overlooked in the popular press. Probing the "upsides of influence" is another critical stop on the journey to reconsider lobbying. Many reading this book may hold a sour or jaded attitude about lobbyists and the advocacy industry. Those views are understandable based on the discussion above about public perceptions, coverage in the media, and the statements of many elected officials. All contribute to an extremely negative view of lobbying in popular culture. But getting under the influence requires challenging some of these myths with an alternative perspective. Although one may not believe it, there is an "upside to advocacy." Interest groups and lobbyists—for all the pounding they take in the popular press—play an increasingly important and in many ways positive role in the American public policy and electoral processes.

Speaking of the role of trade associations in lobbying congressmen, one scholar notes,

> Congressmen themselves regard these national associations as valuable in enabling them to arrive at a clearer understanding of the facts concerning the opinion and the interests of a specific group. Where an association represents a recognizable and clearly defined membership, it is welcomed. If a Washington lobbyist can speak authoritatively for a given number of voters upon a definite issue, the legislators find it easier to arrive at some conclusion as to what the people want."[31]

And while this view is far from dominant over the past century, E. Pendleton Herring concludes his classic work *Group Representation before Congress* with this positive observation and evaluation:

> They [lobbyists or interest groups] represent a healthy democratic development. They have been forced to take the political structure as they found it. Entirely extra-legal and non-constitutional, they have been much maligned and misunderstood. They are part of our representative system, yet due to their heritage from the old lobby they bear the taint of illegitimacy. There is no turning back. These groups must be welcomed for what they are, and certain precautionary regulations worked out. The groups must be understood and their place in government allotted, if not by actual legislation, then by general public realization of their significance.[32]

Most today do not subscribe to Herring's benign conclusions. One notable exception in the popular media is syndicated columnist Charles Krauthammer. He suggests lobbyists change their name to "Redress Petitioners" because these advocates practice some protected by the First Amendment like "speech" or "religion." But not everyone has the time or expertise to "petition the government for redress of grievances," Krauthammer argues. "Lobbyists are people hired to do that for you, so that you can actually stay home with the kids and remain gainfully employed rather than spend your life in the corridors of Washington," he writes.[33] There are some other aspects of lobbying and organized interest that bolster both Herring and Krauthammer's views. First, interest groups and lobbyists help organize citizens and give voice to their concerns, helping people and organizations navigate through the government labyrinth. Advocacy in America began with "lobbyists" representing individuals, not groups.[34] Many of these nineteenth-century advocates helped with veterans claims related to the Civil War or other matters tied to Reconstruction for wealthier individuals. But soon the congressional agenda became clogged with hundreds of individual claims and demands related to the post-Civil War period. Groups began forming to process these issues. These organized efforts helped the legislative process operate more efficiently because Congress could address these concerns on a combined basis instead of individually.

As public policy became more complicated throughout the nineteenth and twentieth centuries, mimicking the growth and expansion of the country, organized interests played an increasingly important role in providing information to lawmakers to help the system work more efficiently. Lawmakers and other policymakers now make thousands of decisions every year, and they often do not know the impact of their actions on local constituencies or the country as a whole. Lobbyists and interest groups routinely help policymakers sort through a variety of questions. In the 2003 debate about the Medicare drug benefit, lawmakers wanted to create a private sector option to the traditional government-run health care program for seniors. Lobbyists from the managed care industry played a role advising lawmakers on how to structure the legislation to involve the maximum number of private plans so that senior citizens would enjoy the maximum number of choices and the benefits of price competition. Similarly, as Congress moved to enact pension reform legislation in 2006, lobbyists from companies with large unfunded pension liabilities provided estimates of how various alternatives would affect workers, retirees, and the solvency of pension plans. In both cases, Congress lacked the data and policy analysis capability to determine the precise impact of their actions. Interest groups had the data and the expertise to pass on to lawmakers.

Consider another contemporary example. During the 2006 debate surrounding the rewrite of the current telecommunications statute, lawmakers were asked to give telephone companies a different way of securing a local franchise to provide video services and compete with cable companies. How would such a move affect telephone companies, cable companies, residential customers, and the local tax base? These were all critical and important questions. Yet without organized interests preparing analyses, making projections, and communicating their views, how were lawmakers supposed to make these judgments? In the modern world, decisions are too complex and numerous and relate to too wide an array of issues to expect elected representatives to make decisions without some additional impact analysis and supporting data—from all interested parties. Are the advocates biased in the information they present? Maybe. But lobbyists provide lawmakers with more information that they had without the advocates' input.

Lawmakers can evaluate and ask more questions—and through this process, ultimately make better public policy decisions. In an increasingly complex and changing public policy environment, lobbyists add information to the process and improve the decision-making culture. Even if the information from two competing groups presents conflicting conclusions, lawmakers can evaluate it and ultimately use it to make more informed decisions.

Interest groups also lobby and bargain with each other, not just with public policymakers. This is an important and overlooked nuance about the American process, particularly as it relates to Congress. Often lawmakers, seeking not to offend one side or the other in a political debate, will ask the warring interest groups to negotiate their differences and bring back a consensus proposal. This is a very different view of the public policy process and lobbyists' role than presented by conventional wisdom or the "textbook" Congress, yet it happens all the time. On issues such as telecommunications legislation, the Clean Air Act, and asbestos litigation reform legislation, lawmakers often ask warring sides to "work it out." After the two sides "reach a deal," Congress ratifies the agreement through legislation.

Recently, the Senate spent months negotiating legislation aimed at asbestos litigation reform. Yet instead of lobbyists pressuring lawmakers to vote a particular way, Senators prodded advocates from the insurance industry, the trial bar, and labor unions to reach an agreement on issues related to the overall cost of the program and caps on damages. Lawmakers served as monitors of the process and refereed the negotiations. Once the various sides reached an agreement, the Senate leadership planned to bring the legislation to the floor and pass the consensus plan. In this particular case, no agreement was ever reached and the legislation died when the 109th Congress adjourned at the end of 2006. But on thorny issues related to environmental, energy, and telecommunications policies in the past two decades, Congress often has ratified agreements brokered between interest groups. Lobbyists are often policy midwives in the birth of many legislative offspring.

They can also help assemble communities of interest. Advocacy organizations and lobbyists organize forums where lawmakers can speak to citizens intensely interested in a specific subject. Many groups sponsor annual "fly-ins" or other Washington-based seminars that provide lawmakers an opportunity to meet with citizens concerned enough about an issue to make a trip to Washington. Every year groups ranging from health insurance executives, to school teachers, to county executives, to water well drillers come to the nation's capital to hear from lawmakers outlining the agenda in DC and how it affects their association, industry, or profession. These meetings become valuable opportunities for lawmakers and citizens to meet face to face and discuss the intersection of the congressional agenda and a particular group's concern. "Some of these events are major productions," Bob Rusbuldt said. "The Independent Insurance Agents & Brokers of America has had a legislative conference in Washington for 30 years, drawing every President of the United States, Speaker of the House, Senate Majority

Leader, and others to address nearly 2,000 insurance agents from every state. Then they go out and meet every member of Congress."

Lobbyists can also spur greater political and governmental participation by American citizens. This type of advocacy depends on motivating citizens to take some kind of action. Corporations, labor unions, environmental interest groups, and trade associations routinely communicate with their employees or membership on a host of political and public policy matters and try to spur their advocacy involvement or political participation.

Consider the managed care industry. It consistently comes under fire from liberal members of Congress opposed to private sector involvement in traditionally government-run health care programs, such as Medicare and Medicaid. Individual companies in this industry, as well as the trade associations that represent them, routinely send out information to their members, their employees, and their customers about how Congress or other policy forums affect their business. Some of these managed care companies regularly organize beneficiaries or even doctors who participate in their health plans to come to Washington and engage in grassroots lobbying. Joining these activities requires the employees to get educated about the policy and the process in Washington. As a result of lobbyists and advocates encouraging their participation, these employees or beneficiaries of health care concerns learn about how Washington works and how they can have an impact. It's "political participation 101," and it gets these individuals involved in grassroots lobbying and the process of government.

PACs also stimulate greater levels of political participation. Giving money to political candidates has long been considered an important form of political participation in America.[35] PACs solicit financial resources from company employees, union members, or trade association members and encourage more participation in the political process through this financial mode.

PACs also provide useful information about the electoral process. Most PACs publish a regular newsletter, for example, updating contributors about key races and contribution decisions made by the PAC. They regularly communicate with their employees about public policy developments and how changes in legislation and regulation affect their company, union, or issue interest. In doing so, corporate employees, union members, or trade association participants learn about the voting decisions of lawmakers and which ones support their cause, and the PAC invests money in these particular campaigns. "Our employees know more about legislative issues, electoral politics, and how it all affects their company and their livelihood due to the communication they receive from our firm's PAC," according to a PAC manager at a Fortune 50 pharmaceutical company.

When it comes to evaluating the role of these campaign financing entities, perspective matters—where you stand depends on where you sit. One person's nefarious special interest money tool is another's access to vital information about how government impacts their company or their job, an interest about which they care deeply.

Beyond lobbyists' organizing and mobilizing roles, there is another upside of influence. In a public policy process growing increasingly large and complex, most organized groups need someone to guide them. "None of the real rules are written down," a Democratic lobbyist observed. "Average people and companies need translators and people to help them through the process. We're kind of like the 'seeing eye dogs' of American public policy," he said.

FOUNDATIONS OF MODERN LOBBYING—A BROADER PERSPECTIVE

By now it should be apparent that lobbying is a large, misunderstood, and dynamic enterprise and in many ways, central to the American public policy-making process. But the dominant narrative about lobbyists tells a different and incomplete story. Dubious characters, no doubt, have been engaged in questionable behavior throughout the history of advocacy. But this generalization is true in any vocation. And the overwhelmingly negative perception of lobbyists and interest groups diverts attention from some of their positive contributions to the American public policy and electoral processes. Just as conventional wisdom overlooks the upsides to influence, it also overlooks some non-obvious ways interest groups and lobbyists conduct their business. Before moving on to the causes and consequences of change in the advocacy industry, we reconsider lobbying from a broader perspective and how it operates beyond its sleazy, pressure-group reputation.

Where, when, and how lobbying occurs is a multidimensional phenomenon. Too often, however, descriptions of advocacy and interest-group behavior focus only on a narrow set of pressure tactics. A broader view is necessary, and an illustration from another part of the political science discipline may be helpful. Scholars argue that the concept of political participation has multiple "modes" (voting, contacting lawmakers, giving money, working on campaigns, etc).[36] Lobbying is no different. For example, many ordinary citizens engage in lobbying activities without even thinking they are involved in the influence-peddling business. Writing a letter to a congressman because your employer or church asked you to do so, paying dues or membership fees to a union or environmental interest group, signing a petition and contributing to a PAC all constitute ways ordinary citizens participate directly or indirectly in lobbying activities.

Much of the writing about interest groups emphasizes only the influence mode. One of the dominant themes of earlier research about advocacy focuses on the pressure side of lobbying—how interest groups persuade. And while that's an important dimension, the activities of professional advocates manifest themselves in many other "modes" as well. A lobbyist for a teachers union attends a hearing to learn more about Congress's education policy agenda for the year. An advocate representing an environmental interest group goes to a press conference and adds his organization's name to a group supporting a new bill imposing tougher emissions standards on the auto industry. A representative from a telecommunications trade association meets with a media consultant to design a new series of advocacy ads. A lobbyist for the railroad industry writes an opening statement for her CEO the night before a Senate hearing on freight regulation. The American Hospital Association's director of government affairs meets with a lawmaker who wants input on the best way for hospitals to broaden the use of electronic medical records. The top lobbyist at a business trade association meets with a polling firm about conducting a new survey about Americans' attitudes toward free trade. A pharmaceutical lobbyist participates in a think tank forum analyzing policies to reduce the price of prescription drugs.

These are not just hypothetical examples of exotic behavior by lobbyists. They are real-life illustrations that occur everyday in the advocacy industry. Indeed, most professional interest advocates spend only a fraction of their time engaged in the behavior most commonly defined as lobbying. Instead of handing out money and plying lawmakers with drinks, lobbyists engage in a diverse set of activities aimed at advancing their client or organization's public policy objectives. The breadth of activities is very different than suggested by conventional wisdom or scandalous and sensational headlines often associated with lobbying. These are intoxicating myths, but they bear little resemblance to the practices plied by today's advocacy industry.

No barriers to entry is another unique feature of the industrial organization of American advocacy and the culture of lobbying. Almost anyone can "speak" for a group, whether consumers, senior citizens, or environmentalists. A more sophisticated understanding of lobbying recognizes the emergence of what might be called "institutionalized mediating organizations." These self-styled advocates for particular causes—American Association of Retired Persons (AARP), Friends of the Earth, National Education Association—are interest groups that claim to speak for a constituency, such as senior citizens, environmentalists, or teachers. But do they? A better understanding of lobbying and interest-group activity recognizes the unique and open character of the American system allows these groups to form and make claims about whom they represent, when the reality may be quite different.

AARP involved itself in many aspects of the 2003 prescription drug debate, including taking positions on behalf of seniors related to complex policy questions like whether the government should negotiate directly with pharmaceutical companies over drug prices and how many private plans could offer coverage in certain geographical areas. These are not the kinds of complex questions a typical 70-year-old man or woman might know about—yet AARP "speaks for them."

Interest groups' causes sometimes shape the reputation of their lobbyists. In Christopher Buckley's spoof on the advocacy industry, *Thank You for Smoking*, the three main characters represent the tobacco, alcohol, and firearms industries. When the trio of lobbyists meets for their regular luncheon, they refer to themselves as The Merchants of Death. Similarly, a Washington lobbyist tells a story—mentioned in the beginning of this chapter—which may be apocryphal, but still makes the point. His third grader came home from school one day and reported a friend had said his father was "not a lobbyist," because he worked for the Environmental Defense Fund and just talked to Congressmen about protecting the environment. Influence peddling in the name of environmental protection is presumably the more acceptable sort.

Finally, the dominant narrative about lobbying, developed in America over the past 200 years, often exaggerates the real political power of interest groups. Contrary to most media accounts, more resources, organizational skills, competence, connections, and so on do not always guarantee success in the lobbying process. While there is a considerable amount of emphasis on the successes of so-called powerful lobbyists and well-organized interest groups, these entities have their share of losses as well. How and why lobbyists "lose" is infrequently explored and not well understood. More attention to the fact that interest groups are not omnipotent may help ordinary citizens view them as less sinister forces as well. Two prominent scholars highlight this point by referencing a *Washington Post* story quoting a knowledgeable advocate who says the, "Dirty little secret about high priced Washington lobbyists (is) . . . they lose a lot".[37]

This insight is largely missing in most scholarly and media depictions of lobbying. Fixed influence or "subgovernment" models of policymaking emphasize how private interests, in largely closed policymaking settings, usually get what they want. These models also suggest a more static model of policy development.[38] But the closed, static process, "private interests always win" paradigm outlined in many accounts of lobbying doesn't seem to fit the real world of advocacy today. The process has changed, but unfortunately our views of it have not.

SUMMARY

This chapter argues no "golden age" of lobbying—a period when advocacy was viewed as a noble or even benign undertaking—ever existed. It demonstrates that lobbyists' image malaise is an enduring crevice etched deep into the American political landscape. The Framers always envisioned factions as both part of the problem and the solution to how citizens express their preferences and grievances to the government, an idea some in the pluralist school of political science embrace, but others vigorously challenge.

Beginning shortly after the Civil War and through the 1970s, trade associations were the dominant force in American lobbying. Classic texts on interest groups underscore this point by only highlighting the lobbying activities of advocates for groups like the Chamber of Commerce, labor unions, the National Association of Manufacturers, and other member level groups.[39] Individual companies and specialized lobbying firms did not emerge as a more dominant force until post-1970. Throughout that over 100-year period, the reputation of lobbyists and their work remained highly suspect in the minds of most Americans as it does today. But little attention has been given to some of the upsides of influence—the positive contributions of interest groups in elections or the public policy process. This chapter outlines a variety of activities that demonstrate how lobbying enhances both citizens' participation and the quality of the lawmaking process.

Finally, lobbying and interest groups are viewed through too narrow of a prism. Most scholarly and media attention focuses only on pressure tactics and scandalous anecdotes. It also tends to exaggerate the real power of interest groups in American politics. Pendleton Herring recognized this fact in his classic text on lobbying when he observed that many bills would pass with or without the pressure of lobbyists.[40] But beyond some notable exceptions, the trajectory of research and press coverage both reinforces lobbyists' image problems and also limits our understanding of the role these advocates play in the public policy and electoral processes. Getting under the influence requires looking at the activities and impact of interest groups from a broader perspective.

With these foundational ideas in mind, we've started down the path of reconsidering lobbying. Now it's time to move to the heart of this volume—describing the causes and consequences of the changing lobbying world. In the next chapter, evidence for this change is presented. Compared to the trade association-based, pre-1970s model, the lobbying world has undergone dramatic transformation over the past 30 years. Next we explore how lobbying has changed and why it has at an increasingly rapid velocity. The advocacy industry is structurally much larger and tactically complex than suggested by conventional wisdom. Chapter 3 continues to get under the influence, reconsidering the lobbying world by describing this growth and complexity in more detail.

NOTES

1. This was quoted in Connor McGrath, *Lobbying in Washington, London, and Brussels: The Persuasive Communication of Political Communication* (Lewiston, NY: Edwin Mellen Press, 2005), 5.
2. A likely apocryphal story often repeated among Washington lobbyists, especially those who often clash with environmental interest groups.
3. Quoted in Pendleton Herring, *Group Representation before Congress* (Baltimore, MD: Johns Hopkins University Press, 1929), 35.

4. Ibid.
5. C.B. Libsen and S. Lesher, *Vested Interests: A Lobbyist's Account of Washington Power and How it Really Works* (Garden City, NY: Doubleday, 1977), 3; McGrath, *Lobbying in Washington, London, and Brussels*, 4.
6. Ibid. Lobbyist David Rehr quoted, 4.
7. Ibid. 6.
8. Ibid.
9. Ibid. M. Pertschuk quoted, 6–7.
10. Ibid. Well-known Democratic Washington lobbyists as quoted, 7.
11. McIver J. Weatherford, *Tribes on the Hill: The U.S. Congress Rituals and Realities*, Revised Edition (Massachusetts, MA: Bergin and Garvey Publishers, 1985), 133.
12. Federalist Papers (New York, NY: Longman, 2004).
13. Ibid. 10.
14. See, for example, Ernest Griffith, *Impasse of Democracy* (New York, NY: Harrison-Hilton Books, 1939).
15. Berry and Wilcox, *The Interest Group Society*. 4th ed. (New York: Pearson–Longman, 2007), 158.
16. Larry Sabato, PAC Power, 1984, quoted in Mark J. Rozell, Clyde Wilcox, and David Madland, *Interest Groups in American Campaigns: The New Face of Electioneering* (Washington, D.C.: CQ Press, 2006), 4.
17. Ibid. 4–5.
18. Grant McConnell, *Private Power and American Democracy* (New York, NY: Knopf, 1966).
19. Kenneth M. Goldstein, *Interest Groups, Lobbying and Participation in America* (Cambridge, UK: Cambridge University Press, 1999), 22.
20. David Truman, *The Governmental Process* (New York, NY: Alfred Knopf, 1951), 66–107.
21. Ibid. 76.
22. Ibid. 75.
23. Ibid. 21.
24. Gary Mucciaroni, *Reversals of Fortune: Public Policy and Private Interests* (Washington, D.C.: The Brookings Institution, 1995), 10.
25. Rozell, Wilcox, and Madland, *Interest Groups in American Campaigns*.
26. Scott H. Ainsworth, Analyzing Interest Groups: Group Influence on People and Policies (New York, NY: W.W. Norton, 2002), 103.
27. Ibid.
28. Weatherford, *Tribes on the Hill*, 116.
29. Ibid. 104.
30. Patrick O'Connor, "Downtown Firm Acquires Down Home Shop," *Politico*, June 28, 2007. Accessed online (www.politico.com).
31. Herring, *Group Representation Before Congress*, 243.
32. Ibid. 268.
33. Charles Krauthammer, In Defense of Lobbying, *Washington Post*. Friday, February 29, 2008 p. A 19.
34. Ainsworth, *Analyzing Interest Groups*.
35. Sidney Verba and Norman Nie, *Participation in America: Political Democracy and Social Equality* (New York, NY: Harper and Row, 1972).
36. Ibid.
37. Berry and Wilcox, *The Interest Group Society*, 115.
38. Lee A. Fritchler, *Smoking and Politics*. 2nd ed. (Englewood Cliffs, NJ: Prentice Hall, 1975).
39. Indeed Herring's title *Group Representation Before Congress* demonstrates the dominant view at the time—group or trade association level influence.
40. Herring, *Group Representation Before Congress*, 246–247.

CHAPTER

3

THE NEW ADVOCACY INDUSTRY—GROWTH AND INSTITUTIONALIZATION IN THE LOBBYING WORLD

With all the lobbyists in Washington today, I hire a few just so they don't lobby against me.

Government Relations Executive

In 1968 I was number "68." I was the sixty-eighth lobbyist registered with the Clerk of the House that year and that was about it. (According to the Clerk of the House in 2007 there are over 30,000 registered lobbyists.)

Tommy Boggs—Washington Lobbyist

Lobbying in America has fundamentally changed during the past 40 years, but our understanding and perceptions of it still lag far behind. This chapter focuses specifically on some key aspects of this transformation—the tremendous growth and institutionalization of the advocacy world since the 1970s. What was once an ad hoc collection of individuals or associations is now a full-blown industry, complete with its own trade, professional, and membership groups.[1] Practices once carried out informally are now more structured and systematic—the ad hoc has become organized. And just as institutionalization affects the practices and composition of public entities such as Congress, it also has impacted the private lobbying world over the past 40 years, creating bigger and more elaborate structures, as well as different modes of behavior.[2]

Today's style, structure, and substance of lobbying stand in stark contrast to advocacy practices in the 1950s and 1960s, then heavily dominated by peak associations such as the American Medical Association, the National Association of Manufacturers (NAM), the Chamber of Commerce, and the AFL-CIO.

These changes did not occur in a vacuum. They are a direct result of other dynamic currents in Washington that produced a more structurally diverse and tactically varied industry. Indeed, examining changes in the external environment of interest groups and lobbyists is important in better understanding the role these groups and individuals play in American government. Too often journalists and academics focus only on the impact lobbyists have on public policy and not on the way changes in the advocates' world affect how they pursue and structure their jobs. So how has this world changed? Continuing our reconsideration of lobbying, let's next turn to documenting the expansion and growing complexity of the advocacy industry in America over the past half-century.

THE SIZE OF THE INTEREST GROUP/LOBBYING WORLD IN EARLIER STUDIES

Interest-group studies hold a venerable history in political science. Many classic texts in group theory provide some potentially useful estimates about the size of the advocacy universe and its role in American public policymaking. We begin our examination of changes in the advocacy industry by reviewing the findings from the older literature and piecing together various estimates and descriptions of the lobbying industry's size and scope. Unfortunately, deciphering historical information about the character and complexion of interest groups and lobbying in America requires a bit of sleuthing. But regardless of the shortcomings of using multiple disparate sources, with a small amount of detective work, the mosaic of growth in the advocacy industry becomes clear.

Lobbying was a much smaller enterprise before World War II. Political scientist E. Pendleton Herring writes that in the 1920s there were "well over 500 lobbies at work in Washington." Herring also observes there were "over one hundred trade associations" in Washington.[3] He reached these estimates by imprecise means, such as looking through phone books for names of associations, but they are about the only numbers available and provide a rough baseline of the size of the lobbying world. Even earlier scholars recognize the limits and challenges of quantifying the number of Washington representatives and lobbyists. Herring concludes, "Certain difficulties are encountered, however, in attempting to count them one by one. It has never been done, and it is safe to say that it will never be done with entire success. They are too many and too changing to submit to the statistician."[4]

About 50 years later, by 1977, the number of Washington-based trade associations had increased to 1,300, according to published sources.[5] Not necessarily a boom in a half-century. Yet just three years later—in 1980—the estimate had increased by over 30 percent to 1,700.[6] Lobbying, like politics, is always changing and transforming, but the velocity of that transformation shifted into mach speed in the late 1970s and 1980s.

One study of a 1981 lobbying directory found that 40 percent of the groups had formed since 1960, with the greatest growth between 1970 and 1980.[7] Political scientist Frank Baumgartner reinforces this point by showing the number of trade associations more than doubled between the mid-1960s and the 1990s, although growth had leveled off by 2004.[8] Not only were there more trade associations in general, but also the proportion headquartered in Washington DC and with a lobbying mission grew exponentially. One study estimates the proportion of national associations with their headquarters in DC rose from 21 percent to 31 percent between 1970 and 1984.[9] According to Berry and Wilcox, "During this time, many trade associations felt it was necessary to move to Washington so that they could focus more on lobbying, and Washington replaced New York as the city with the most trade groups."[10]

Corporate America also joined in the lobbying growth game during this same period. One scholar estimates that before 1920, only one corporation had a permanent DC lobbying outpost. By 1978, the number grew to 175, and by 2004, more than 600 had Washington offices.[11] Other scholars show a similar pattern. For example, one reports the number of major corporations operating offices in Washington increased from 50 in 1961 to 545 in 1982.[12] And in 2006, the corporate investment in Washington continued with companies such as Google, Valero Energy, Herbalife International, Walgreens, and GoDaddy.com each deciding to form their own DC lobbying offices for the first time.[13]

In addition to growth in trade associations and corporate Washington offices, spending on lobbying also grew. One estimate suggests overall spending on federal lobbying nearly doubled between 1999 and 2005 from about $116.3 million per month to $200 million per month. This same journalist found that there were twice as many registered lobbyists in 2006—about 30,000—compared to just six years earlier.[14] But registered lobbyists form just a small portion of all those involved in the lobbying industry, which also includes media consultants, pollsters, fund-raisers, and grassroots firms. Combining all of these ancillary and support services—each of which has grown—produces a much bigger advocacy industry beyond just registered lobbyists.

These data come from disparate sources and measure various aspects of the advocacy industry, but they all point to the same conclusion—the lobbying industry ballooned over the past 40 years, experiencing its own advocacy "baby boom" of sorts. Others came to the same conclusion over a decade ago:

> Despite reservations inherent in all data, all available evidence points in the same direction, namely that there are many more interest groups operating in Washington today than in the years before World War II . . . there are

good reasons to believe that far-reaching changes took place during the past 30 years in the system of interest groups in the United States, a conclusion shared by virtually all recent observers.[15]

Some dimensions of growth leveled off during the 1990s, such as the number of corporate Political Action Committees (PACs) and the percentage of Fortune 500 companies with Washington lobbying offices. This slowdown, however, is more an artifact of trends like industry consolidation through mergers and acquisitions or sheer saturation. During this same period, however, other elements, such as e-advocacy consultants, professional fundraising firms, and grassroots organizers, emerged and contributed to the growth of the overall advocacy industry.

THE WASHINGTON REPRESENTATIVES BOOK AND OTHER EVIDENCE OF GROWTH

Another valuable source of data on the lobbying industry is the so-called "Washington Representatives book," published annually since 1977.[16] It demonstrates the same mosaic of change, only in different hues. Most major law firms, lobbyists, trade associations, and corporate Washington offices purchase this annual publication both to check out the competition and as a source of new client prospecting. "If Microsoft has a problem on the Hill, you check out the Washington Representatives book to find out who lobbies for them and whether or not they need additional help," one veteran lobbyist with a major public affairs firm in DC said. It lists registered lobbyists and their clients, and then lists all interest groups—such as corporations, trade associations, non-profit advocacy groups, and labor unions, among others—and who is registered to lobby on their behalf. Unfortunately, it does not list other components of the advocacy industry such as media relations, grass roots, polling or communications. It also relies on self-filing by individuals and organizations. No one is compelled by law or regulation to pass their information on to this publication. Still, each year an updated Washington Representatives book provides an invaluable source of information about which lobbyists represent various interests. It includes a cross-sectional snapshot of the people and organizations engaged in the lobbying industry in any given year. It is the bible in the church of lobbying.

Reviewing the books longitudinally provides a clear picture of the growth and change in the advocacy world. Counting the number of Washington representatives and advocacy organizations listed each year and comparing the number over time indicates that while the pace of growth has slowed in recent years, since 1977 the number of individuals and organizations listed in Washington Representatives has tripled, with the fastest growth occurring from the late 1970s to the early 1990s (Figure 3-1).

FIGURE 3-1 THE GROWTH OF THE WASHINGTON LOBBYING
INDUSTRY—NUMBER OF INDIVIDUALS AND ORGANIZATIONS IN WASHINGTON
REPRESENTATIVES BOOK 1977–2006.

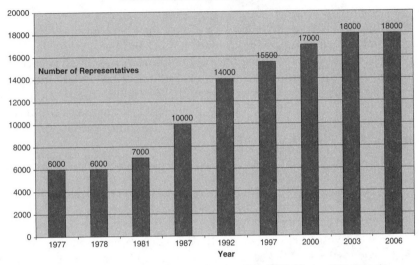

Source: Figures taken from *Washington Representatives*, 1st–30th ed. (Washington, D.C.: Columbia Books Inc., 1977–2006).

The book also reveals growth in other ways. Since the Washington Representatives book lists organizations and their lobbyists, a bigger advocacy industry should also mean more total pages in each volume. Viewing the data this way shows a similar but even more dramatic pattern. As Figure 3-2 demonstrates, the number of pages is over seven times larger in 2006 compared to 1977.[17]

The advocacy industry has also grown increasingly specialized. As noted in the previous chapter, associations did the primary lobbying in the first part of the twentieth century through World War II. In the past 40 years, there has been a trend toward more specialization—individual firms and organizations choosing to rely less exclusively on peak associations and instead institutionalizing and growing their own government affairs structures internally. Analyzing the Washington Representatives book over time confirms this trend. Figure 3-3 compiles the number of subspecialties listed for three major industries—telecommunications, energy, and health care.

As with the other overall trends, growth in these sub sectors occurred rapidly during the 1970s and 1980s. Some industries, such as health care, have continued to grow, while others, such as telecommunications and energy, have leveled off. Part of the slowdown evidenced in these latter two industries, discussed in more detail below, is a function of industry consolidation, mergers, and acquisitions among companies in these sectors

FIGURE 3-2 THE GROWTH OF THE WASHINGTON LOBBYING INDUSTRY—NUMBER
OF PAGES IN THE WASHINGTON REPRESENTATIVES BOOK 1977–2006.

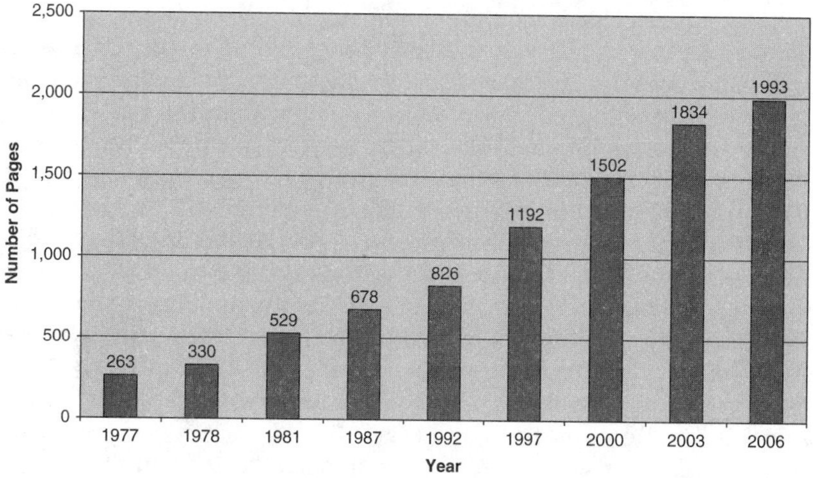

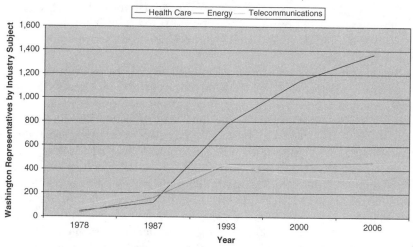

Source: Figures taken from *Washington Representatives*, 1st–30th ed. (Washington, D.C.: Columbia
Books Inc., 1977–2006).

during the 1990s. Health care, on the other hand, has seen the opposite
trend. More companies have been formed during the last 40 years,
and health care spending—both in the public and private sectors—has
continued to expand. Similarly, as public spending has increased, so have

FIGURE 3-3 THE GROWTH OF THE WASHINGTON LOBBYING INDUSTRY—
AN EXPANDING NUMBER OF LOBBYING SUBSPECIALTIES (HEALTH CARE, ENERGY,
AND TELECOMMUNICATIONS 1978–2006).

Source: Figures taken from *Washington Representatives*, 1st–30th ed. (Washington, D.C.: Columbia
Books Inc., 1977–2006).

the rules, regulations, and legislation—all requiring additional government relations attention.

The increasing specialization of lobbying and government affairs is a major reason why the advocacy industry has grown so rapidly over the past four decades. And not only have subspecialties burgeoned within industries in terms of a Washington presence, but this proliferation has stimulated secondary demands for a host of ancillary services like public relations, law, grassroots advocacy, and media consulting. Former Congressman Bob Walker, now the CEO of Wexler-Walker, a venerable DC lobbying firm, recently explained these trends in lobbying as paralleling transformations in the U.S. economy.[18] He describes lobbyists as starting out as "hunters and gatherers," looking for information in a highly relational and access-based environment. Then lobbyists moved to an "agriculture" era, when they grew their own information by adding analyses and interpretation to legislation and regulation. Next the system underwent its own "industrial revolution," as new products and services like grass roots, polling, and public relations were added. We are now in what Walker calls "the information age," where specialized information and knowledge about process and public policy is key.

The Public Affairs Council in Washington DC, is another valuable source of information concerning more recent trends in the advocacy industry. The Council houses an organization called the Foundation for Public Affairs that conducts ongoing studies of trends in corporate public affairs. Interestingly, the founding of this organization during the 1950s provides a metaphor for the growth of the lobbying industry. According to Brian Hawkinson, executive director of the Foundation for Public Affairs, it was President Eisenhower and some corporate executives who played a role in the organization's creation. "President Eisenhower saw the growth of organized labor lobbying as a potential threat to corporate interests," Hawkinson explained. "The Public Affairs Council was formed to help corporations respond."

Business interest groups responding to real or perceived threats to their competitive position—either from intra-industry competitors or outside threats, such as labor unions, consumer groups, non-governmental organizations (NGOs), governmental actions and regulations—all can spur changes in the size, scope, and structure of business interests and their lobbyists. The Public Affairs Council has monitored these trends over the past decade, noting changes in how corporations organize and staff to meet these new challenges. These studies offer a unique window on how institutionalization of the interest group universe has unfolded in this important sector of lobbying.

In a survey of about 400 companies conducted every other year since 2000, the Public Affairs Council has asked corporate Washington offices to categorize their annual budgets in Washington in $500,000 increments, from less than $500,000 to over $7.5 million. The surveys demonstrate growth in the advocacy industry even during just a six-year period. For example, the number reporting spending "$4 million or more increased from 17 percent to 26 percent between 2000 and 2006."[19] The 2006 study also finds 42 percent of corporations report increased spending and use of outside lobbyists and consultants since 2000. The Public Affairs Council notes that these outside lobbyists "supplement" existing staff rather than replace them—another sign of the overall growth of the advocacy industry.[20] They also find that 42 percent project their use of outside lobbyists to expand, which points to even more growth ahead in the advocacy world.

Lawyers are part of the growth calculus too. It would be hard to imagine a growing advocacy industry without an accompanying rise in the number of attorneys. And during the past 40 years, a surge in the legal community has unfolded almost in lockstep with increases in other areas of lobbying. One recent estimate notes the number of Washington lawyers expanded from 11,000 in 1972 to around 63,000 in 1994, nearly a sixfold increase in just over 20 years. The number then ballooned to 81,000 by 2005—nearly 25 percent more in about a decade.[21]

Corporations, trade associations, and other interest groups use lawyers for a variety of purposes in the advocacy world. Some law firms have so-called government affairs practices. These individuals are usually former members of Congress, legislative or executive branch staffers, and sometimes even "non-lawyers" who lobby on Capitol Hill. They provide strategic government relations advice, set up meetings with lawmakers and staff, and do many of the traditional functions of a lobbyist. Other practice areas in these firms might have specialists in various policy areas who could provide policy advice, draft legislation, or craft regulatory filings.

In 2007, as the new Democratic majority commenced a lobbying oversight agenda, many law firms added practice groups focused specifically on helping interest groups navigate congressional investigations. The pharmaceutical, managed care, energy, and student loan industries were in the crosshairs of numerous congressional investigative panels. Former staffers from congressional committees with active oversight agendas were added to the ranks of major law firms to provide this much-needed lobbying expertise. This change in law firms is another—often overlooked—part of the growth of the lobbying industry.[22] How changes in partisan control of Congress affected the oversight agenda is explored in more detail in Chapters 4 and 5.

As the advocacy industry has grown and the external environment of interest groups has continued to change, the myriad services these lawyers provide, from lobbying, legislative drafting, legal advice, and regulatory filings, have also grown in importance and size.

PUBLIC INTEREST GROUPS/NON-GOVERNMENTAL ORGANIZATIONS

Most of the evidence in this chapter demonstrating interest group growth focuses on corporate or business-oriented trade associations and the lobbyists they deploy. But other segments of the advocacy world also have proliferated during the last 40 years, including citizens groups and public interest groups. Some have referred to this as the rise of "movement politics."[23] Consumer groups and environmental organizations, such as the Consumers Union and the Environmental Defense Fund, burgeoned during this period, challenging corporate and business interests with calls for higher taxes and more regulations to advance their particular agendas. As we shall see later in this volume, the growth of public interest groups has been both a cause and an effect of greater activism by business too. As the voices of consumer and environmental groups grew louder, as the scope of conflict expanded, businesses often responded with even greater investments in the government affairs and lobbying arena.

Non-governmental organizations also have become another challenge with which business groups contend. These organizations pressure corporations to spend more on environmental remediation, raise worker salaries, and stop outsourcing jobs. Corporate interests during the 1990s in particular felt the impact of the growing number of NGOs and decided beefing up their government affairs efforts was one way to contend with this threat.

Interest group scholar Jack Walker notes this pattern of mobilization and countermobilization. "Most of the groups formed in the 1950s and 1960s were dedicated to liberal causes, but they were matched almost immediately by conservative counter movements that grew even stronger in the 1970s and 1980s."[24] A prominent Democratic Washington lobbyist notes that some of the growth in lobbying during this period was reciprocal or symbiotic. "It's hard to separate the growth in business lobbying from public interest groups. They kind of fed off each other. Businesses changed their approach in Washington because of the growth of public interest groups in the safety and environmental area, for example. And the public interest groups expanded because of what business was doing." Galbraith's notion of countervailing power was on display again as business responded to public interest groups.

THE RISE OF THE POLITICAL ACTION COMMITTEE

The proliferation of PACs offers another indication of the burgeoning growth and institutionalization of the advocacy industry. PACs, like many other aspects of the lobbying industry, grew as a direct result of strategic political decisions by interest groups mixed with judicial, regulatory, and legislative changes. During the early 1970s, right before and after Watergate, Congress passed the Federal Election Campaign Act (1971) and some major amendments to that act (1974). The Federal Election Commission followed up these bills with its so-called Sun-PAC decision in 1975, a major ruling clarifying certain legislative ambiguity. And the Supreme Court finalized this framework for a time with its *Buckley* v. *Valeo* decision in 1976. The legislative, regulatory, and judicial decisions in several ways defined how interest groups could contribute and participate in federal elections. Corporations had been barred from using their own treasury funds for direct contributions to federal candidates since the Tillman Act passed in 1907. What was unclear was whether businesses, or labor unions for that matter, could use their own treasury funds to administer PAC. Several unions had PACs in the late 1960s, but very few corporations followed suit.

As Figure 3-4 shows, the total number of PACs grew significantly during roughly the 15-year period between 1974 and 1989. Like some other aspects of the lobbying industry, PACs growth skyrocketed during the 1970s and 1980s and then leveled off. As with the slowdown in the number of Washington representatives in certain industry subspecialties mentioned earlier in this chapter, some of the leveling off during the 1990s occurred due to pure saturation, industry consolidation, and mergers where two or three corporate PACs may have been combined into one.

The telecommunications industry provides a good example. Right after the AT&T divestiture in 1982, seven new Regional Bell Operating Companies

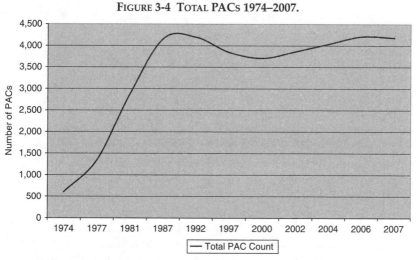

FIGURE 3-4 TOTAL PACs 1974–2007.

Source: Figures taken from the Federal Election Commission, http://www.fec.gov/press/press2007/20070710paccount.shtml.

were spun off—so one company in effect became eight (Ma Bell and its seven new babies). Yet over the past 25 years, these eight have consolidated back into three—AT&T (combined with Ameritech, Bellsouth, Pacific Telesis, and Southwestern Bell), Verizon (the product of two other merged baby Bells, Nynex and Bell Atlantic), and Qwest (the new name for U.S. West). This consolidation means eight PACs in the 1990s became three by 2007. Consolidation in the energy, financial services, and technology industries caused similar fluctuations in the numbers.

Banking, financial services, and securities firms also underwent consolidation, which made the number of PACs appear smaller. For example, during the 1990s corporate mergers such as J.P. Morgan with Chase, Wells Fargo with Norwest, Deutche Bank with Alex Brown, and Citigroup with Salomon Brothers/Smith Barney contracted the overall number of PACs. But the bottom-line pattern in PAC growth, like other measures of the advocacy industry, shows they proliferated and were used as a campaign finance tool by increasing numbers of interest groups.

Federal Election Commission data reveals another interesting difference between corporate and labor PACs. While labor involvement in campaign finance also grew during the 1970s, the rate of growth, as well as the overall number of union PACs was lower. Two main factors account for these differences. First, the universe of large businesses with the resources and incentives to form PACs is bigger. There are more telecommunications, defense, banking, chemical, energy, transportation, and retail—to name a few—business interests than large organized labor unions. Second, labor's issues tend to affect all union members in a similar way. For example, legislation related to paying a particular wage level to federal contractors would have similar effects on many unions. Less diversity of interests means many smaller unions could rely on larger groups like the Teamsters or AFL-CIO to make political contributions for them. Still, as the figure demonstrates, unions did increase their involvement in PACs, they just did it at a slower rate than did business.

Prior to the PAC growth during the 1970s and 1980s, lobbyists and interest groups used to approach campaign finance in an ad hoc, unorganized manner. Some lobbyists might raise money for lawmakers with whom they were particularly close. A business would gather contributions for a congressman or senator who served on a key committee overseeing the company's industry. But there was little structure, strategy, or organization underlying these activities. Once the legal and regulatory environment clarified in the 1970s, PACs, particularly among corporations, proliferated quickly. PACs provided businesses a way to operate in campaign finance and government relations in a much more systematic and institutionalized manner. Companies hired full-time PAC directors and staff. These individuals could determine the lawmakers most helpful to the company based on voting analyses, then develop specialized giving plans maximizing and targeting contributions. Most importantly, they could educate employees about the importance of contributing to the PAC and organize internal fundraising drives, maximizing the amount of money in the corporate coffers available for distribution.

This more systematic approach to both raising and giving money, educating employees about the role of government and policy in the affairs of the business, and mobilizing corporate political participation all grew during the 1970s and 1980s, representing a fundamentally new form of involvement by business in the electoral and policy process.

PAC growth reshaped the lobbying world in another way due to a confluence of events. On the money side of campaigns, changes in federal law limited individual contributions while the cost of elections continued to rise. This meant lawmakers in Congress had to spend a lot more time raising money. At the same time, as the congressional power structure became more decentralized (See Chapter 4), PACs offered members of Congress with heightened demands for money a new national fundraising platform. Washington lobbyist Bert Carp underscores this point:

> Congressmen and senators used to raise money primarily from their states and districts. But as the demands for money grew, and the supply from big donors became more limited, PACs and lobbyists provided a national fundraising resource for elected officials. You used to have to rely on your constituents or maybe a committee chairman to help you raise money. PACs set members free from that, but also had the unintended effect of making lobbyists more important than ever in the money game.

Related to the growth in PACs, and the voracious demands for money among elected officials, was the growth of another cottage industry in Washington—the professional fund-raiser or fundraising firm. Often individuals in these organizations cut their teeth as party fund-raisers for the various national committees, such as the Republican National Committee, the Democratic National Committee, and their respective congressional campaign committee arms. And while these firms are not technically part of the lobbying industry, they are related. Lobbyists, for example, may work closely with fund-raisers to build new relationships or cement old ones. And as the advocacy industry institutionalized, it opened the door for the growth of specialized fund-raisers and money-raising organizations. One veteran lobbyist with a well-established bipartisan firm put it this way, "In the old days, lobbyists used to raise money for members of Congress on their own. As the business grew and got more complicated, the professional fund-raiser is another service a lobbyist can use to help him do his job more effectively."

In the 1970s, very few if any specialized fundraising firms existed. By 2007, there were dozens of individuals and firms—almost all dedicated to one partisan camp or the other—helping lawmakers and lobbyists in the money chase. It's another illustration of the growth and institutionalization of the advocacy industry in the past 40 years.

Republican fundraising consultant Tom Hammond recalls, "When I first started in the business 20 years ago, in the mid-to-late 1980s, there were very few people who did fundraising full time. I can only think of two or three. Normally the congressman's chief of staff on a part-time basis did the money-raising job. But today the whole process is much more formal and sophisticated. Now there are 20 or 30 individuals or firms that work in this area. They are full-time, professional fund-raisers for hire."

Most of the growth in professional fund-raising occurred immediately after the sharp rise in PACs during the 1980s and the Republican takeover of Congress in 1994. "Most of the people who do fundraising fulltime raise money from PACs," Hammond explained. "Before PACs existed, the number of professional fund-raisers was much smaller. It's almost like as the number of PACs grew, the cadre of people trying to raise money from them did too."

The Republican Congress in 1994 also raised the ante, according to several long-time observers. Before the GOP takeover, it was common for a PAC to give $250–$500 to an incumbent. Once Republicans won the majority—and wanted to hang on—the numbers increased considerably. "The whole mentality changed after 1994," Hammond says. "They wanted to hang on to their majority, and the fundraising operations went into high gear. The congressional leaders also pushed hard for members to raise money," he said. The data supports his observation. For example, as the Democrats' 40-year reign of Congress was coming to an end, PAC contributions increased at a 6 percent clip between the 1990 and 1992 campaign cycles and then grew more modestly by only 2 percent between the 1992 and 1994 cycles. After the GOP took over the majority in 1994, however, the ramp-up quickly commenced. PAC contributions soared by 16 percent between the 1994 and 1996 cycles, and increased again by 8 percent between the 1996 and 1998 cycles. And between 1998 and 2000, the rate of growth of PAC contributions ballooned by double digits, increasing by 14 percent. Republicans knew they had to work hard to raise money to protect their majority. And the new cottage industry of fundraising firms helped them do just that for the next 12 years. Figure 3-5 supports this Republican fund-raiser's conjecture. After Republicans took control of Congress following the 1994 election, the rate of increase in fund-raising by the National Republican Congressional Committee (NRCC) swelled.

Better linkages and coordination between these professional fund-raisers and lobbyists also grew during this period. For example, while most

FIGURE 3-5 REPUBLICAN FUND-RAISING GROWTH AFTER CAPTURING
CONGRESSIONAL MAJORITY IN 1994.

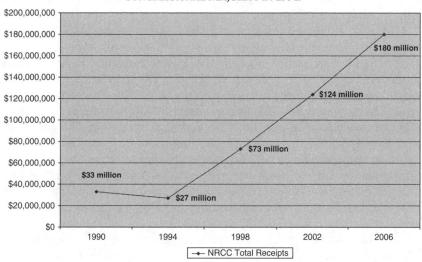

Source: Figures taken from the Federal Election Commission, http://www.fec.gov/press/press2007/partyfinal2006/repfederalye06.xls.

fund-raisers are hired by members of Congress to build their campaign coffers, some government relations departments of interest groups have begun hiring them to help coordinate their fundraising and contributions with the advocacy mission of the organization. Many expect the connections between professional fund-raisers and lobbyists only will continue to get closer in the years ahead.

All of these factors combined to spawn a number of new firms specializing in raising money from PACs and for members of Congress and their leadership PACs. Like many aspects of the interest-group world, campaign finance institutionalized over the past 40 years. The proliferation of specialized fundraising firms is just another example of the growth of the advocacy industry in Washington.

THE RISE OF GRASS ROOTS—ORGANIZING THE GROUND WAR

Another indicator of growth in the advocacy industry has been the increased reliance on grassroots lobbying. Interest groups have become more adept at mobilizing citizens—or at least conveying the perception of voter participation—to help their lobbying campaigns. Measuring grassroots advocacy is difficult because unlike direct lobbying or PACs, grassroots activities are governed by very few rules. For example, grassroots firms or the interest groups that hire them do not report expenditures in the same way traditional lobbyists do with the Congress.

However, analyzing references to the phrase "grassroots lobbying" in the press is one way to document the growth in this practice. Back in the 1970s, the term was hardly mentioned in publications that cover Washington closely, such as *The New York Times*, *The Washington Post* or *National Journal*. Yet from about the late 1980s to the mid-1990s, the same time lobbying was burgeoning in other areas, mentions of the phrase "grassroots lobbying" exploded.[25] One scholar notes that "after slowly rising throughout the 1980s, the number of articles mentioning grassroots lobbying tripled in the early 1990s."[26] He goes on to demonstrate that growth in grassroots tactics by corporations and trade associations account for most of this increase. The Public Affairs Council also reports a dramatic increase in the number of attendees at its annual conference on "grassroots government relations techniques."[27] Many businesses are also institutionalizing this form of advocacy. As this same scholar describes it, ". . . most Fortune 500 companies now have full-time grassroots organizers and detailed plans of action that they can implement when needed. Efforts that were once ad hoc have now become permanent and official divisions of many corporations."[28]

Moreover, reliance on grassroots lobbying—by corporations, trade associations, and unions—has also spawned a cottage industry of independent grassroots consultants who help identify and mobilize citizens for interest-group clients. One scholar notes, " . . . a whole new cadre of consultants who specialize in orchestrating mass participation has cropped up. Professional directories from *Campaigns and Elections* magazine show that the number of grassroots firms has grown every year and that more than 150 firms now specialize in stirring up mass participation."[29]

Firms like Bonner & Associates and DCI provide a range of grassroots services to clients, utilizing a host of former campaign operatives who understand the mechanics of organizing and motivating volunteers to write, call, visit personally, or e-mail lawmakers. "We left campaigns behind, but we brought the campaign mentality with us," a veteran political operative remarked. These firms can add political support to a client's legislative initiative.

Some of the demand for grassroots advocacy comes from elected officials seeking political cover and support for their positions. "If you want to protect your funding you need a march on Washington to demonstrate support," a lawmaker recently told a lobbyist for a major health care company. Grass roots can give literal "legs" to such a march, making advocacy more ambulatory. This connection is explored in more detail in a future chapter, examining the strong linkage between the *supply* of grass roots and the *demand* from elected officials.

Grassroots advocates are also growing increasingly sophisticated in their use of the Internet as an organizing and mobilization tool. "We used to think of the Internet primarily as an advertising device," a former Republican Party official said. "Now 'point and click' can mean thousands of messages to a congressman's office or generate people to walk the halls of Congress." Chalk up the growth of grassroots firms as evidence of another component of the burgeoning Washington advocacy establishment.

INCREASING THE SUPPLY OF ADVERTISING

Hill staffers, lawmakers, and other public officials inside the Beltway are major consumers of information in specialized print and online publications. *Roll Call, The Politico, The Hill, CongressDaily,* and *National Journal* are just a few of the major outlets that are "must reads" among the most informed policymakers. These publications focus just on the Washington world. Well-read advocates and policymakers also need to keep up with *The Washington Post, The Washington Times, The New York Times,* and of course other online publications and influential blogs.

Over the past two decades, the media universe has fragmented and grown larger. The broadcast networks now compete with Fox News, CNN, MSNBC, CNBC, and even with some Internet sites, such as Drudge Report or Daily Kos. So the number of outlets viewed by influential political eyes has changed as well. Americans under 30 now say they get the bulk of their political news from comedy cable shows like *The Daily Show*. As the number of viewers migrates to other forms of media, so do the advertisers. And the fragmented media world provides opportunities not only to sell products, but also to push a lobbying message or an interest-group image campaign. Moreover, after identifying communities of interest, these advocacy campaigns can encourage and provide specific avenues for citizen action. Welcome to the new world of advocacy advertising—another growth sector in the institutionalized lobbying world. "We used to have to rely on *The New York Times, The Washington Post* or the major broadcast networks to get out our message or to set the agenda," one former senior communications advisor to the House Republicans recalls. "Now the world is completely different. You can both start stories or set the agenda in numerous places—online, print, and on cable, or broadcast. These same venues need to be monitored and sometimes responded to as well. There are just a lot more places to play offense or defense," he says.

And these new outlets also create myriad opportunities for creative approaches to advertising—which in turn generate new opportunities and growth for businesses in this area. Part of the growing lobbying world centers on specialized media firms that work on everything from paid media production of broadcast, cable, print, and online ads to strategies about the best way to target and deploy this content. In the new media world, deciding where to advertise is just half the battle; getting people to take action is now part of the equation too. The number of firms engaged in this area of advocacy, the amount of money spent, and the sheer volume of advertising all illustrate the growth and change in this part of the advocacy industry.

Mobil Oil Corporation (now Exxon-Mobil) pioneered experimentation with the concept of advocacy advertising, running the equivalent of short stories on selected subjects that merged advertising, news, policy, and lobbying. The Mobil Oil ads would run on the op/ed pages of major papers like *The New York Times* and discuss everything from tax policy, to environmental regulations, to energy policy, and much more. Others soon followed suit in the new, fragmented media world. Figure 3-6 displays an example of the kind of advocacy advertising that has become popular over the past two decades.

The Annenberg Public Policy Center issued a report in 2005 estimating that over $404 million was spent on Washington-based broadcast and print issue advocacy during the 108th Congress.[30] And that figure is almost four times larger than the amount spent on inside-the-Beltway issue advocacy advertising in the previous Congress (Annenberg reports $105 million was spent on inside-the-Beltway issue advertising in the 107th Congress).[31] The latest Annenberg report also notes that business spending heavily dominated the totals. "Business interests outspent citizens-based advocacy groups by more than five to one."[32] Both reports suggest that the side with the greater amount of spending tends to prevail. Yet, while the Annenberg studies imply a causal relationship between resources on issue advertising and advocacy success, the nature of this linkage and the conditions under which it is as powerful as suggested deserve further investigation.

Another way to measure the changes and growth in advocacy advertising is to simply count the number of issue-oriented ads in publications like *National Journal*. A review of that publication during the past 30 years reveals dramatic growth as well. For example, there were no issue ads between 1969 and 1977. In 1978, four issue ads ran, primarily funded by defense companies like McDonnell Douglas or Rockwell International. But from the late 1970s until 2007, the number of issue ads grew dramatically. As Figure 3-7 demonstrates, issue ads in *National Journal* grew like the advocacy industry in general. These ads reflect the growing tactical variety deployed by lobbyists during this period. And it's another piece of evidence pointing to the dramatic growth in the advocacy industry.

The advent of the Internet age since the 1990s has also created a cottage industry of growth, including firms that monitor blogs for advocacy purposes

FIGURE 3-6 ADVOCACY ADVERTISING BY THE ENERGY INDUSTRY.

Investing in America's energy future

By 2030, experts predict that the world will require about 40 percent more energy than it did last year. Growth in developing countries will drive most of this increase, but energy demand is expected to increase in the United States, too.

ExxonMobil is helping meet these needs by continuing to make massive investments in future energy development — about $280 billion worldwide over the last 20 years, which *exceeded* our total earnings during that period. In the last five years alone, we have invested over $80 billion, including about one third in North America.

Today, for example, we are unlocking the natural gas potential of Colorado's Piceance Basin; investing in Gulf of Mexico production and in the world's largest liquefied natural gas (LNG) project, which will help supply the U.S. market; and growing our U.S. refinery capacity.

Such projects help increase and diversify energy supplies available to American consumers. This strengthens energy security. More energy from more places mitigates the impact of a disruption in any one country or region.

Investing in new technologies that reduce the environmental impact of our global operations is a priority, also. Such investments, for example, have led to drilling technology improvements that result in smaller footprints; have reduced energy use and emissions at our refineries and chemical plants; and have improved the fuel economy of the cars our customers drive.

And we are working with leading research institutions to identify breakthrough technologies that can deliver energy with dramatically lower greenhouse gas emissions.

Stable and impartial tax policies are critical to companies looking to invest on such a scale. ExxonMobil's total U.S. tax expenses for the past five years were nearly $60 billion, *exceeding* our U.S.-based earnings during that period by more than $20 billion.

As the U.S. economy grows, so will Americans' energy needs. Government can help meet these needs by ensuring reliable and impartial rules for all energy investments. We are committed to meet these needs through continued investments in energy supplies and ever cleaner technologies that help secure America's economic future.

Russia/Caspian   Latin America/Other
                                    8   3
                                             North
Asia Pacific/   25   America
Middle East   14

                15
Europe   17
                          Africa

ExxonMobil Investment 2002-2006
($US Billion)

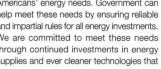

ExonMobil
Taking on the world's toughest energy challenges.™

Source: www.exxonmobil.com/corporate/news_opeds_20070726_investing.aspx

FIGURE 3-7 ADVOCACY ADVERTISING GROWTH 1969–2007.

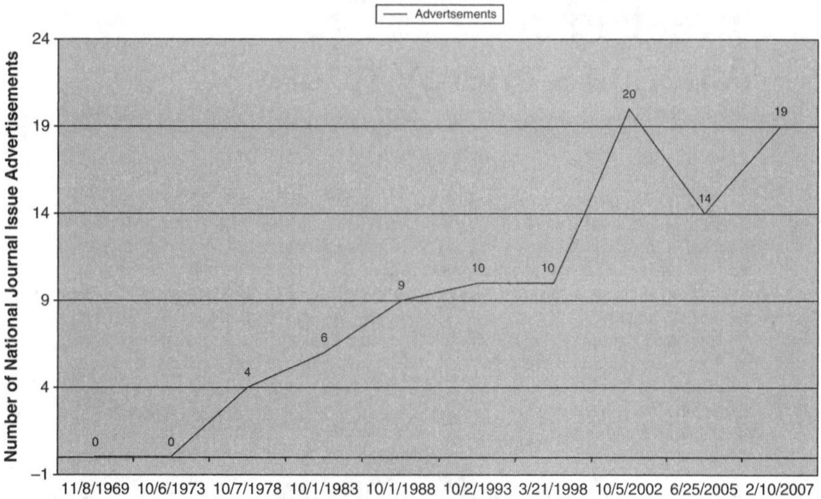

Source: Figures counted by author in the *National Journal.*

and others that specialize in new media consulting, focusing on advertising in online publications or using the Internet to organize and deploy "e-advocates." "It's hard to imagine a major lobbying campaign that doesn't include an e-advocacy component, including online advertising on web-based publications and blogs," Pete Snyder, founder and president of New Media Strategies, a company at the cutting edge of the e-advocacy field, says. "The Internet is the world's largest focus group. Legislative campaigns need to take advantage of what's being said in these conversations," according to Snyder. Like so many other areas of American life, the growth of the Internet has had a profound effect on the way the lobbying business operates. In fact, some believe Internet applications of lobbying may be among the fastest growing subspecialties in the advocacy world.

One recent study of the political influence of blogs notes that nearly all congressional offices now read them.[33] We also know that blogs possess an inordinate amount of political power compared to their relatively small number of readers because blogs shape the stories, attitudes, and agendas of media elites and other political activists.[34] Advertisers—particularly advertisers with an advocacy focus—now want to target these readers. That is why Internet display advertising increased by 17.3 percent between 2005 and 2006, the fastest growth of any kind of advertising during that period.[35] Estimates of online advocacy advertising are difficult to find, yet anecdotal information confirms that in percentage terms, this mode of advertising is the fastest growing segment of the field.

Snyder also argues that lobbying applications on the Internet are the fastest growing segment of his business. "Most public relations firms in DC, for example, will now tell you they monitor blogs/Internet," he said. That is a new service that didn't even exist five years ago. He also estimated that between 50 and 60 firms are now in the "online intelligence" business. Most of these offer services related to advocacy, informing lobbyists and interest groups what is being said about their issues. It's another critical piece of the burgeoning advocacy industry.

SUMMARY

Veteran Washington lobbyist Tommy Boggs told a group of Washington representatives, lawyers, and trade association executives at the Bryce Harlow Foundation Award dinner in 2007 that about 40 years earlier, he ambled down to the Office of the Clerk of the House of Representatives and registered as a lobbyist for the first time. "I was number 68," he recounted. "Their were only 68 lobbyists registered in the House at that time." As of this writing, the number of registered lobbyists stands at more than 30,000 and growing every day. Mr. Boggs's story contributes only one piece in this mosaic of growth. The number of "registered lobbyists" is just a small portion of the total number of individuals dedicated to the advocacy industry.

This chapter sketches a broad portrait of advocacy and lobbying growth—one that should lead to a reconsideration of the true size and scope of the advocacy world. It argues that interest-group behavior is a dynamic process responding to evolving government rules and structures, the behavior of competitors, and technological changes.

Lobbyists started representing individuals in the earliest days of the republic, but later in the eighteenth century and into the nineteenth century, interest groups and lobbying became more synonymous with peak associations such as the Chamber of Commerce, the National Association of Manufacturers, the American Federation of Labor, the American Medical Association, and the Cotton Council. In the post–World War II period, but particularly during the 1970s and 1990s, interest groups and lobbying became much more specialized and institutionalized. During this period, rapid growth occurred in the number of Washington representatives, trade associations in DC, and more specialized lobbying enterprises. Pharmaceutical companies abandoned sole reliance on the Pharmaceutical Manufacturers Association and formed a corporate Washington presence. Firms like Pfizer, Merck, and Johnson and Johnson invested more in creating individual DC offices. Oil companies no longer just used the American Petroleum Institute, and instead Shell, Exxon-Mobil, and Texaco created their own Washington offices, formed PACs, and hired outside lobbyists to help them pursue and promote their individual interests. Some indicators of growth were most dramatic during the 1970s and 1980s—such as the number of PACs and corporate Washington offices—and then slowed more recently due to saturation or consolidation. But other dimensions of the advocacy world continued the torrid growth pace, such as Internet advocacy, media consulting, grass roots, and professional fundraising firms.

But what led to this growth and individual involvement in the government relations process? Why couldn't firms rely exclusively on their industry groups to represent them anymore? And why are there more interest groups in general now in Washington? Part of the explanation lies in the broadened scope of conflict created by the sheer number of new entrants in the lobbying environment. As one group of scholars suggests, "The emergence of organized representation of citizen interests and the counter mobilization of business injected many new conflictual issues into legislative deliberation."[36] Lobbying is a dynamic enterprise and exhibits many of the characteristics of a Cold War arms race. When one side takes an action or adopts a new tactic or institutionalizes an activity, their opponents in the policymaking process usually respond or even try to "one-up" their competitors by trying new, bigger, and even more ingenious tactics. Interest groups, like copycats, emulate each other, and always try to do a little more. The beat goes on and the advocacy song continues—and the lobby world gets bigger.

Changes in Washington itself—its size and activism, fragmentation and polarization—the competitive environment interest groups face and transformations in media and technology all have contributed to the institutionalization and new complexity of the lobbying industry in Washington. These all represent areas where our thinking about advocacy deserves reconsideration. To extend former Congressman Walker's analogy, the lobbying world has undergone an "information-age" revolution, while our perceptions and understanding are stuck in the industrial age. In the next three chapters, we continue to probe under the influence by tracing these changes and how they all have contributed to growth and change in the advocacy industry.

NOTES

1. The American League of Lobbyists, the American Soceity of Association Executives, and the Public Affairs Council all represent various aspects of the new lobbying industry.
2. For a similar change in Congress see Nelson Polsby, "Institutionalization in the U.S. House of Representatives," *American Political Science Review* 62 (1968): 144–168.
3. Pendleton Herring, *Group Representation Before Congress* (Baltimore, MD: Johns Hopkins University Press, 1929), 99.

4. Ibid. 19.
5. This estimate is from David C. King and Jack L. Walker, "An Ecology of Interest Groups," In Jack L. Walker, ed. *Mobilizing Interest Groups in America: Patrons, Professions, Social Movements* (Ann Arbor, MI: University of Michigan Press, 1991), 62. The original estimate King and Walker cite is from Pendleton Herring, *Group Representation Before Congress* (Washington, D.C.: The Brookings Institution, 1929).
6. Ibid. 62.
7. K.L. Schlozman and J.T. Tierney, *Organized Interests and American Democracy* (New York, NY: Harper and Row, 1986), 75–76.
8. Frank R. Baumgartner, "The Growth and Diversity of U.S. Associations: 1956–2004: Analyzing Trends Using the Encyclopedia of Associations," Working paper, March 29, 2005. Cited in Jeffrey M. Berry and Clyde Wilcox, *The Interest Group Society*, 4th ed. (New York, NY: Pearson Longman, 2007), 16.
9. Ibid. 17.
10. Ibid.
11. Ronald G. Schaiko, "Making Connection: Organized Interests, Political Representation, and the Changing Rules of the Game in Washington Politics," In Paul S. Herrnson, Ronald G. Shaiko, and Clyde Wilcox, eds. *The Interest Group Connection*, 2nd ed. (Washington, D.C.: CQ Press, 2005).
12. David Yoffie, "Interest Groups v. Individual Action: An Analysis of Corporate Political Strategies," 1985 Working paper, Harvard Business School, quoted in Heinz et al. *The Hollow Core: Private Interests and National Policymaking* (Cambridge, MA: Harvard University Press, 1991), 375.
13. Jeffrey H. Birnbaum, "Washington's Once and Future Lobby," *The Washington Post*, September 10, 2006, B01.
14. Ibid.
15. King and Walker, "An Ecology of Interest Groups," 64.
16. Washington Representatives, published annually since 1977 (Washington, D.C.: Columbia Books).
17. The book has not changed in any major ways stylistically, so the page number comparison from year to year is valid.
18. Jeanne Cummings, *The Politico* interview with Bob Walker on transformations in lobbying industry, August 14, 2007.
19. The Public Affairs Council, Final Reports, 2000, 2003, 2006. Corporate Washington Office Benchmarking studies.
20. 2006 Public Affairs Council Corporate Government Relations Washington Office Benchmarking Project. P. 3.
21. Jeffrey M. Berry and Clyde Wilcox, *The Interest Group Society*, 4th ed. (New York, NY: Pearson Longman, 2007), 18.
22. Jim Snyder, "Corporations Prep for Inquisitive Oversight," *The Hill*, December 6, 2006.
23. Berry and Wilcox, *The Interest Group Society*, 21.
24. Jack L. Walker, *Mobilizing Interest Groups in America: Patrons, Professions, Social Movements* (Ann Arbor, MI: University of Michigan Press, 1991), 37.
25. Kenneth M. Goldstein, *Interest Groups, Lobbying and Participation in America* (Cambridge, UK: Cambridge University Press, 1999), 24.
26. Ibid. 24.
27. Ibid. 25.
28. Ibid.
29. Goldstein, *Interest Groups, Lobbying and Participation in America*, 25.
30. The Annenberg Public Policy Center report, *Legislative Issue Advertising in the 108th Congress*, March 16, 2005.
31. The Annenberg Public Policy Center report, June 19, 2003.
32. Ibid. Annenberg Study press release, March 16, 2005.
33. T. Neil Sroka, "Understanding the Political Influence of Blogs: A Study of the Growing Importance of the Blogosphere in the U.S. Congress," *Institute for Politics, Democracy and the Internet*. The Graduate School of Political Management. The George Washington University, April, 2006.

34. Daniel Drezner and Henry Farrell, The Power and Poltics of Blogs. Paper presented at the American Political Science Association Convention, August 2004. Accessed the paper online.
35. Report by TNS Media Intelligence, March 13, 2007.
36. Thomas L. Gais, Mark A. Peterson, and Jack L. Walker Jr. "Interest Groups, Iron Triangles and Representative Institutions," In Jack L. Walker Jr. ed. *Mobilizing Interest Groups in America: Patrons, Professions and Social Movements* (Ann Arbor, MI: The University of Michigan Press, 1991), 134–135.

GOVERNMENTAL GROWTH
AND THE ADVOCACY INDUSTRY

When the government starts dictating to you the size of your toilet seat, you better get someone here to cover your—.

Former lobbyist and White House aide Tom Korologos[1]

Few would consider a full-time policy analyst churning out issue briefs about energy markets, or a researcher focusing on the best way to cover the uninsured, a part of the lobbying world. Nor are pollsters or media specialists commonly viewed as influence peddlers. Yet they are now all often integral components of the advocacy universe. But why? Lobbying today requires many new tactics and strategies due to significant shifts in the government environment. More people, increased use of specialists, creative tactics, and new advocacy structures are just some of the ways the lobbying industry has transformed due to the changing world in Washington.

This chapter explores the relationship between a bigger, more complex, open, fragmented, and increasingly activist federal government and the lobbying industry. How has government changed and what are repercussions and consequences of these transformations on the advocacy world?

The first half of the chapter outlines changes in the legislative and executive branches of government such as

- An evolving seniority system in Congress.
- The proliferation of subcommittees in the House.
- The growth of congressional staff.
- A more activist Congress, conducting an increasing number of hearings and passing more complicated legislation.
- A changing regulatory environment.
- A more open, accountable system due to "sunshine" laws.

Taken together, these alterations in government have created a new kind of Washington Establishment. And these shifts in the external environment of interest groups have induced a host of changes in the advocacy world.

The second half of the chapter explores the consequences of these transformations on lobbying and interest groups. These consequences include

- New government-induced risk and rewards for interest groups.
- The rise of new issues and decline of others.
- Increased conflicts over new rules between interest groups and lobbyists seeking competitive advantage.
- The creation of multiple "entry points" for lobbyists.
- Changes in the congressional oversight agenda.
- Opportunities for policy entrepreneurs.
- The need for more policy specialists in the interest-group world.

The growth of the Washington Establishment—to borrow a phrase from political scientist Morris P. Fiorina—impacts the lobbying world in some obvious and non-obvious ways. At one level, new rules, laws, and policy changes require attention from interest groups because they simply add costs (new taxes or regulations) that organizations seek to avoid, or at least try to predict and influence. But the growing Washington Establishment also has a more complex impact. Over time, new laws and policies create temporary winners and losers. Incumbent interest groups try to maintain their status quo advantage, while others attempt to change it. In many industries and policy sectors, the Washington Establishment sets the ground rules determining who can compete, where, when, and how. Washington is a place where the terrain is complex, dynamic, and often uncharted. Lobbying in this environment, as we shall see later in this chapter, is a complicated game of information and intelligence gathering about the behavior of potential competitors and then taking steps to respond. For example, labor seeks to trump management with new workplace rules, environmental activists try to shift more costs to business, and cable firms advance policies to keep telephone companies out of the cable business. In other words, as the government grows in size and influence it does more than impose new taxes, costs, or regulations—that's only part of what government does and what interest groups try to shape. It also sets the ground rules for competition, triggering a constantly shifting give-and-take dynamic between actors in the advocacy industry. A government with more staff, decentralized decision making, and increased complexity also induces shifts in the interest-group world. These additional impacts of government growth are also explored later in this chapter.

GOVERNMENT FACILITATION OF LOBBYING GROWTH

Recent political science research confirms that government policy changes draw lobbyists to Washington.[2] Groups mobilize in Washington in response to the growth of activities of government. One recent study concludes with this parsimonious observation: "Groups do not automatically form and come to Washington; there must be demand for them. Government creates that demand."[3] In other words, one of the reasons there are so many lobbyists is because there is *so much government*. And the increased size and tactical complexity of the advocacy world is directly correlated to a more intricate government policymaking environment.

But the advocacy world is also reciprocal—lobbyists also cause the government to expand. Some scholars conclude, "The growth and proliferation of interest groups has long been considered a major cause of growth in the size and scope of the U.S. government."[4] How the lobbying world produces changes in government is discussed in more detail in the final two chapters of this book. For now, however, I focus on the first part of the reciprocal relationship—how changes in Washington alter the structure, style, and substance of lobbying.

The revolution in the advocacy world over the past 40 years corresponds almost perfectly with growth in Congress and the federal government in general. Part of the job of advocacy is to influence, predict, and understand the public policy universe, and that cosmos has exploded in size and scope over the past 40 years. As the challenges and circumstances interest groups faced changed, so did the advocacy world. I begin by reviewing some of the transformations in the legislative and executive branches of government in Washington and then turn to a discussion about how congressional and bureaucratic growth has impacted the world of lobbying.

CHANGING CONGRESSIONAL ENVIRONMENT

AN EVOLVING SENIORITY SYSTEM

Some of the most dramatic reforms and changes in Congress occurred in the early 1970s, around the same time the lobbying world began its rapid growth.[5] Most of these modifications can be organized under the general theme of decentralization and greater numbers of people involved in the decision-making process. The late Dan Dutko, a well-respected Democratic lobbyist, used to tell his colleagues:

> If you knew one subcommittee chairman as a lobbyist really well and he would take care of you, you were fine. You could ask him for a favor and if you did one in return you could get a lot accomplished. That all changed during the 1970s. The old world of "I scratch your back and you scratch mine" did not exist any more. There were too many people involved in the process now. Now there were too many staff, too many subcommittee chairs, and too many places in the process where a bill could get derailed.

His point is reinforced by another well-known Washington lobbyist, Charls E. Walker, who said,

> It used to be if it was a tax matter and you had lined up Sam Rayburn and Wilbur Mills and whoever was the minority leader on Ways and Means, you were home free. . . . Now with the reduction in power of committee chairmen, and with the open markups, these technical amendments immediately get labeled—the "E.F. Hutton amendment" or the "Ross Perot amendment." And if it's the least bit controversial, each member wants to know how it will affect his constituents. So you've got to work the whole committee, and maybe the whole floor.[6]

Prior to the 1970s, strict adherence to seniority dictated the choice of committee leaders. When that seniority system broke down, it opened the committee and subcommittee chairs to new potential advocacy pressures, enhancing the role for more lobbyists and interest groups – a great example of how political reform lead to the unintended consequence of empowering the advocacy world.

One of the most dramatic departures from strict adherence to the seniority system occurred in January of 1975 when three Democratic full committee chairs—Edward Herbert of Louisiana, chairman of the Armed Services Committee; W.R. Poage of Texas, chairman of the Agriculture Committee; and Wright Patman of Texas, chairman of the Banking Committee—were all dumped by a group of insurgent Democrats first elected in 1974.[7]

This change had a significant impact on the advocacy world. From the standpoint of interest groups, it was like swatting a beehive with a baseball bat. More lawmakers were now emboldened and empowered to swarm around an interest group's business. And this new, decentralized, and increasingly uncertain world required a response. The advocacy industry's reaction was to expand and professionalize. It enlarged, adding investments in personnel and other political resources to cover all the new lawmakers involved in the process and to reduce and manage the uncertainty created by the new disequilibrium in the system.

PROLIFERATION OF SUBCOMMITTEES

Along with changes in the seniority system, the number of subcommittees grew during the 1970s as well. And with new subcommittees came new "chairmen," with all their accompanying power. One lobbyist used to joke, "There are so many subcommittee chairman now every time I pass a member of Congress I say, 'Hello, Mr. Chairman,' and I'm right most of the time."

The decentralization and growth of power centers in Congress during this period is well documented. One study notes that as a result of post-Watergate reforms, power was decentralized and power centers were expanded to bring in more junior members. The number of standing subcommittees in the House increased by 25 percent to 151. The number went up in the Senate as well, by more than 10 percent. The number of House members chairing committees or subcommittees rose from 131 in 1972 to 150 in 1975.[8] This study also notes a dramatic expansion in resources at the subcommittee level during the same period.

From an interest-group perspective, more subcommittees meant more potential threats, opportunities, and increased uncertainty. It represented a change in equilibrium for the advocacy world. And as we shall see time and time again, disequilibrium in the lobbying environment usually leads to changes in structures and substantive methods of interest groups.

GROWTH OF STAFF

All of these new subcommittees required additional staff. And all of these new personnel needed something to do. The proliferation of congressional employees is one of the most dramatic changes in government in the second half of the twentieth century. Figure 4-1 illustrates the growth in the number of House and Senate employees since 1947. Again, the bulk of the increase occurred during the 1970s. From the late 1940s to the late 1970s, the number of House and Senate staff grew fivefold, with a 30 percent increase from 1972 to 1976 alone.[9] More staff meant more hearings, more investigations, more bills introduced, and just more people for lobbyists to get to know and influence.

FIGURE 4-1 GROWTH IN THE NUMBER OF CONGRESSIONAL STAFF 1947–2001.

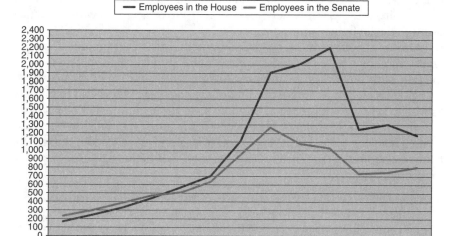

Source: Norman J. Ornstein, Thomas E. Mann, and Michael J. Malbin, *Vital Statistics on Congress 2005–2006* (Washington, D.C., Congressional Quarterly, Inc. 2006).

FIGURE 4-2 GROWTH IN FEDERAL MONEY ALLOCATED FOR CONGRESSIONAL
OPERATIONS—SIZE OF THE LEGISLATIVE BRANCH APPROPRIATIONS BILL 1947–2000.

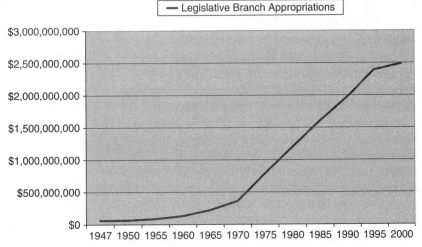

Source: Norman J. Ornstein, Thomas E. Mann, and Michael J. Malbin, *Vital Statistics on Congress 2005–2006* (Washington, D.C., Congressional Quarterly, Inc. 2006).

Analyzing the size of legislative budgets is another way to note the growing power and resources of lawmakers and their staff. Figure 4-2 tracks the growth of legislative branch appropriations during this period. Again, the pattern of expansion is clear. These funds were used to enhance the capabilities of Congress in a variety of areas, including more resources for personnel, travel, investigations, and hearings. And like other structural changes in Congress, this new level of legislative activism caused ripples through the lobbying community.

More and better-educated staff, along with legislative personnel empowered with larger budgets, also required more sophisticated information on the part of the advocacy community. As the public funding of the legislative branch increased, the private funding of the advocacy world had to increase as well to keep up and respond. I outline some of the new tactics of advocacy in more detail in Chapter 7. However, Democratic lobbyist Kim Bayliss, a former House staffer and now a partner at Dutko Worldwide, makes this comment about the relationship between more and better-educated staff, and the lobbying world:

> Information used to play less of a role in lobbying before the growth of staff. In the old days lobbying was based on favors. Today it's based on information and analysis. The person with the best facts usually wins. So if you want to win in the lobbying game, you better have your facts right. With all these new staffers demanding information, the need for lobbyists to provide it grew as well.

FIGURE 4-3 GROWTH IN THE NUMBER OF CONGRESSIONAL HEARINGS.

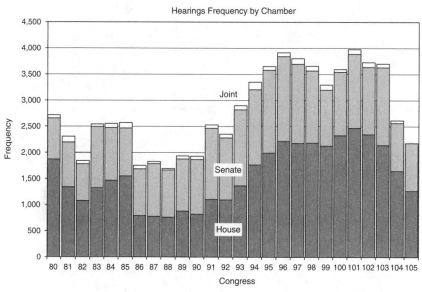

Source: Policy Agendas Project, Center for American politics and public policy, University of Washington.

The increased supply of subcommittees and legislative personnel created increased demand for congressional hearings, oversight, and investigations. As Figure 4-3 demonstrates, the number of these hearings grew during this period of unsettled change in Congress, creating a host of new vulnerabilities and opportunities for interest groups and lobbyists.

Finally, the legislation enacted by Congress grew increasingly complex, producing a host of new mandates, rules, programs, and bureaucratic directives. One way to measure the growing intricacies of the legislative process is to look at the number of pages per statute enacted. For example, between 1948 and 1998, the average page per statute increased from 2.5 pages to 18.4 pages. Figure 4-4 demonstrates this move toward greater complexity.

Sally Murphy, vice president of government affairs for the Wine Institute and previously a corporate lobbyist and a Senate aide, underscores this point:

> The legislation Congress used to pass was never this complicated. We used to work on much broader statutes with far fewer directives to regulatory agencies. That's all changed now. Legislation is much more prescriptive and gives agencies a lot less wiggle room. I think the growth of lobbying may have something to do with that. Interest groups never like to leave anything to chance. So if they can nail down things in a bill, all the better. I think that's the reason legislation has gotten longer and more complex.

FIGURE 4-4 LEGISLATION GETTING MORE COMPLICATED?
NUMBER OF PAGES PER STATUTE 1947–1998.

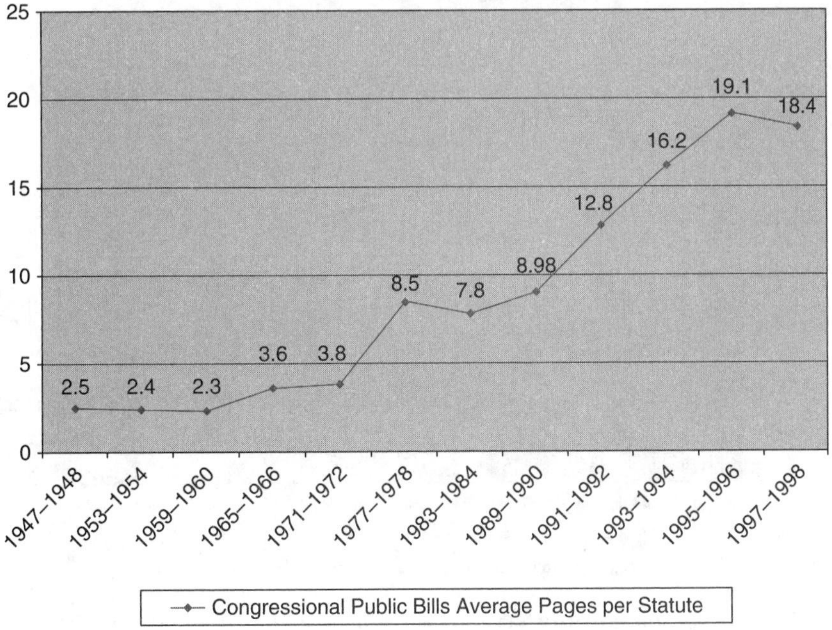

Source: Norman J. Ornstein, Thomas E. Mann, and Michael J. Malbin, *Vital Statistics on Congress 2005–2006* (Washington, D.C., Congressional Quarterly, Inc. 2006).

But Congress wasn't acting alone. Another factor in the equation was growth in the massive regulatory and bureaucratic part of the Washington Establishment.

CHANGING REGULATORY ENVIRONMENT

Burgeoning legislative activities were not the only changing dynamic affecting lobbyists. The growth and power of regulatory agencies during the 1970s and 1980s also contributed to the rise in interest-group activity during this period. A study by the Conference Board found that 71 percent of businesses cited "increased government activity" as one of the reasons to change their government relations efforts during this period.[10] These business leaders increased the size of their government relations initiatives and the budgets dedicated to those initiatives dramatically. Another study found significant evidence that the greater the level of regulation during the 1970s, the more likely a business was to form a PAC as a way to institutionalize its participation in politics.[11]

The increase in regulatory activity was more than perception. Congress during the 1970s and 1980s passed fewer, but longer and more complicated bills with more regulatory requirements.[12] Growth in the number of pages in the *Federal Register* is one way to measure this increase in regulatory requirements. For example, in the 1950s this source of regulatory information ranged from 10,000 to 15,000 pages per year. By the 1970s, the *Federal Register* averaged 50,000 pages per year[13] – about a fivefold increase in just two decades. More interest-group representatives were required to find not only what was included in this vast expansion of regulatory information, but also what could be done to change it or adapt to it.

Figure 4-5 demonstrates this growth in the number of pages in the *Federal Register* measured by decade since 1940.[14]

The *Code of Federal Regulations* offers another way to measure the impact of regulations on interest groups, and it too burgeoned. A study by Susan E. Dudley for the Mercatus Center of George Mason University notes that in total the *Code* now occupies 25 ft of shelf space and in 2003 alone the federal government added 75,795 pages of rules and announcements—the highest annual page count ever. In terms of costs, the same study notes, "Federal agencies appear to impose more than twice the cost on Americans as they did 25 years ago."[15]

Finally, someone must produce all those pages of regulations. A recent study by Paul Light argues the true size of the federal government grew to 14.6 million employees in 2006, a gain of more than 2.5 million since 2002.

FIGURE 4-5 REGULATIONS GETTING MORE COMPLICATED? NUMBER OF PAGES IN *FEDERAL REGISTER* 1940–2000.

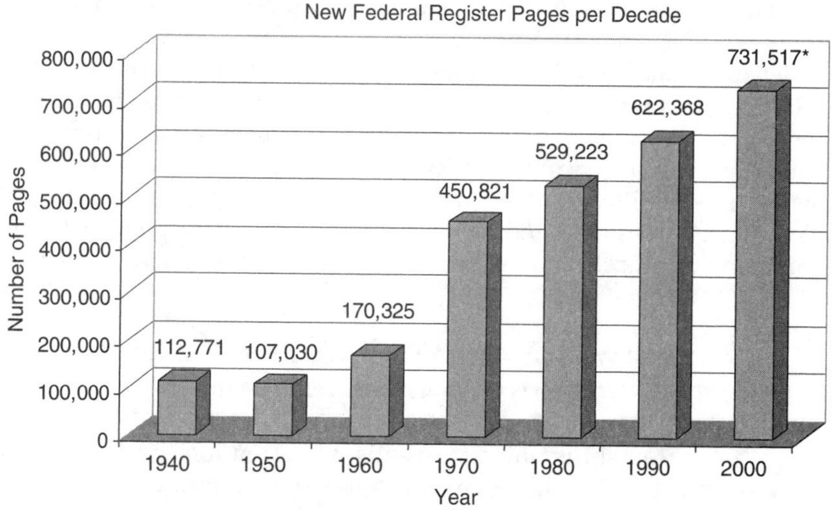

New Federal Register Pages per Decade

Note: *Denotes the projection based on three-year average.

Source: National Archives and Records Administration, Office of the Federal Register.

He argues that this figure, which includes "hidden government" employees like federal contractors, is a more accurate measure of the true size of the federal bureaucracy. However one gauges the particulars, there is no doubt that the federal Leviathan continues to grow.

SUNSHINE LAWS, GREATER OPENNESS, AND ACCOUNTABILITY

During the 1970s and 1980s a host of other changes occurred in Washington that produced more openness and accountability in the process.[16] Yet, ironically, many of these new laws and regulations also stimulated the growth and proliferation of the lobbying industry. Beginning with the Legislative Reorganization Act of 1970, Congress took a variety of steps to open up the process to the public. These reforms included making recorded votes in the House public for the first time (previously votes in the "Committee of the Whole," where the House does most of its work considering and debating amendments, were done by voice vote or "teller votes" where individual members' votes were not recorded). Shortly thereafter, Congress also required recorded votes in committees and opened committee deliberations to the public. Television coverage of Congress also began during this time period. In 1979, House proceedings were all covered live on C-Span for the first time, and the Senate followed suit in 1986. Changes in campaign finance laws during the 1970s also had the effect of opening up the process to the public through new disclosure requirements.[17]

The combined impact of these changes led to even more fragmentation of power in the public policymaking process. These "reforms" expanded the number of actors who could and did influence the process. This meant a greater number of decision makers advocates had to worry about and lobby. And this stimulated demand for more lobbyists and a bigger advocacy industry.

The more fragmented, open, and accountable process meant more potential risks to lobbyists' interests from more policymakers. No longer was Washington exclusively controlled by a small group of people making decisions in "smoke-filled rooms." In the post-reform process, more people could impact the system—and the advocacy community responded. Getting bigger, more organized, and institutionalized was the collective reaction.

LOBBYING: ANOTHER KEYSTONE IN THE WASHINGTON ESTABLISHMENT?

When Washington shifts, interest groups pay attention. In the minds of many advocacy groups, bigger, changing government meant new risks and opportunities. The growing government Leviathan created a host of consequences for lobbyists.

About 30 years ago, political scientist Morris Fiorina wrote a small and now classic book mentioned at the beginning of this chapter called *Congress: Keystone of the Washington Establishment*. Fiorina argues that uncoordinated activism by Congress creates bigger government, like the developments outlined above, and also facilitates legislative electoral safety. He demonstrates how pork barrel spending and casework boost incumbents' political fortunes, while at the same time creating a bigger federal government enterprise. But while Fiorina details some of the same evidence for the rise of the Washington Establishment outlined earlier in this chapter, such as burgeoning congressional staff, the proliferation of subcommittees, more regulations and skyrocketing government spending, he focuses far less attention on the institutionalization and growth of the lobbying industry that moved in tandem with the advent of bigger, more activist government.

Fiorina's assessment seems accurate as far as it goes. Congress indeed facilitated governmental growth and enjoyed the accompanying political benefits associated with pork barrel spending and casework. Yet, since he wrote his book 30 years ago, another piece of the Washington Establishment emerged in reaction to these inside-the-Beltway transformations—the modern advocacy industry. Changes in Congress, the bureaucracy, and general government activism resulted in growth and professionalization of the lobbying world. Lobbying may not be "the keystone" of the federal establishment, but it's now part of the bedrock of Washington.

But what are some of the specific implications of the rise of the Washington Establishment for lobbying? And why would these transformations cause the advocacy industry to change in structure, style, and methods? The next section lays out some examples of how altering the structure and scope of government affected the advocacy world.

NEW GOVERNMENT-INDUCED RISKS OR REWARDS

At a very basic level, bigger, more active government has created a new atmosphere of heightened risks, vulnerabilities, and rewards. New taxes, environmental regulations, workplace and safety rules, labor mandates, and financial reporting requirements are just some of the changes affecting business, labor, and other interest groups in America. The larger government instituted multiple forums filled with new and unknown hazards and opportunities.

Some of the risks are relatively straightforward. Any kind of change, for example, that costs an interest group's members more money—in terms of new taxes, higher compliance costs, or other government filing or disclosure requirements—demands close attention. And as documented above, these costs were substantial and growing during the 1970s and 1980s. Trying to shape the outcomes of these new public policy actions was critical to many interest groups. During the 1970s, for example, Congress created the Environmental Protection Agency (EPA) and the Occupational Safety and Health Administration (OSHA), and the executive branch formed its own new regulatory entities through executive orders. The effects of these new government agencies in imposing new costs and other burdens on interest groups are clear. They make the cost of doing business more expensive and force firms to change their operations.

Analyzing energy and environmental policy during the 1970s and early 1980s—the same period when congressional staff, subcommittee fragmentation, and activism ballooned—reveals a torrent pace of lawmaking with major new implications for a host of interest groups ranging from business to labor unions to environmental activists. Some major new statutes passed in this policy domain during those years include the Clean Air Act of 1970, the Water Pollution Control Act Amendments of 1972, the Safe Drinking Water Act of 1972, the Energy Policy and Conservation Act of 1975, the Clean Water Act of 1977, the Comprehensive Environment Response, Compensation and Liability Act (the so-called Superfund program), and the Windfall Profits Tax. It was a decade that potentially cost some industries hundreds of billions of dollars and offered interest groups fresh opportunities, as well as risks, for their agendas.

The advocacy world responded by trying to manage these risks and uncertainties by gathering information and attempting to shape the process. Institutionalization – and getting bigger – was a rational response to these new vulnerabilities. The ever-evolving policy domain and changing issue agenda continually create demand for a new supply of lobbyists. Charting how new issues evolve and old issues decline represents graphically why new advocates and interest groups constantly emerge on the Washington scene (Figures 4-6 and 4-7).

The telecommunications industry witnessed some of the greatest upheaval during the 1970s and 1980s as well.[18] For example, in 1974, the U.S. government initiated an antitrust suit against AT&T, the country's largest telecommunications firm. The government alleged that the company unfairly used its monopoly power to block potential competitors in long distance and telecommunications equipment by denying access to AT&T's network. For eight years, Congress and other policymakers sought to address the situation.[19] Finally, in 1982, AT&T entered into a consent decree that broke the company up into seven smaller operating companies, and these so-called Baby Bells provided only local telephone service. The original AT&T could still manufacture communications equipment and provide long distance service in a more deregulated environment, but it was no longer in the local telephone business.

The uncertainty and evolving nature of government policy in the communications industry was a boon for the advocacy industry during the

FIGURE 4-6 THE DECLINE OF OLD ISSUES IN CONGRESS.

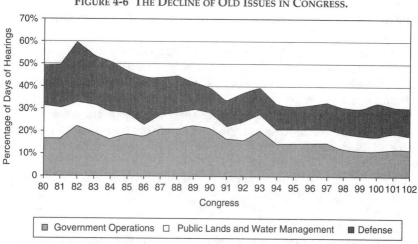

Source: Frank R. Baumgartner, "Social Movements and the Rise of New Issues." Paper Presented at the Conference on Social Movements, Public Policy, and Democracy. University of California, Irvine. January 11–13, 2002. Data from the Policy Agendas Project, Center for American Politics and Public Policy. University of Washington.

1970s and 1980s. Prior to the consent decree in 1982, potential competitors to AT&T, such as MCI in the long distance sector and a host of companies in the communications manufacturing industry, all geared up to shape legislation and potential new regulations. Labor unions and telecommunications

FIGURE 4-7 THE RISE OF NEW ISSUES IN CONGRESS.

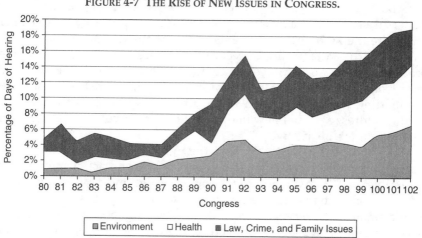

Source: Frank R. Baumgartner, "Social Movements and the Rise of New Issues." Paper Presented at the Conference on Social Movements, Public Policy, and Democracy. University of California, Irvine. January 11–13, 2002. Data from the Policy Agendas Project, Center for American Politics and Public Policy. University of Washington.

"users coalitions" all got into the game as well to protect their interests and gain knowledge of the potential implications of government policy on their members.

After the breakup in 1982, each of the seven new "Baby Bells" created its own Washington office, government relations department and PAC, and hired a host of outside consultants, creating one of the largest booms in the lobbying business in decades. All of these changes were a direct result of government policy. Moreover, before the ink was dry on the consent decree, advocates began the process of trying to change it, attempting to gain a new competitive advantage by promoting legislation to alter the status quo. This dynamic process of interest groups trying to reshape laws and regulations to their own competitive advantage is another critical way public policy change shapes lobbying growth.

COMPETITIVE ADVANTAGE—THE LOBBYING EQUIVALENT OF THE HATFIELDS AND MCCOYS

Costly new government rules, regulations, and uncertainties are only part of the equation. A bigger government has other implications for the lobbying community. New rules, agencies, and policies often create forums where competitors or adversaries can seize the upper hand. A bigger, more complicated government environment simply creates more opportunities for these adversarial conflicts to take place at any time. In this new environment, nothing is fixed or permanent. Change is always a possibility. And as one lobbyist who used to work with the House Republican leadership said, "If you're not on offense, you're probably on defense." These are the lobbying equivalents of the Hatfields and the McCoys— feuding parties attempting to secure their share of policy spoils. Sometimes the fights occur out of spite and revenge, other times they are unprovoked. But more expansive government, with more actors, provides the feuding parties increased opportunities to brawl and creates the need to address a host of new known and unknown vulnerabilities. A few illustrations are instructive.

Both the pharmacist lobby and the groups representing those who manage pharmacy benefits have increased in size and activism in the last several years. Why? Changing government rules and policies offer both sides the opportunity to tilt the competitive landscape and increase the level of uncertainty for everyone involved. As a way to help control the rising price of prescription drugs, a new cottage industry has formed over the past decade: pharmacy benefit managers. These entities help businesses and insurance companies manage the cost of drug coverage. During the debate leading up to passage of the Medicare Modernization Act in 2003, and throughout its implementation, a major battle brewed between these two players in the health care industry. On one hand were the local pharmacists, whose livelihood depends on regular interaction with consumers dispensing prescriptions. On the other were pharmacy benefit managers, attempting to reduce the costs of prescription drugs for their clients. Particularly for consumers receiving regular prescriptions, mandating more mail order availability and 30-to-60-day supplies of medications would be a cost-saving device. But while more mail order would mean lower costs, it also would produce fewer visits to the local pharmacy—squeezing pharmacists' profits as a way to reduce overall health care costs. In this case, how the rules were structured could help one group at the expense of another. The size and involvement of the government created a forum where one interest group could attack another. Both sides of this debate have beefed up their lobbying arsenals to promote and protect their economic interests—not just from the government, but also from other interests seeking to use public policy to harm them.

Railroads and chemical companies engage in a similar fight. Railroads offer the most efficient way and in some cases the only feasible way to ship chemicals around the country. Chemical companies, facing competitive pressures, constantly look to reduce their costs. In 1980, Congress passed the Staggers Act, essentially deregulating the rates freight railroads can charge their customers. Railroads argued that regulation had set artificially low rates of return, hampering their ability to make the kind of capital investments necessary to continue providing high quality, efficient services. Yet in some areas of the country, shippers only have access to one railroad. The Staggers Act did provide a remedy to these shippers, allowing them to file a grievance with the Surface Transportation Board at the Department of Transportation. Some shippers have been unhappy with the procedure and have urged Congress to impose rate regulations on the freight railroad industry.

In this legislative conflict, railroads try to protect the status quo, while shippers attempt to use the public policy process to enhance their business position in the form of cheaper short-term transportation rates. As the Washington Establishment has grown, the risks, potential rewards, and points of potential influence have grown exponentially. The railroad industry has made substantial investment to protect their position from the onslaught of the shippers. For their part, the shippers view the policy process and its many points of entry as a place to address their grievances and lower their transportation costs. A more complex, permeable, and diffuse public policy process increases the risks, rewards, and uncertainties—and the advocacy industry responds by investing more and getting bigger.

Telecommunications and cable companies face a competitive battle similar to that seen in the health and transportation sectors. Telephone companies serve as the primary vehicle for voice communications, while cable dominates in the video sphere. Both want to get into each other's business and view the public policy process as the place to do it. Cable companies built their franchises for video on a community-by-community basis, nationwide. Telephone companies don't want to repeat this costly and time-consuming process, and in 2006 these firms proposed a national franchise of sorts that would allow them to build in any community. Cable firms opposed the legislation, knowing the measure would hurt cable from a competitive perspective.

These brief illustrations all provide variations on a familiar theme. Competitors use the public policy process to enhance their own position, typically by proposing asymmetric rules intended to hurt the other guy. Again, a bigger, more active, diffuse, and permeable policy process gives them the means and the motive to do just that.

This pattern repeats itself over and over again in today's public policy process. Banks fight brokerage houses over getting into each other's business. Media content providers want to extract higher fees from communications firms that carry the material. Energy producers want cheaper ways to transport their raw materials or finished products. And those who use energy want cheaper sources of supply. As government has grown in complexity and size, the opportunities to advance these goals through lawmaking or regulation have increased exponentially; and so have potential vulnerabilities. As a veteran Republican lobbyist observed, "If you don't have a seat at the table you could be eaten for lunch." In sum, the lobbying industry has grown not only because of the potential for new costs and regulations from government, but also because the larger Leviathan set ground rules that competitors and incumbents tried to use to their advantage.

Washington strategist Patrick Griffin sums up this point very well:

> Something shifted during the 1980s when it came to the role of the government in a lot of these areas. It used to be that interest groups played more defense than offense—which also had implications for the number and types of tools lobbyists used. There was a lot more emphasis on just protecting the existing status quo. But over the last 20 years or so, Washington became a potential *profit center*. Business and other interest groups now viewed Washington as a place that could affect the bottom line. And this had huge implications for how the game was played and the level of resources interest groups deployed.

MULTIPLE ENTRY POINTS

The proliferation of subcommittees and the fragmentation of policymaking caused another important change in the lobbying world. In the past, when congressional barons reigned supreme, the path to influence was fairly well demarcated. Powerful committee chairs could rule through intimidation and tightly hold the reigns of power. But in today's lobbying world, there is more than one route to influence the process—both within the committee process, because chairmen are less powerful today than in the past, and outside the committee process, where a congressional panel's work is now vulnerable to attack from other committees, activist members, or party leadership. A former Republican leadership aide, who worked on Capitol Hill from the 1970s through the 1990s, describes the breakdown of a strong committee process and its effect on lobbying this way, "There are now multiple entry points into the legislative process. In the old days there were fewer people involved. Today, there are more subcommittee chairs and more members empowered to make a difference. This is one of the biggest implications of the diffusion of power that occurred in the 1970s." A Republican lobbyist sums it up, saying, "Now you have to always be on guard. It's as if no decision is ever final. You get a provision in a bill and some member of the committee can swoop in and try to take it out. After you survive the committee process, someone from the leadership can try to change it. In the old days a deal was a deal. Now it's like the appeal process is unending."

In 2007, legislative opponents of government-sponsored-enterprise companies like Freddie Mac and Fannie Mae discovered the implications of multiple entry points and the diffusion of power. The Bush administration and House Financial Services Chairman Barney Frank (D-MA) struck a deal that would give these companies' regulators more power to limit the size of the portfolios of mortgage-backed securities Freddie Mac and Fannie Mae own. In the old days, few would challenge a delicately negotiated arrangement between the White House and a powerful committee chair. Yet, lobbyists for the two companies did not relent. They persuaded four House members from Mr. Frank's own committee to challenge the deal by offering an amendment to scuttle it. Commenting on the seemingly unending process of appeal, *The Wall Street Journal* wrote, "Just when you think they're defeated, Fannie Mae and Freddie Mac arise in Congress to kill any attempt to clean up their dangerous habits. This week's scary movie comes as an attempt to blow up a carefully negotiated deal between Treasury Secretary Hank Paulson and House Financial Services Chairman Barney Frank."[20] In a more fragmented system, vulnerabilities and opportunities like this spring up like legislative dandelions.

The use of creative and unorthodox parliamentary tools is another expanding part of the advocacy arsenal in a system with multiple entry points. Some scholars have written about the more frequent use of novel procedures in the lawmaking process.[21] Increasingly, lobbyists, especially former staff turned advocates, use their experience from Congress to help engineer these new parliamentary tactics. Lobbyists and lawmakers are both adaptive creatures—and evolution in the legislative food chain moves quickly. When one interest group successfully scuttles an opponent's legislative initiative with a new and creative procedural move, others quickly emulate the tactic.

A former House GOP leadership aide turned lobbyist says, "I think the biggest surprise for me over the past 10 years has been the increasing importance of procedure. It's critical to now know procedure. It can save clients or give them new opportunities."

Examples from the House of Representatives demonstrate how lobbyists can use procedure at various stages in a more fragmented legislative process. Lobbyists sometimes work with allies on the Hill and use the committee referral process as a way to alter legislation. Over the past decade, lobbyists who opposed the telecommunications policies produced by the House Energy and Commerce Committee would petition the House Judiciary Committee to seek jurisdiction over the issue. Staff from the Judiciary Committee would routinely appeal to the House parliamentarians and the Speaker's office about these jurisdictional concerns. By convincing the Speaker and the parliamentarians that a provision in an Energy and Commerce bill treaded on the Judiciary Committee's jurisdiction, it could trigger a subsequent referral of the bill to the Judiciary panel and potentially reshape or stall the legislation. Republicans in the House changed the rules regarding referrals during the mid-1990s, but the general point remains the same. As power became more fragmented during the 1970s through the 1990s, the referral process became another entry point and an increasingly used tactic of the lobbying world.

Challenging legislation later in the process, such as in the Rules Committee or by challenging a rule on the House floor, is another popular tactic in a more fragmented process. Lobbyists now routinely ask lawmakers to petition the House Rules Committee to make certain amendments in order. If they are successful, the amendments could (if adopted) disrupt fragile compromises reached earlier. If an amendment is not made in order, it sometimes allows interest groups the opportunity to urge lawmakers to vote against the legislation. Either way, in the post-1974 House, it has become easier and more common for lobbyists to ask lawmakers to ambush or amend legislation at various points in the process, ranging from committee referral decisions very early in the game to late-stage procedures, such as the structure of the rule governing consideration of legislation on the House floor. As the system fragmented, and more lawmakers and staff felt empowered to participate, lobbyists adapted and used the legislative procedure to affect the process in the House.

And the House is not the only place where lobbyists use procedure in a more fragmented process. Greater use of "holds" on bills and nominations in the U.S. Senate provides another example of an "entry point" lobbyists exploit. Interest organizations now routinely request Senators place anonymous holds on legislation that the organizations oppose. While holds have always been part of the culture of the U.S. Senate, their use has become more common in recent years.

Holds offer a particularly effective tactic when Senators use them late in the process. When time is at a premium and the legislative calendar packed, interest groups opposed to a particular bill or advocates who want to produce some kind of action on an unrelated item may ask Senators to put holds on bills or nominations in order to build leverage in the legislative process. One congressional scholar underscores the power of holds during end-of-session time crunches: " . . . one Senator placed a hold on the Export Administration Act so he could try to attach his home equity loan amendment to it."[22] It's impossible to know for sure, but the chances that an interest group and a lobbyist asked the Senator to impose that hold are very high.

PARTISAN CONTROL AND THE OVERSIGHT AGENDA

The Democratic takeover of Congress following the 2006 election and the new majority's interest in oversight is another institutional change that sent ripples through the lobbying world. Democrats complained between 2001 and 2006 that the Republican majority in the House did too little on the oversight front. Democrats controlled a slim majority in the Senate from June of 2001 until January of 2003. But other than that 18-month period, Republicans maintained the majority in the Senate too.

While some disagree that the Republican oversight effort was lackluster, most acknowledged that the new majority would focus new energy on investigations in both the House and the Senate beginning in 2007. Pharmaceutical makers, managed care companies, defense contractors, and insurance companies were among those with the bull's-eye on them. Law firms and lobbyists with backgrounds in congressional investigations saw a surge in demand. Many law firms beefed up their practices specializing in investigations, hiring former staffers from the Hill and other lawyers to meet these new demands. "Our white collar crime and investigations practice has been the fastest growing part of our business this year," a lawyer/lobbyist with a major Washington law firm observed in 2007.

Some consider the oversight process a no-man's-land between a "court of law and the court of public opinion."[23] A recent article in *The Hill* newspaper put it this way:

> Jack Quinn, a counsel to then-President Clinton—and thus someone familiar with congressional inquiries—said he has also heard from clients about what Democrats are likely to be looking for. His firm, Quinn Gillespie & Associates, isn't a law firm, but has still guided health care, financial services, and telecommunications clients through the public battering that can often accompany congressional investigations. 'We have already heard from corporate clients that are concerned they might be in the crosshairs,' Quinn said. Quinn Gillespie recently hired Kevin Kayes, a chief counsel to (then) Senate Minority Leader Harry Reid (D-NV). Kayes is expected to help with the firm's investigations practice.

So once again, changes in the government environment – in this case partisan control of Congress – the advocacy world to adapt as well, adding new people, structures, expertise, and services, just as they have in the past.

OPPORTUNITIES FOR POLICY ENTREPRENEURS

Another implication of larger government and more staff has been the emergence of policy entrepreneurs—lawmakers, congressional staff, and other government officials who promote new ideas that can either help or hurt the welfare of interest groups. Policy entrepreneurs often generate new ideas, policy proposals, oversight requests, and investigations. Each of these initiatives can hold a host of implications for interest groups, enhancing or hurting their competitive positions, costing or saving money, or even affecting a company's reputation within its industry or among its customers. Additional staff, subcommittees, and a greater number of power centers all create the means for mischief or positive change. Interest groups must monitor and often try to influence these developments. Prior to the 1970s, when committee chairs ran their panels like fiefdoms, policy entrepreneurs had fewer opportunities to generate new ideas or initiatives. But as the changes in government have unfolded, the number of policy entrepreneurs has grown as well, which in turn has altered the way interest groups operate. The lobbying world have responded by getting bigger more professionalized and sophisticated in their advocacy efforts and the tools deployed.

BOOSTING THE NEED FOR POLICY SPECIALISTS

Increasing policy complexity also has produced repercussions in the advocacy world. As demonstrated earlier in this chapter, the number and length of regulations has ballooned during the past four decades. So has the average length of bills enacted into law. Life in Washington has become more complex, more complicated. A slap on the back, a stiff drink, and a good cigar no longer produce the desired results in the persuasion game. As congressional staff have become more specialized and substantive, the advocacy world has had to respond in kind. The lobbying world has changed by hiring more specialists and experts of its own. Some corporations have created their own policy development departments or hired issues managers. It is not unusual for corporations and trade groups to coordinate closely the efforts of internal policy development staff with their hired lobbyists. The health care industry is a good example. Organizations like the American Hospital Association, American Medical Association, and America's Health Insurance Plans all now have extremely sophisticated internal policy divisions. The insurance, pharmaceutical, energy and banking industries have done the same, as have a host of public interest groups and labor unions. These positions at advocacy organizations were either much smaller or nonexistent in the 1960s and 1970s because the demand for this type of expertise from policymakers was much lower.

SUMMARY

An expanding, decentralized, and activist government Leviathan clearly has rocked the lobbying world over the past 40 years—creating growth, more professionalism, and the institutionalization of various advocacy functions within interest groups. Increasingly, the government has become a risk as well as a potential profit center—a nuance we need to add to our list of reasons why lobbying deserves reconsideration. "From the standpoint of regulated industries you might hear, 'I'm going to introduce a bill to ruin your business—so talk me out of it," a lobbyist who has worked in Washington for three decades recalls. That has required a big change in attitudes, as well as strategies and structures, including forming Washington offices for interest groups, hiring lobbyists, forming PACs, and significantly boosting engagement in the public policy and electoral processes. "And again, from a business perspective, this was all happening during the rise of public interest lobbying for a whole variety of causes," he said.

And while all this new activity has led to lobbying growth, it also has constrained advocacy power. The growth of the lobbying world didn't necessarily produce more influence for individual interests. The changes generated a more nuanced effect. More money, more lobbyists did not necessarily mean interest groups achieved whatever they wanted.

Additional decision-makers in the process affected the lobbying world in other ways as well. The smaller, more closed system was split wide open by changes in the seniority and committee system. More lawmakers and staff involved in shaping policy mean increases in interest group and lobbying activity. These changes have implications for how lobbying is structured, as well as for the types of tactics and tools lobbyists deploy. But an enlarging, decentralized government has not been the only transformation in the environment of lobbyists. Other factors have contributed to the emergence and contours of the advocacy industry as we know it today. Outlining these changes and their implications for the lobbying industry is the next step in getting under the influence and reconsidering the advocacy industry.

NOTES

1. Quoted in Paul Taylor, "Lobbyists Lose the Game, Not the Guccis," *The Washington Post*, July 31, 1983, A12.
2. Beth L. Leech, Frank R. Baumgartner, Timothy M. Lapira, and Nicholas A. Semanko, "Drawing Lobbyists to Washington: Government Activity and the Demand for Advocacy," *Political Research Quarterly* 58(1) (March, 2005): 19–30.
3. Ibid. 19.
4. Ibid.
5. For a good review of the causes and consequences of changes in the House, see David W. Rohde, *Parties and Leaders in the Post Reform House* (Chicago, IL: University of Chicago Press, 1991).
6. Taylor, "Lobbyists Lose the Game, Not the Guccis."
7. See Tim Groseclose and David C. King, "Committee Theories Reconsidered," In Lawrence C. Dodd and Bruce I. Oppenheimer, *Congress Reconsidered*. 7th ed. (Washington D.C.: CQ Press), 204.
8. Norman Ornstein, Thomas Mann, and Michael Malbin, *Vital Statistics on Congress* (Washington, D.C.: The American Enterprise Institute Press, 2002).
9. Ibid. 13.
10. Phyllis S. McGrath, *Redefining Corporate-Federal Relations* (New York, NY: Conference Board, 1979), 1. This study was cited in Jeffrey M. Berry and Clyde Wilcox, *The Interest Group Society*, 4th ed. (New York, NY: Pearson Longman, 2007), 27.
11. Gary J. Andres, "Business Involvement in Campaign Finance" (Chicago, IL: Unpublished Ph.D Dissertation, The University of Illinois-Chicago, 1983); and Gary J. Andres, "Business Involvement in Campaign Finance: Factors Influencing the Decision to Form a Corporate PAC," *PS. Spring*, Vol. XVIII, No. 2 (Washington, D.C.: The American Political Science Association, 1985).
12. Ornstein, Mann, and Malbin, 15.
13. Ornstein, Mann, and Malbin, 13
14. Ten Thousand Commandments: An Annual Snapshot of the Federal Regulatory State. Clyde Wayne Crews, Jr. The Competitive Enterprise Institute, 2006.
15. Susan E. Dudley, "The Hidden Tax of Regulation," The Mercatus Center, George Mason University January 5, 2004.
16. For a good review of these developments, see the House Rules Committee website, http://www.rules.house.gov/archives/jcoc2bn.htm.
17. The developments in campaign finance laws are discussed in more detail in Chapters 5 and 7.
18. For a detailed history of the legal and political developments leading to the AT&T breakup, see Steve Coll, *The Deal of the Century: The Breakup of AT&T* (New York: Simon and Shuster, 1988).
19. Ibid.

20. *The Wall Street Journal* Editorial, May 10, 2007, A16.
21. See, for example, Barbara Sinclair's Unorthodox Lawmaking for a comprehensive description of these changes in more recent years.
22. Walter J. Oleszek, *Congressional Procedures and the Policy Process*. 6th ed. (Washington DC: CQ Press, 2004).
23. Jim Snyder, "Corporations Prep for Inquisitive Oversight," The *Hill*, December 6, 2006.

CHAPTER 5

PARTISANSHIP AND THE
ADVOCACY INDUSTRY

Partisanship has gotten out of hand in Washington at every level. The goal used to be to just win—beat your political opponents, shake hands and move on. Now the goal is to destroy them—politically and personally.

Democratic U.S. Senator

This is a tribal town now. You're either Red Sox or Yankees.

Scott Parven, Democratic Lobbyist[1]

Partisanship defines contemporary American politics, and polarization shapes every vestige of the Washington landscape. Political scientists debate the causes and consequences of the permanent campaign mentality and polarization with vigor and regularity. While its origins and effects are still a little murky, the spike in partisanship in Washington is undisputed. I call the link between polarization, the permanent campaign, and lobbying "the electoral/advocacy complex." Understanding the impact of partisan polarization on interest groups and advocacy is another critical piece of reconsidering lobbying.

Political scientists Nolan McCarty, Keith T. Poole, and Howard Rosenthal write in their 2006 book, *Polarized America* : "In the middle of the twentieth century, the Democrats and the Republicans danced almost cheek to cheek in their courtship of the political middle. Over the past thirty years, the parties have deserted the center of the floor in favor of the wings. In the parlance of punditry and campaign rhetoric circa 2004, American politics have polarized."[2] And while there is lively debate about whether polarization is just confined to elites and politicians, or whether it spreads to voters in general, the growth of congressional polarization is certain.[3] David Hobbs, a former House leadership aide and head of White House Legislative Affairs agrees. Asked about some of the biggest changes he has seen in Washington over the last 20 years, he puts the growth of partisanship at the top of his list. Hobbs believes a more closely divided Congress breeds more partisanship. "It's easy to be fair and nice when at the end of the day you win by 60 votes in the House," he says.

But how does increasing partisan polarization and the permanent campaign mentality in Washington affect lobbying? Considerably, I maintain, but that impact remains largely unexplored.

This chapter dissects four major dimensions of the relationship between partisanship and lobbying:

- Closer links between congressional leadership and lobbyists.
- Closer links between party organizations and lobbyists.
- Advent of boutique lobbying firms.
- How partisanship empowers and strengthens interest groups and lobbyists.

The increased partisan environment confronted by interest groups and lobbyists caused ripple effects through the advocacy world. Polarization changed lobbying; precisely how is investigated below.

POLARIZATION, PARTY LEADERSHIP IN CONGRESS, AND LOBBYING

One of the consequences of polarization is the growing importance of legislative party leadership. The power of leadership has ebbed and flowed throughout the history of Congress. Prior to the 1880s, it was relatively feckless. Writing in 1885 Woodrow Wilson described legislative operations as "committee government."[4] But not long after Wilson published his classic text, legislative leaders asserted themselves more into the operation of Congress, particularly in the U.S. House of Representatives.[5] Centralized power grew to an apex under Speakers such as Thomas Brackett Reed and Joseph Cannon in the late nineteenth and early twentieth centuries. But over time, many in the House rebelled against the autocratic style of these leaders and pushed back. During the first half of the twentieth century, lawmakers recoiled against tyrannical leaders and power became more decentralized again in the House. The uprising against leadership created a relatively long period of decentralized power in Congress. Some describe this as a period of moving "from hierarchy to bargaining."[6] Scholars note that the post-Watergate reforms in the Democratic Party gradually consolidated power back to the leadership after this relatively long period of committee rule that began in the early twentieth century. Following the 1994 election, Republicans in the House continued this trend toward moving power back into the hands of congressional leaders, as Speaker Newt Gingrich and his team consolidated and strengthened party control even more.

This ebb and flow of leadership power has important implications for lobbying. Students of advocacy should know that the leaders' grip on power, whether weak or strong, will affect interest-group tactics. In more recent years, the lobbying industry responded accordingly as centralized power swung back to the hands of congresional leaders again.

Political scientists Gary Cox and Mathew McCubbins argue that as polarization increased during the 1990s, rank-in-file members of Congress voluntarily empowered their party leaders to craft more unified party positions. Central to their thesis is the notion that a political party's "brand" is a public good. That is, all members are affected positively or negatively depending on the rising or falling fortunes of their party—regardless of what individual lawmakers do on their own initiative. " . . . if a party's reputation improves or worsens, all members benefit or suffer together, regardless of whether they contributed to the improvement or worsening,"[7] they write. Moreover, compiling a favorable record of accomplishment, or what Cox and McCubbins call "team production," is key to improving the party's brand. But achievement means overcoming a series of cooperation and coordination problems. The most common solution to a collective action problem means delegating power to a central authority.[8]

As partisanship increased during the 1990s, "team production" became more critical than ever. Lawmakers responded by doing what Cox and McCubbins's "responsible party" theory suggests: they delegated increasing amounts of authority to congressional leadership. This change affected both Congress and interest groups. Here are a couple of examples.

Consolidated party leadership increased in the House after Republicans won the majority in the 1994 election. Following the Republican takeover of Congress in January of 1995, Speaker of the House Newt Gingrich consolidated power in a number of ways. He had to ensure the House delivered on its promises to finish the *Contract with America* on time. The *Contract* included 10 bills the GOP campaigned on during the 1994 election, including popular measures such as a balanced budget, welfare reform, term limits for members of Congress, tax cuts, and regulatory reform. Republicans promised they would bring up votes on all these matters in the House or "you could throw us out of office." This required a more hands-on approach on the part of the leadership to process legislation through committees and to the floor. House Republican leadership task forces held daily coordinating meetings, planning when legislation would get introduced, marked-up in committee, and then scheduled for floor consideration. "The Leadership completely dominated the process during the *Contract*," says a Republican lobbyist who worked on the Hill in 1995.

A trend toward interest groups hiring lobbyists with close ties to the new congressional leadership was one of the first responses of the advocacy community. "If lobbyists wanted to make changes to the legislation, they had to work with the leadership. And most smart interest groups at the time were looking to hire lobbyists with close ties to the leadership." The new

Republican majority created a renewed sense of disequilibrium in the lobbying world, a powerful shift similar to the transformations produced by the post-Watergate congressional reforms. The advocacy world responded by changing its structure, style, and substantive methods—taking steps to improve information gathering and reduce uncertainty.

While most interest groups certainly hoped to gain influence with the new majority by hiring Republican lobbyists there were clearly other motivations. Gathering intelligence, understanding the decision-making process, and reducing uncertainty in this new environment were all critical determinants as well in hiring those with strong GOP ties. Information became a currency as valuable as influence, and Republican lobbyists in 1995 had a wealth of it. The same phenomenon occurred after Democrats to over the majority in Congress following the 2006 midterm elections. "I'm getting hired principally as a 'translator,' " a former House Democratic leadership aide who is now a public affairs consultant said in 2007. "Business groups don't know how to talk to Democrats, because they haven't really had to deal with them for the past 12 years," he observed. "Now they do, and I help them understand the new majority."

Interest groups need help analyzing, interpreting, and responding to these new conditions. Hiring lobbyists who can decode and predict the meaning of these shifts and restore some sense of equilibrium is a valuable asset in the advocacy world. These partisan lobbyists don't "control" the process by writing amendments as the press likes to suggest, but they can help explain leadership's motivations and predict their next steps—all valuable currency in the advocacy economy. And as the power of partisanship grew during the 1990s and as the reach of leadership expanded, lobbyists with close ties to the new power centers became an increasingly valued commodity.

Strong party leaders also led to another change in the lobbying world— separate venues for advocacy outside the traditional committee process. Again, Speaker Gingrich's approach to legislation in the mid-1990s provides a good example of the expanded purview of the leadership. Gingrich believed legislative accomplishments were both important for his party and his responsibility as leader. He would not let committee chairs' obstinacy or egos stand in the way of GOP legislative wins. In effect, he created a second forum to formulate and arbitrate differences on legislation. Bob Rusbuldt, president and CEO of the Independent Insurance Agents & Brokers of America, underscores this dynamic:

> Everything changed after the 1994 elections. Before Republicans took over, the best lobbyists had strong relationships with committee chairs. Now knowing the leaders is just as—or even more—important. This shift from the dominance of committee chairs to the dominance of elected party leaders is the biggest change in Washington I've observed in the last 20 years.

The House Republican leadership during the 1990s consistently proved this lobbyist right. Speaker Gingrich's style meant there were two forums for lobbying every bill—the committee and the leadership. Sometimes an entire measure was rewritten after a committee reported the bill because lobbyists convinced the leadership it was a bad piece of legislation. The 1996 telecommunications legislation offers a good example. Lobbyists for local telephone interests were unhappy with the legislation crafted by the House Energy and Commerce Committee, viewing then-chairman Thomas Bliley of Virginia as more of a friend to their rivals, such as long distance businesses AT&T and MCI and a host of small local competitors unhappy with the rates local phone companies charged for access to their network of residential and business customers. Once the bill was reported from the committee, lobbyists for local phone interests immediately focused on the second forum—the offices of the Republican congressional leaders, especially Speaker Gingrich's. They charged the bill would move the telephone industry back toward "reregulation," a concept despised by many economic conservatives in GOP circles—especially new majority leader Speaker Gingrich, who prided himself as a champion of deregulation in the tradition of President Ronald Reagan.

After heavy lobbying from the Bell Companies, Gingrich announced he would not bring a "reregulatory bill" to the House floor and it had to be changed. Working with the leadership, Bell Company lobbyists made changes in the bill and received assurances that certain amendments making further modifications were in order. This process would not have occurred during a period of weaker congressional leadership and less partisan polarization. But the Republican leadership possessed the means to make such a change, and it dramatically impacted how interest groups approached the process.

This two-track power structure also worked in favor of legislation that lobbyists convinced leadership was meritorious. If the leadership liked a bill, they could jump-start the committee process or clear the way for expedited floor consideration. The leadership became like a separate legislative court. They could either breathe new life into a bill or give it a death sentence.

Rusbuldt adds,

> Before 1994 the process was less political and less ideological. Committee chairmen were all powerful and created fiefdoms. You wanted to know Dan Rostenkowski (former Democratic chairman of the House Ways and Means Committee), not Tom Foley (former Democratic Speaker of the House). The committee chairs would give some legislative things to Republicans from time to time, because they were just not that political. Even the lobbyists were less political. They were more interested in power than ideology. You got the sense that most lobbyists would be comfortable with Republicans or Democrats in charge. *They just wanted to know whoever was in charge.* After the Republicans took over in 1994 that all changed and there was a fundamental shift in power. The leadership now called the shots and they often checked

your party pedigree at the door. It was really hard for a Democratic lobbyist to get anything done with the new leadership. They were shut out. They had no access.

The days of committees exclusively calling the shots were over in this new era of strong centralized leadership. This hyper-partisan environment was more reminiscent of the late nineteenth century and early twentieth century when Speakers ruled with iron fists. And it was a dramatic departure from the pre-polarized era prior to the 1990s when committee chairs held a lot more sway. During the 1990s, it was not unusual for members of the Speaker's or majority leader's staffs to show up at a committee markup and give instructions about how the leadership wanted a bill to turn out. "We saw the Speaker's staff at our markup today," a committee aide said. "They usually don't show up in the committee room. That tells me this bill is a leadership priority," he said. The savviest elements of the interest-group world understood the implications of this power shift and would heavily lobby the leadership in this new environment.

I remember a couple of circumstances during my days working in the White House Office of Legislative Affairs for George H. W. Bush when Speaker Foley was asked to arbitrate a conflict between two powerful committee chairs. He used to say, "It's not my problem. They have to work it out." In one major dispute between Energy and Commerce Chairman John Dingell and House Ways and Means Committee Dan Rostenkowski, Speaker Tom Foley looked at his two chairmen and said, "The two of you have to resolve this."

In contrast, in a more polarized era, when feuds between committees stalled the legislative process and a party's substantive accomplishments, leadership stepped in—providing interest groups a new venue for lobbying. For example, during consideration of financial services reform legislation in the late 1990s, House Republican Conference Chairman John Boehner of Ohio negotiated jurisdictional and policy differences between the House Energy and Commerce Committee and the House Financial Services Committee, shepherding the legislation to successful enactment. Without ignoring the committee members in this process, many lobbyists also petitioned to Boehner because of his pivotal role in the process. This unprecedented amount of leadership involvement in the dance of legislation changed the way lobbyists approached the lawmaking tango.

As leadership consolidated power during the 1990s, some interests actually hired two different types of lobbyists: one that understood the committee process and another equipped with good ties to the leadership. The practice of interest groups retaining an individual or a firm with "close ties to the leadership" became a common strategy. How polarization contributed to the growth of "partisan" lobbying firms is discussed in more detail later in this chapter.

Despite the myriad reasons for heightened interest-group demand in hiring lobbyists with close ties to the congressional leadership, most observers continue to focus only on the role of advocates *influencing* the process. The attention in the media on lobbyists drafting legislation is an example of how this emphasis on "influence" is overblown. The real impact of lobbyists in a partisan age is different than secretly writing new laws in the cubbyholes of the Capitol. That only happens on TV.

Critics of the Republican majority during this period charged the GOP allowed K Street lobbyists actually to write legislation in the Capitol—a charge with dubious authenticity, but one that quickly became part of the conventional wisdom in Washington. "Lobbyists writing legislation in the Capitol"—usually invited to participate by the "evil Dick Cheney"—became part of the media and Democratic mantra leading up to the 2006 congressional elections—another illustration (they charged) of the "culture of corruption." Elizabeth Drew typifies much of the writing about lobbyists and Republicans during this time period:

> Corruption has always been present in Washington, but in recent years it has become more sophisticated, pervasive and blatant than ever. A friend of mine who works closely with lobbyists says, 'There are no restraints now; business groups and lobbyists are going crazy. *They're in every room on Capitol Hill writing legislation.*' (emphasis added)[9]

Political scientists also reported that "outside groups had unprecedented access to bill drafting" during the early days of the Republican majority in 1995.[10]

This allegation was not only overstated, but far less nefarious than suggested by the sensational headlines. It is common practice for interest groups, particularly those who employ former staffers with substantive legislative drafting expertise, to make suggestions about a bill's technical language. Despite breathless charges from the media and Democrats, Dick Cheney and the Republicans did not invent the practice. Lawmakers often welcome this help as a way to ensure they are accomplishing their intended objectives. It's a highly common practice in Washington and is not unique to the Republicans of the mid-1990s. Indeed, in 2007, after Democrats took control of the House, a Republican staff director of a major House committee reinforced this point:

> Labor union lobbyists are now drafting legislation for the Democrats. I know it because the Democratic staff is showing me the same documents the unions showed me last year. The Democrats are working with their labor union allies the same way we worked with business lobbyists. The only difference is the press used to write a lot about business lobbyists giving us their ideas in legislative language. They just seem to ignore it when labor does the same thing with the Democrats.

In the real world of lobbying, both Democrats and Republicans rely on expert outside allies to draft legislation to make sure it comports with lawmakers' objectives. They want to ensure it's technically and substantively sound. Lawmakers would likely reach the same policy conclusions with or without the lobbyists' help—it just may take them longer and their final product likely would include unintended errors. The fact that some lobbyists write legislation is undisputed. The conclusion that this behavior suggests "inordinate influence" is an exaggeration. But in this hyper-partisan age, those kinds of allegations are commonplace and expected when it comes to lobbying.

Drafting legislation in the backrooms of Congress is not the real reason interest groups hire Republican or Democratic lobbyists with close ties to the majority party leadership during an era of increased partisanship. The central reason lobbyists with close ties to the Republicans were hired in the mid-1990s and Democrats were in such demand during 2007 was their ability to help interest groups gather information, reduce uncertainty, and restore some equilibrium as changes in the institutional environment of Congress occurred. *As the Democratic consultant argued above—groups need "translators" and trusted former staff that can help shape the agenda of the interest group to fit the majority party's goals.*

PARTISANSHIP AND THE GROWTH OF REVERSE LOBBYING

Growing demands on lobbyists to help promote partisan agendas is yet another consequence of polarization. In recent years, as partisanship became a more dominant fixture in Washington, advancing party-backed legislation ("team production" in the words of Cox and McCubbins) became a central goal for both Republicans and Democrats in Congress—and lobbyists were called upon more frequently to assist in these efforts. Asking interest groups to help pass legislation backed by congressional parties turns traditional advocacy on its head. It's a phenomenon some label "reverse lobbying."[11] Instead of interest groups asking lawmakers for help, in this case it's the elected officials doing the "asking." Once again, the *Contract with America* period offers a unique perspective into how growing partisanship has created new opportunities and challenges for lobbyists.

In 1995, Republicans united two disparate parts of their electoral coalition—business interests and social conservative groups. Lobbyists representing the Chamber of Commerce, the National Association of Manufacturers, and the National Federation of Independent Business joined with social conservative groups like the Eagle Forum (conservative activist Phyllis Schlafly's organization), National Right to Life and Sixty Plus (a conservative senior citizen organization). These groups met along with a host of veteran Republican lobbyists and GOP House leadership staff to organize the "outside" infrastructure and lobbying campaign supporting the *Contract with America.* This ad hoc coalition mobilized thousands of grassroots contacts supporting all parts of the *Contract.* "Social groups and business groups came together with one condition, they had to support all the bills in the *Contract,* not just the ones that pertained to their organization," a former GOP leadership aide said. Republicans on the Hill mobilized support for their agenda using the resources of these lobbying organizations and individual advocates. It was a powerful example of how strengthened party leadership deployed their clout to activate support for their agenda. The lobbyists enjoyed the access and goodwill it built for them and their organizations. The legislative leaders benefited from the instant reservoir of political support for their agenda.

In this example of "reverse lobbying," congressional leadership organized these groups. Instead of lobbyists petitioning lawmakers, it was the elected officials asking for help promoting their agenda. Many of the groups had little direct interest in the legislation. National Right to Life traditionally did not lobby on balancing the budget or tax cuts, while the Chamber of Commerce usually didn't advocate the social conservatives' agenda. Yet in this case, passing the *Contract* and helping the Republican leadership united them. Many of these interest groups, whether business-oriented or socially conservative, believed their goals were enhanced if the Republicans succeeded. In many ways, *partisan success* was every bit as important as a means of influence as contacts and relationships—the traditional modes of advocacy. Interest groups working with congressional parties realized the added benefit of building their lobbying contacts. Hence, they welcomed the requests for reverse lobbying from the new GOP majority and willingly joined the effort.

Yet, turning advocacy on its head was not a completely new legislative exercise. Its seeds were planted in the late 1980s and early 1990s as partisan polarization rose. Democrats developed an interest-group coalition of their own during this time. It was less structured and institutionalized than the GOP's efforts in 1995, but lobbyists representing labor unions, environmental groups, the trial bar, and liberal public interest groups were called upon with increasing frequency. For example, during several major votes in 1991 and 1992, Speaker Tom Foley and Majority Leader Richard Gephardt organized representatives from many of these groups to lobby when the House considered legislation critical to the Democrats. Even though many of these interests had little pending directly in the measures, ensuring success for the Democrats was important to them. Party mattered more as polarization heightened and these groups wanted to see the Democrats succeed. The leadership "reverse lobbied" these groups and received a needed dose of manpower and lobbying resources. Sometimes the lobbyists provided intelligence on how a lawmaker might vote. Other times their presence and involvement just sent a signal. A Democratic lobbyist with ties to the congressional leadership recalls, "Labor believed that it was important for the Democrats to win. On important votes they were often asked by the leadership to show up at the Capitol to send a signal—'this vote counts, for labor and the Democrats.'"

More recently, congressional Democrats in 2007 engaged in reverse lobbying on the State Children's Health Insurance Program (SCHIP), a critical party initiative. As the Capitol Hill newspaper *Roll Call* reported,

> Senior House Democrats are turning to K Street to help them sell an ambitious expansion of children's health insurance. It is a textbook, if rarely seen, example of Congressional operatives turning the tables on lobbyists— Democratic leaders pressuring downtown interests to provide them air cover for their plan. The campaign still is in its formative stages, but the majority party already has sought funding from a broad cross-section of downtown groups, including those representing drug companies, doctors, hospitals, labor unions and patients. They want lobbying organizations to fund a multimillion-dollar media blitz for the widely popular State Children's Health Insurance Program.[12]

In this particular case, Energy and Commerce Committee Chairman John Dingell of Michigan called trade association leaders asking for their help funding the advertising blitz. And the lobbyists wanted to avoid having their ox gored as a way to pay for SCHIP expansion. "Everyone is nervous about becoming a pay-for, so we all know it's in our best interest to help out," said one person familiar with the discussions.[13]

These are all examples of why political scientists Richard L. Hall and Alan V. Deardorff call for a broader definition of lobbying. They argue that how we view advocacy needs to expand. Instead of thinking about it only as either "exchange" (vote buying) or "persuasion" (information signaling), they suggest another model: legislative subsidy. Describing this subsidy as a "matching grant of policy information, political intelligence, and legislative labor to the enterprises of strategically selected legislators,"[14] they also argue, "the proximate political objective of this strategy is not to change legislators' minds but to assist natural allies in achieving their own, coincident objectives."[15] Another observer analyzing lobbying during a much earlier period comes to the same conclusion. J. McIver Weatherford, in his book *Tribes on the Hill*, writes, ". . . lobbyists play a permanent part in the congressman's career as information broker." Weatherford references an article former President John Kennedy wrote while a member of the U.S. Senate:

> As John Kennedy described them, 'lobbyists are in many cases expert technicians and capable of explaining complex and difficult subjects in a clear, understandable fashion.' Among the specific tasks lobbyists perform Kennedy listed preparing briefs and legislative analyses, as well as writing legislation. They keep detailed score cards on past voting records of other

members, as well as important political information on the other members' supporters. And these facts and figures are laced with appropriate bits of inside gossip, which may be of even greater importance than the technical information.[16]

This broader view of lobbying helps us better understand how and why advocates do what they do in the real world. Interest groups in the example above did not "lobby" Chairman Dingell. Instead, he "lobbied" them. In effect, asking for a subsidy to help enact a shared legislative agenda.

POLARIZATION AND EARMARKING

The relationship between partisanship and lobbying has also come into clear focus with the rise of earmarks over the past decade. One of the ironies of the Republican majority between 1995 and 2006 was its heavy use of government spending and earmarking as a way to gain political favor. Despite being a party based on principles of fiscal conservatism and smaller government, Republicans opened up the spending spigot as a way to curry favor with local constituencies and help GOP members win reelection. As a party it was important to win. More spending was the vehicle to do that, and the lobbying world came along for the ride. But in the end the strategy backfired—at least for the Republican Party.

"We spent like drunken sailors," one former Republican House staffer turned lobbyist says. He is right. Not only did overall federal spending skyrocket in the last several years of the Republican majority, but so did the number of earmarks. According to a Congressional Research Service (CRS) analysis, the number of earmarks authorized by Congress in appropriations bills alone increased from 4,155 in 1994 to 15,887 in 2005—an increase of 282 percent. Others provide even higher estimates. Citizens Against Government Waste (CAGW) estimates there were 1,439 earmarks in 1995 and 13,997 in 2005, an increase of 872 percent. Different definitions of earmarks account for this variation but the trend is clear—directed spending ballooned during the Republican majority.[17] Much of this increase in spending was directly related to the aftermath of the terrorist attacks on September 11, 2001, the wars in Iraq and Afghanistan, and the new Medicare prescription drug benefit. Non-defense, non-entitlement spending was actually more constrained. But these details were lost on the public, who viewed the big rise in government spending by a Republican Congress and a Republican president bad management at best and hypocritical at worst.

"Despite our 'conservative' principles, we thought we could 'buy' the majority," one former GOP House leadership laments. "It didn't work out that way." Or at least not forever—every binge has its hangover. The Democrats wove an effective tapestry, conflating Republican spending and earmarks on projects like "a bridge to nowhere," with ties to lobbyists like the infamous Jack Abramoff mentioned earlier. They spun a "culture of corruption" theme that linked wrongdoing by a few Republican members of Congress into the tangled web of political deceit. Perceptions of corruption and inordinately close ties to lobbyists were one of the factors that led to Republican defeat in the 2006 election.

The rise in earmarking also led to growth in the lobbying business. In another example of what Galbraith might call "countervailing power," once some interest groups saw others achieve earmark success, they decided to hire lobbyists too. "I had a university come to me," one lobbyist recalls. "They told me, 'We noticed other universities are hiring lobbyists to get earmarks. We want to do the same." And in a more partisan age, interest groups sought out Republican lobbyists between 1995 and 2006 to help convince the majority to add more spending. GOP members, thinking the additional directed spending could help maintain the majority by enhancing accomplishments and "team production," willingly complied with these requests, even though more federal spending was at odds with their conservative philosophy.

Earmarks suffer from misperceptions among citizens and changing attitudes in the minds of lawmakers in Washington. It wasn't that long ago that "pork barrel" spending was viewed as a staple of smart congressional politics and worn as a badge of honor by elected officials. "Pork barreling," along with casework and lawmaking are the three central roles of members of Congress according to one leading political scientist.[18] Yet, that all has begun to change in the last few years.

Seeing a political opening in 2006, Democrats tied the GOP's big-spending ways and ties to lobbyists seeking money around the Republicans' political necks. The Democrats used earmarks as a noose. And it worked. Many believe the Republicans' disregard for fiscal restraint in the last couple of years before the 2006 election cost them their congressional majority.

Since returning to the minority in 2007, Republicans have begun doing most of the talking about ending earmarks. Lobbyists have had to make a big shift in their strategies and tactics, not only because of the new majority, but also because many GOP lawmakers now eschew the process of earmarking in general. Republican appropriators still ask for and get earmarks, but in lower amounts and with less frequency.

A former Republican "cardinal" (chairman of an appropriations subcommittee) put it this way in early 2007: "I talked to the new (Democratic) chairman last week, and he said, 'Look, you always treated me well when I was in the minority, and I will do the same with you.' I take him at his word and he will treat me okay. It's some of the more junior Republican members of the committee that will get cut back. But they'll be okay too." In 2008, House Republicans sought to rebuild their brand as the party of fiscal discipline by advocating an outright ban on earmarks. The senate rejected that proposal.

There is no doubt, however, that for those lobbyists who work specifically with the appropriations process, the new scrutiny on earmarks and the change in party control will result in major adjustments in how they conduct their business. But most agree it will cause a change in emphasis, who gets lobbied, and who does the lobbying, rather than a whole-scale change in the process of getting an earmark. Keep in mind Congressman James Moran of Virginia's comments about the Interior appropriations bill under his chairmanship: "When I become chairman, I'm going to earmark the shit out of it," he told constituents.[19] Like lobbyists' reputation problems, some things never change.

Much could be written about the politics of earmarking in general. Yet as the practice pertains to lobbying in a partisan world, a few more observations are in order. First, this kind of congressionally mandated spending takes on many forms in addition to the traditional dollop of cash from the appropriations committee. For example, in the 2007 House-passed SCHIP bill, Democratic lawmakers, eager to win a majority of votes, made changes in the Medicare law that reclassified cities for payment purposes. Taking a city, town, or county and reclassifying it into a higher payment area is one way to target more money to a congressional district without appropriating more funds. Also, in the 2007 energy bill passed by the House, Republicans charged that billions of dollars spent to guarantee renewable energy bonds were nothing more than "green pork." Here again, using the tax code to redirect federal revenue flows through the tax code is just an earmark by another name.

Earmarked spending can manifest itself in many ways. Lobbyists and their allies in Congress possess a variety of options to promote directed spending. Whether it is through the appropriations process by changing formulas in authorization or entitlement legislation or through the tax code, directing particularized benefits to members is a popular device to garner legislative support. And in an era of growing partisanship, providing these benefits – even through unorthodox means – is a growing practice.[20]

Looking at the FY 2008 appropriations process, all the negative publicity heaped on earmarks by Democrats in 2006 and then by Republicans in 2007 is having some effect. The Office of Management and Budget (OMB) in 2007 instituted a tracking procedure for future earmarks, using FY 2005 as a baseline. According to the OMB, the total number of appropriations earmarks for FY 2005 was 13,492. For FY 2008 (these estimates are subject to change) the number of appropriations earmarks dropped to 6,651, less than half the total from three years earlier. The Bush Administration proposed cutting earmarks in half again in its 2009 budget.

From a lobbying perspective, many believe earmarks are on the decline due to negative publicity—at least in the appropriations process. But as mentioned above, lawmakers and lobbyists can direct federal spending in other ways—through tax policy and the authorization process. One media account sums up what lobbying insiders in Washington all know: " . . . the taboo has not stopped either Democrats or Republicans from continuing to seek these expenditures while calling them something else. Members of Congress are now resorting to less obvious tactics that allow them to get money to favored beneficiaries without acknowledging support for what others consider to be earmarks."[21] The article goes on to review some of the new tactics utilized by lawmakers and lobbyists, including holding hearings to cajole and pressure executive branch officials, using special procedures to hide earmarks in spending bills, as well as letters and phone calls to bureaucrats to solidify spending commitments.

Indeed, in 2008 Washington lobbyists were abuzz with rumors of lawmakers engaging in "phone-marks" or "phone-pork," whereby lawmakers or their staff call executive branch agencies to gain assurances that money will be spent in a particular way even without a congressional earmark.

These practices continue, and lobbyists persist in shaping, learning and reporting information about directed federal spending for their clients. Yet it's now the Democrats in the congressional majority who have reasserted control over the budget purse strings. And while the tactics of earmarking are changing, the underlying goals of some interest groups seeking earmarks and lawmakers trying to accommodate remain the same.

LOBBYING AND PARTY ORGANIZATIONS IN A POLARIZED AGE

Another consequence of increased partisanship is the blurring line between the politics of campaigns and the politics of public policy.[22] Lobbyists have always been involved in the money game, but in the past decade lawmakers and lobbyists have become more closely and formally intertwined and integrated in party organizations as well as lawmakers' own political operations. For example, members of Congress now play a much larger role raising funds for national party groups, such as the Republican National Committee (RNC) and the Democratic National Committee (DNC), and congressional campaign arms, such as the National Republican Congressional Committee (NRCC) and the Democratic Congressional Campaign Committee (DCCC). It's not unusual for the respective campaign committee chairs in the House and Senate to brief their members at weekly caucus meetings on the status of party fundraising efforts. That type of close monitoring and coordination between a party's political operations and its weekly legislative agenda-setting meetings were unheard of in the 1960s and 1970s, according to many Washington veterans. "We bring a scored card about how members are helping with party fundraising efforts to our caucus meeting every week," a Hill leadership aide remarked.

Moreover, this pressure on lawmakers to help the party flows down to the interest group community as well. Most lobbyists—Democrat and Republican alike—will say the pressure from lawmakers to assist party organizations has grown dramatically during this era of increased partisan polarization.

So-called "leadership PACs"—federal campaign committees intended to raise money and contribute funds toward winning seats in the House or Senate—have proliferated during this period and represent one of the consequences of the electoral/advocacy complex. Increasing demands for money from party organizations and leadership PACs ripple through the lobbying world as well. As with other changes in the external environment of interests groups, when the money game changed, so did the demands on advocates.

Obviously, the role of lobbyists in fundraising could be the subject of entire books. Yet one general conclusion about money, politics, and advocacy is in order: increasing the need for financial resources among politicians has the unintended effect of empowering lobbyists. The 1971 Federal Election Campaign Act and subsequent amendments limited the amount of individual contributions. The reform meant lawmakers had to spend more time raising money—and lobbyists became the channel for many of these contributions.

In other words, well-intended campaign finance reforms have had the *unintended* consequence of increasing the interactions between lobbyists, lawmakers, and staff—a new linkage that can sometimes produce very messy results, particularly in a more partisan age. Lobbyist Bert Carp has seen this unintended part of reform first hand:

> One of the biggest unintended consequences of campaign finance reform, is that it increased the amount of interactions between lobbyists and members of Congress. And not only between members and lobbyists, but between lobbyists and the staff. Before these reforms I never remember attending a fundraiser with policy staff in attendance. Now it happens all the time. What it does is put more people in the situation to make difficult policy and political decisions that used to be relegated only to the member of Congress. I ran into a young staffer a few years ago who said, "Hey I missed you at our fundraiser." That just never used to happen in the past and it creates a whole host of real and potential problems.

Two other critical changes in campaign finance produced by partisan polarization are the ascent of leadership PACs and the rise and fall of so-called "soft money." Both of these developments have produced major shifts in the way interest groups engage with money and elections. The implications of these two factors for lobbying are explored below.

PARTISANSHIP, LEADERSHIP PACS, AND LOBBYING

Leadership PACs have lurked in the weeds of Washington politics for many years. Made legal and clarified through a series of Federal Election Commission (FEC) and Supreme Court decisions as outlined in Chapter 2, PACs in general and leadership PACs in particular first became popularized by presidential candidates such as George H.W. Bush during the 1980s and then Senator Robert Dole in the 1990s. These entities became vehicles for presidential candidates to raise and spend money on political matters, make contributions to lawmakers to build political support, and also pay for travel and other campaign-related expenses. During the 1990s, however, as polarization grew in Washington, lawmakers—and of course the lobbyists and interest groups enabling them—adopted leadership PACs for their own purposes. Like many other changes in the political and interest-group world, this transformation had a "viral" nature to it. As one group or individual adopts a successful tactic, the practice spreads to others. The growth of PACs—and for the purposes of the discussion here, leadership PACs—was no exception.

Some leaders are honest and transparent about the goal of these entities—to hang on to majority status in order to keep their leadership positions. Plain spoken, down-to-earth, former Speaker Dennis Hastert is a good example. His PAC went by the initials "KOMPAC"—Keep Our Majority PAC. But many members use leadership PACs principally to promote themselves and their own ambitions inside the institution. In a more polarized age, lawmakers are expected to give money to their colleagues and party organizations as a way to secure better committee assignments and win leadership positions. With leadership PACs, lobbyists become key allies in raising and dispersing these funds.

Figure 5-1 below demonstrates the rapid growth of leadership PACs over the past decade among members of Congress—more than doubling in sheer number in fewer than 10 years, with contributions nearly quadrupling during the same period. Like a political virus without a vaccine, PAC adoption among congressmen and senators has spread aggressively.

The growth of leadership PACs has affected the lobbying world in several ways. First, it has further strengthened the links between the interest groups and the electoral ventures of lawmakers. Congressmen and senators interested in maintaining their majority status or moving out of the minority use leadership PACs to help vulnerable lawmakers and viable challengers within their party. Making contributions to colleagues also helps legislative leaders gain or maintain coveted posts or committee slots in the congressional hierarchy. And lobbyists work with lawmakers in these endeavors, aligning lobbyists more closely than ever with the electoral aspirations of these elected officials and their parties. Savvy and successful PAC managers in the business community are explicitly reminded to build leadership PAC contributions into their overall contribution strategy.[23]

FIGURE 5-1 GROWTH IN THE NUMBER AND TOTAL CONTRIBUTIONS
OF LEADERSHIP PACs 1998–2006.

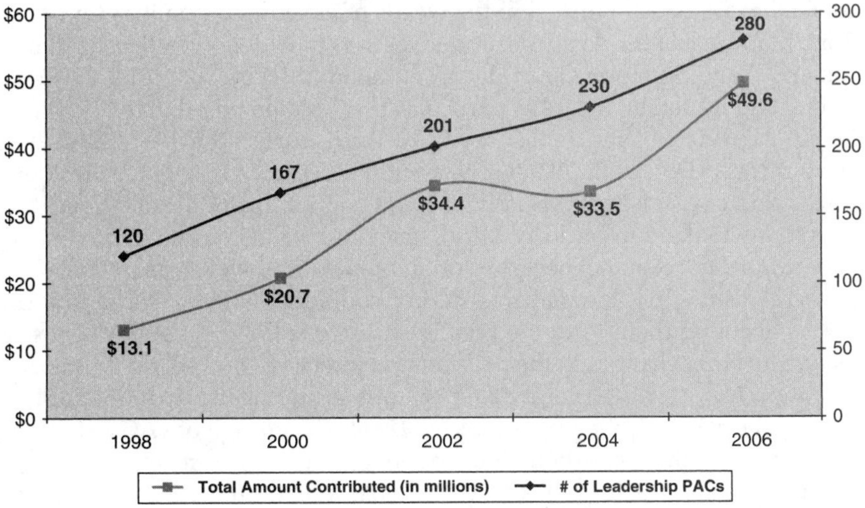

Source: http://www.fec.gov/press/press2004/20040202paccount.html

Second, it is not unusual for lobbyists to hold formal positions with congressional leadership PACs. Many include "steering committees" of lobbyists to help with strategy and fundraising tactics. Some even bring in lobbyists to hold positions, such as "treasurer," in lawmakers' leadership PACs. Like other dimensions of the electoral/advocacy complex, these relationships have blurred the lines between lobbyists working with lawmakers in the public policy context and their activities focused on electoral endeavors. The degrees of separation have become non-existent, making the relationship between lobbyist and lawmaker more partisan in the process. In recent years, lobbyists playing formal roles in leadership PACs have drawn increased scrutiny and criticism, leading some advocates to scale back their positions.

The Center for Public Integrity in 2005 conducted a study of such practices and found at least 39 members of Congress listed lobbyists as treasurers of their campaign committees or leadership PACs. And since 1998, at least 79 lawmakers had used lobbyists to serve in that capacity.[24] One lobbyist oversaw the leadership PACs of prominent senators such as Democratic leader Harry Reid of Nevada, Senate Finance Committee Chair Max Baucus of Montana, and Senate Health and Education Committee Chair Edward Kennedy of Massachusetts.[25]

While the practice remains legal and continues, some lawmakers quietly ousted lobbyists from these formal roles due to scrutiny following the Abramoff lobbying scandal in 2005–2006. "I think it's a little too cozy," said Melanie Sloan, head of Citizens for Responsibility and Ethics in Washington DC.[26] During this time, lawmakers such as Reid and Kennedy decided to dump registered lobbyists as the treasurers of their campaigns. However, despite these rather superficial changes due to negative publicity, advocates still play an increasingly important informal role in the strategies and tactics surrounding the burgeoning number of leadership PACs.

PARTISANSHIP AND THE RISE AND FALL OF SOFT MONEY

While the 1970s and 1980s brought an era of rapid growth for government relations staff of corporations and trade associations, the 1990s witnessed an increased connection between lobbyists, lawmakers, and party organizations—the electoral/advocacy complex. And no single factor contributed to the intermingling of these forces more than the use of soft money.[27]

Bob Rusbuldt, who has been on the front line of these changes over the past 20 years summarizes the transformations this way:

> If the post-Watergate reforms took the undisclosed cash out of politics and led to more legal forms of campaign finance, like PACs, the growth of soft money and how it changed lobbying and then changed again with McCain-Feingold in 2002 was the other big transformation in the lobbying world over the past 30 years.

Indeed, soft money did alter lobbying during the 1990s, and then Congress changed the picture again with the Bipartisan Campaign Reform Act (McCain-Feingold) in 2002. If the 1990s conceived an era of increased partisan polarization, soft money was one of the midwives. It provided another channel by which lobbyists and interest groups could navigate and congeal their ties to political parties—further strengthening the electoral linkage in the advocacy process.

According to the Congressional Research Service (CRS), "soft money" are funds raised by national parties from sources and in amounts otherwise prohibited by the Federal Election Campaign Act (FECA).[28] FECA, first enacted in 1971 and then amended numerous times during the 1970s, limited the amount interest groups (PACs) and individuals could contribute to the national parties. When national political parties raise funds from those sources in amounts otherwise prohibited by FECA, and then transfer these funds to state parties for grass roots, party building, overhead or issue ads, and campaign law calls these funds "non-federal" or "soft money."

During the 1980s and early 1990s, most political parties took a relatively cautious approach to using soft dollars. For example, the Republican National Committee and the Democratic National Committee used these resources raised from corporations, trade associations, and unions for their so-called "building funds," aimed at upkeep and purely administrative purposes. The approach was so cautious, during my days working in the government relations department of a major telecommunications company, soft dollars were viewed as an inferior type of contributions. When speaking to party officials, if given a choice between a hard dollar and a soft dollar contribution, the hard dollars (which could be used directly for federal races) were always preferred. It was like the difference between a Pontiac and a Porsche—most would accept both, but prefer the Carrera.

That attitude began to change with the proliferation of issue ads during the 1990s. According to CRS, "Unlike communications that expressly advocate the election or defeat of a clearly identified candidate, many lower courts have interpreted Supreme Court precedent as deeming issue ads constitutionally protected First Amendment speech, which cannot be regulated. Hence, issue ads may be paid for with soft money."[29] During this time, both parties increased their use of "issue ads". By the late 1990s, they became a dominant form of assistance to incumbents and challengers. Without expressly advocating the election or defeat of candidates, issue ads could say things like "Tell Congressman Smith to stop raising taxes." Or "Thank your Congressman Jones for protecting Medicare and Social Security." And as issue ads became more attractive and valuable, so did the "soft money" needed to fund them.

This changing view of soft money came about as the courts clarified the definition of what kinds of ads "expressly advocate" the election or defeat of a candidate. Political parties became more confident that issue ads could be written in such a way as not to fall into the prohibited "express advocacy" category. In *FEC v. Furgatch*, the Ninth Circuit presented a three-part test to determine whether a communication may be considered issue advocacy.[30] The FEC in 1996 also promulgated its own regulations defining "express advocacy." Then, as CRS notes, both circuit courts and the FEC itself moved to even more limited and narrow interpretations of "express advocacy" in the next couple of years. And as CRS concludes, " . . . regulation of fewer types of communications are being upheld as constitutionally permissible and therefore, more 'issue ads' are permissibly funded with soft money."

And as parties tested the limits of the law, the amount of soft money spent continued to balloon. CRS reports that the amount of soft money spent by Republicans grew 224 percent between the 1992 and 1996 election cycles. For Democrats, the amount of spending surged 271 percent during the same period. Lobbyists and interest groups were called on increasingly to raise large sums of soft money to help refill coffers drained by the new demand for issue ads.

And as Figure 5-2 demonstrates, the growth of soft money reached its apex right before passage of the Bipartisan Campaign Reform Act of 2002 (BCRA). The 2004 and 2006 election cycles—and especially the role of lobbyists in raising "soft money"—changed dramatically as a result of this legislation. Issue ads that used to be run by national party committees

FIGURE 5-2 NATIONAL PARTY NON-FEDERAL (SOFT MONEY) DISBURSEMENTS 1992–2006.

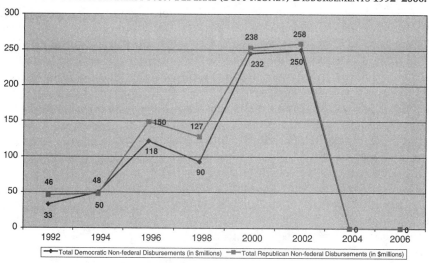

Source: www.fec.gov/press/press2002/20021218party/nonfederalsummary.xls

continued but were now funded by so-called 527 organizations.[31] 527 organizations will again change the relationship between lobbyists, lawmakers, and the electoral process, most observers believe, but the exact nature of those transformations remains in flux.

Two other points regarding the rise and fall of soft money deserve mention. First, in June of 2007, the Supreme Court changed the issue advertising landscape again with its *Wisconsin Right to Life* v. *FEC* decision. The Court's actions are outlined in more detail in Chapter 7, but this is another illustration of how the landscape of soft money continues to evolve. Essentially, the court held in a narrow five-four decision that BCRA's call for a blanket ban on hard money-funded issue ads 60 days prior to an election was too broad and violated the free speech rights of citizens. This loosening of BCRA when it comes to issue ads is described in more detail later, but for now it is important to note how the changing nature of law makes the relationship between issue ads and lobbying a very dynamic enterprise.

Second, BCRA did unravel the closeness between political parties and lobbyists to some extent. The heavy pressure on advocates to raise "soft money" for political parties abated with the passage of this bill. But now 527 organizations are filling the void. Critics say there is just as much or more money churning through the system, only it is moving into less public venues than political parties. In the view of many, BCRA did more to hobble political parties—and weaken the link between parties and lobbyists—than to reduce the amount of money in the political system. Lobbyists' ties with 527 organizations is an area ripe for further investigation.

POLARIZATION AND PARTISAN LOBBYING FIRMS

Polarization also spawned another species in the lobby genus—the partisan lobbying firm. These entities come in two varieties—the "partisan" and the "bipartisan." Due to the increasing importance of partisanship, firms that either specialize in lobbying Republicans or Democrats, or alternatively advocacy firms that emphasize they cover "both sides of the aisle," using teams of partisan lobbyists, also grew during the past two decades. They both fill an important niche in the polarized world.

Partisan firms like Barbour Griffith & Rodgers (Republican), Fierce and Isakowitz (Republican), Avenue Solutions (Democrat), and Capital Strategies (Democrat), successfully market their strong ties to their respective parties in Congress. They are lobbyists for their clients, but in many ways political confidants to public officials and political parties. Their knowledge of the process, close personal ties to lawmakers or key administration officials, and keen strategic aptitudes place them among the most skilled advocates in Washington. They are also nearly indispensable among lawmakers and other political figures in Washington as trusted advisors often helping direct "reverse lobbying" campaigns. In a polarized age, the value of and need for individuals and firms like this—for all the reasons suggested above—continues to grow.

A variation on this theme are the high-powered bipartisan firms. Timmons and Company, The Duberstein Group, Washington Counsel, and the C2 Group are among the top lobbying companies in Washington that employ both partisan Democrats and Republicans in the same firm. Law firms with lobbying practices also like to highlight their strength of former staffers and members of Congress from both sides of the aisle. These lobbying companies and law firms also grasp the importance of the new polarized age and put together teams of individuals to fit their clients' needs. None of the individual lobbyists attempts to play both sides of the political aisle. They are each clearly partisan Democrats or Republicans. But from the clients' perspective, their representation on the Hill or the administration is clearly "bipartisan." They get strong partisan advice, counsel, and advocacy help from some of each side's top partisan lobbyists in Washington—from one bipartisan firm. This partisan blend is another highly successful and common strategy in today's polarized age.

It's particularly effective during shifts in partisan control of Congress. "We noticed after the Democrats took over in January [2007] that some of the Democratic offices wanted us to send in our Democratic lobbyists," said Nelson Litterst of the C2 Group. "I can remember when it wasn't that way. People on the Hill used to be more interested in your issues knowledge or your experience. Increasing partisanship changed that. But working at a bipartisan firm allows us to adjust." Litterst says, "In an era when you have to 'show your party affiliation card' at the door, it's helpful to work at a firm that covers both sides of the aisle."

During the post-World War II period, another structural phenomenon—divided government—also significantly impacted the lobbying world. During the past 40 years, this institutional arrangement has been a lot more common compared to earlier in the twentieth century when unified party control was more the norm.[32] More divided government—in an increasingly partisan environment—has also created the demand for specialization in areas such as lobbying the White House. For example, over the past several years, lobbying companies in Washington with strong ties to the Republican White House, such as Fierce and Isakowitz or Barbour Griffin & Rodgers, have continued to represent clients and provide valuable lobbying services despite a change in partisan control in Congress. Some clients recognize the value of access and insights into the White House policy and decision-making process. These specialized firms know, for example, how the decisions are made by the president's staff to generate a veto or how the Executive Office of the President formulates Statements of Administration Policy (SAPs). Just as the Democratic majority in Congress is more comfortable interacting with lobbyists of their own partisan persuasion, so too are the White House staff. So in periods of divided party control, lobbyists that are known and trusted by executive branch officials can continue to play an important role with interest-group clients, even if the majority in Congress is of another party.

While there is a lot of research on the issue of executive/legislative relations, how lobbyists interact with the White House, in terms of influence and intelligence gathering is less understood.[33] As one long-time Republican lobbyist observes, "People make too big a deal out of Democrats taking control of the Congress in 2007. I tell clients that if you hire me to work the White House, as long as there are 34 solid Republican votes in the Senate or 146 in the House (enough to sustain presidential vetoes) Republican lobbyists who know how to work the White House are extremely relevant, important and powerful."

PARTISANSHIP AND THE DEMOCRATIC MAJORITY

Partisanship continued its strong impact on the lobbying world following the Democrats' takeover of Congress after the 2006 election, witnessed in the scramble in Washington during 2007 to hire lobbyists with close ties to new Democratic leadership. After the Democrats took control, many interest groups felt ill-prepared to deal with the new majority. After 12 years of uninterrupted Republican control of the House (and almost the same number of years in the Senate), the lobbying world had reached an equilibrium of sorts. The 2006 election shook things up.

One widely-read Capitol Hill publication summed up the heightened demand for Democratic lobbyists with an article titled "K Street Just Can't Get Enough Democrats."

It led with this:

> Demand for top-flight Democratic lobbyists is outpacing supply, leaving trade groups, associations, and firms with holes on their staff as they try to make inroad to the new majority. The relatively activist agenda from Democrats appears to be driving business on K Street across the board. The Washington Post reported last month that the number of new lobbying registrations has doubled during the first four months of the year compared with the same period a year ago.[34]

Many of the same adjustments and decisions that occurred in 1995 following the GOP takeover repeated themselves in 2007. I was deeply involved in the lobbying industry during both transitions and drew several conclusions based on personal observations.

First, as suggested above, many segments of the interest-group community chose to move quickly to hire lobbyists with strong Democratic ties. Advocates with close links to the new majority leadership were in high demand. "My phone is ringing off the hook," a former House leadership aide said. "I can't possibly service all this business," he said. Another observer put it this way: "The main reason for the surge is the need of interest groups and corporations to get access to—and understand the thinking of—a new set of Democratic chairmen in Congress and the constituencies that they listen to, such as labor unions, environmentalists and trial lawyers. Hundreds of Democratic lobbyists have been hired for that purpose."[35]

Yet as with the transition to the Republican majority, there was a wide range of sophistication among various interest groups in how they deployed lobbying resources and their level of expectations of what these advocates could accomplish. Some thought all they had to do was to hire a Democratic lobbyist, and it would ameliorate their problems. This was an example of old-school thinking; that somehow just retaining the right person with close ties to the leadership would automatically protect them from negative public policy outcomes. They were sorely mistaken.

At this juncture, it is important to make a distinction about the impact of partisan polarization on various types of lobbying interests. Like most circumstances, one size does not fit all. Partisanship affects some interests differently than others. For example, the change in party control after the 2006 election meant putting some interest groups and lobbyists on offense and others on defense. Just like the election created winners and losers in Congress, it also changed the agendas of interest groups. And in an enhanced partisan era, some groups and their lobbyists were part of the new majority's "team," much like social conservative groups and some aspects of the business community were part of the Republican coalition after 1994, helping with initiatives like the *Contract with America*. Others were clearly on the "outs" with the Democrats. Let us first examine how these less-favored groups responded.

Business interests were among those receiving a frosty reception with the new majority. Companies in the pharmaceutical, insurance, energy, and defense industries, to name a few, were clearly in the crosshairs of the Democratic leadership. The new majority moved quickly with a series of bills and investigations that were potentially extremely negative for these industries.[36] While many firms and trade associations scrambled to add Democrats to their rosters of lobbyists, there was little these advocates could change. The conventional wisdom that interest groups hire powerful lobbyists to "fix" their problems was quickly disproved in the first few months of 2007. One of the dominant misconceptions about lobbying—that interest-group advocates are somehow omnipotent—was clearly exposed as myth. One corporate lobbyist observed, "After the election people panicked and wanted to hire Democratic lobbyists. What we are finding now is that they can't help us change any minds on the Hill (if lawmakers take stands against business). The best they can do is tell us the 'bad' news a little earlier. I'm not sure that that is too helpful."

Still, in the polarized world of Washington, the new Democratic majority leadership, like the Republicans in 1995, was clearly calling the shots. Democratic chairmen in the House, such as Charles Rangel from New York of the Ways and Means Committee and John Dingell of Michigan from the Energy and Commerce Committee, lamented on several occasions that the leadership was trampling on their committees' prerogatives. Rangel complained that Speaker Pelosi was dictating policy on issues ranging from taxes to trade. Dingell objected to Pelosi's plan to create a separate select climate change committee, impinging on the legislative jurisdiction of Dingell's Energy and Commerce Committee. Early in 2007, Speaker Pelosi also put the leadership imprimatur on the committee process, overriding the seniority system and installing her own loyalists as committee chairs and granting key slots on panels to her legislative allies.

As with the Republican takeover in 1995, the Democratic leadership's consolidated power created a strong demand for lobbyists with close ties to the new majority—even if they could not reshape Democratic policies, they could help interpret where they might move next. And while some interest groups and organizations had wildly unsophisticated expectations, others had a more realistic and accurate view of what these advocates could and could not achieve.

Democratic lobbyists representing business interests changed few, if any, minds in the new majority. Their ability to gather information, intelligence, and help interest groups reduce uncertainty was their real value. Contrary to conventional wisdom, even the best-connected lobbyists rarely change legislation, stop negative policies, or forestall investigations, but they can help their interest-group clients know what is coming down the pike a little earlier and help them avoid being completely blindsided. Again, advocacy is not like the manufacturing process. Simply investing in lobbyists could not "buy" or "produce" more favorable public policy production.

On the other hand, lobbyists representing interests more closely linked to the new majority's agenda faired much better and faced a completely different set of challenges. They were on full-time offense, pushing through many provisions stalled during 12 years of Republican rule. These advocates—at least on the surface—looked more "powerful." Labor unions, environmental groups, and the trial bar—and their lobbyists—now had a lot more influence on the process than they did during the Republican majority. In a more partisan age, lobbyists tied to groups allied with the new Democratic majority, such as organized labor, were the new power brokers in Washington. Democrat-oriented groups were considered part of the new majority's "team." Many of these interest groups and their lobbyists had helped all the new Democratic leaders raise money, plot strategy, and provide ground troops in the past election. Now they were reaping the benefits.

Just like the Republicans assembled a group of lobbyists to help pass the *Contract with America*, Democratic leadership organized an outside coalition of labor, environmental, trial bar, and other liberal public interest groups—and their lobbyists—to help push their "Six for '06" first hundred hours agenda. One such group, "Change America Now," is heavily funded by labor unions and makes no secret of their direct linkage between policy and elections. One official from this group noted that they not only want to help pass the Democratic agenda, but also "juice up attacks on Republicans."[37]

While the media never wrote about it this way, the Democrats' efforts working with these groups clearly resembled the infamous "K Street Project" Democrats had decried as an example of the "culture of corruption" pervading Washington under the 12-year Republican rule between 1995 and 2007.[38] In reality, Change America Now is another example of the "reverse lobbying" mentioned above. While the ties are murky, most Washington insiders believe groups like this form in a partisan age with the strong encouragement of congressional leadership—a phenomenon that occurs on both sides of the political aisle.

Again, partisan polarization meant these lobbyists worked even more closely with the Democratic leadership than with the committees producing the legislation. "If you want information about timing or substance about anything related to the Democrats' agenda, you have to talk to the Speaker's office," a Democratic lobbyist said in 2007. "The Speaker's office is writing and scheduling all these bills."

More muscular party leadership in Congress is one of the primary implications of partisan polarization in Washington. And strengthened party leadership has consequences for the way lobbyists operate in this new environment. It also has major implications for the perceived "influence" of lobbyists and interest groups. Partisan control can do more to help the fortunes of particular interests than can legions of well-connected lobbyists. This nuance of the advocacy world is often missed. Some business groups and their lobbyists are going to look a lot more powerful with a pro-business, Republican majority in charge. Democrat-aligned lobbyists representing labor unions, environmental groups, and trial lawyers will seem to have more influence with a Democratic majority. Partisanship and partisan control have an independent impact on lobbying, above and beyond the skills, contacts, and relationships of the individual advocate.

PARTISANSHIP EMPOWERS LOBBYISTS

Partisanship produced another change in the advocacy world—ironically, it empowered lobbyists. Before the era of extreme partisan polarization, more members of Congress talked to each other. As lawmakers spend less time conversing with each other, lobbyists increasingly have become a source of vote counts and general information. "It's gotten so bad you don't want to get caught having lunch with a member from the other side of the aisle," one long-time Democratic lobbyist says, only half jokingly.

During the Republican majority in the House between 1995 and 2007, lawmakers frequently worked a Tuesday–Thursday schedule in Washington, meaning less time for personal interactions in Washington at dinners or other social occasions. They also met far less frequently in bipartisan markups or conference committees compared to the 1970s and 1980s. "The markups are all for show now," the lobbyist says. "It used to be a place where they rolled up their sleeves, talked, joked, got things done—but got to know each other too. In a more partisan environment that doesn't happen anymore."

This change empowers the advocacy community because Democrat and Republican lobbyists still talk to each other. Whether it is in bipartisan firms or when a client hires a team of Democrat and Republican lobbyists, the opportunities for dialogue and exchange of information continue among the lobbyists. "It's then the lobbyists who share this information with their respective sides of the aisle, and that empowers them," the lobbyist concludes.

Lobbyists fill the vacuum created by partisanship. Polarization has strengthened their hand in a process where information—particularly intelligence about what is happening on the other side of the aisle—is a highly valuable commodity.

SUMMARY

Partisan polarization in Congress reached near pandemic proportions by the beginning of the twenty-first century. Many facets of the institution—inside and out—are infected by developments related to the permanent campaign and the increased power of party leaders. And lobbyists are not immune from these transformations. Polarization amplifies the power of congressional leadership, which in turn heightens the demand for lobbyists with strong partisan ties. It also has led to the creation of new campaign finance vehicles, such as leadership PACs, that further blur the lines between the politics of elections and the politics of public policy—involving groups like the RNC, NRCC, DNC, and DCCC more intimately and regularly in the politics of lawmaking. And when new laws like BCRA constrained the use of soft money, resources and lobbyists flowed quickly into new organizations like 527's. These changes, in effect, have created a new electoral/advocacy complex. This places lobbyists more in the center of these party-building mechanisms than ever before.

Polarization has also increased the importance of developing and passing party agendas, like the Republicans' *Contract with America* in 1995 or the Democrats' "Six for '06" in 2007. At the same time, congressional leaders increasingly practice "reverse lobbying," asking allied interests—like the coalitions formed around the *Contract with America* by the Republicans or the "Six for '06" agenda of the Democrats—to help enact initiatives critical to the party's success. Lobbyists gladly contribute to these efforts, believing the access and goodwill their efforts engender with legislative leaders beneficial to their long-term advocacy ambitions. These behaviors provide further support for broadening the definition of lobbying and conceptualizing it as a "legislative subsidy."[39] And congressional leaders are more than willing to accept these "subsidies" as their own success is increasingly tied to promoting a successful party agenda. Finally, polarization has also led to the advent of the partisan lobbying firm—featuring two distinct flavors, bipartisan and one-party firms.

Once again, this chapter shows that examining how changes in the external environment of interest groups "influence" lobbying—instead of looking only at how advocates try to shape the process—provides some rich insights into how the advocacy industry really operates, and why it has changed. Partisan polarization—much like the growth and activism of government outlined in the last chapter—affects the structure, style, and substantive methods of lobbying in some dramatic ways.

The stereotypical lobbyist, who plays both sides of the partisan fence, is now a vestige of a bygone era. In today's more polarized world, partisan lobbyists—Republicans and Democrats with strong ties to congressional leaders, active in party fund-raising activities or helping partisan leaning 527 organizations and often asked to participate in "reverse lobbying"—are now the norm. They work largely with partisans who share their own political stripes on the Hill and in the administration. Polarization has produced a wave change in the advocacy industry. Recognizing and appreciating the more dominant role of partisanship on interest groups is another critical piece of our reconsideration of lobbying. Partisanship can make certain advocates (e.g. business lobbyists during a Republican Congress or labor lobbyists during a Democratic majority) look more powerful than they really are. Just as the President of the United States may look more successful and influential when his party controls Congress, interest groups with close ties to the majority party may appear more powerful when their allies control the gavels. In other words, some business lobbies may appear more influential when Republicans are in power, while labor appears more powerful when Democrats are in control. Polarization also leads to new structures and tactics, like the emphasis of lobbyists on influencing one governmental institution (e.g. lobbying the White House).

But other factors also have reshaped the way the "influence business" works. The next chapter explores fragmentation of the old media and rapid development of the new media age and how they affect the lobbying world.

NOTES

1. Quoted in Tory Newmyer and Emily Pierce, "New Paradigm Has GOP Lobbyists Stumbling," *Roll Call* 7 (June 2007): 18.
2. Nolan McCarty, Keith T. Poole, and Howard Rosenthal, *Polarized America: The Dance of Ideology and Unequal Riches* (Cambridge, MA: MIT Press, 2006), 1.
3. Political scientist Morris P. Fiorina argues that "elites" like members of Congress are polarized but ordinary voters are not in his book, *Culture War? The Myth of a Polarized America*, 2nd ed. (New York, NY: Pearson Longman, 2006).
4. For a brief history of leadership and partisanship in the House, see David W. Rohde, *Parties and Leaders in the Post Reform House* (Chicago, IL: University of Chicago Press, 1991), 1–16.
5. Woodrow Wilson, *Congressional Government* (Boston, MA: Houghton Mifflin, 1885).
6. Joseph Cooper and David W. Brady, "Institutional Context and Leadership Style: The House from Cannon to Rayburn," *American Political Science Review* 75: 411–425. See also chapter 1 of Rhode for a good history of the shifting power of congressional leadership. Cooper and Brady, 1981, 417.
7. Gary W. Cox and Mathew D. McCubbins, *Setting the Agenda: Responsible Party Government in the U.S. House of Representatives* (New York, NY: Cambridge University Press, 2005), 21.
8. Ibid. 23.
9. Elizabeth Drew "Selling Washington," *New York Review of Books* 52(11) (June 23, 2005). Another example of this genre is Nicholas Confessore. "Welcome to the Machine," *Washington Monthly*, July/August 2003.

10. Darrell M. West and Burdett A. Loomis, *The Sound of Money: How Political Interests Get What they Want* (New York, NY: Norton, 1999), 121.
11. See Scott H. Ainsworth, *Analyzing Interest Groups: Group Influence on People and Policies* (New York, NY: W.W. Norton, 2002), 109–113.
12. Tory Newmyer, "Lawmakers Look for Cover Downtown," *Roll Call* (June 18, 2007): 11.
13. Ibid. 16.
14. Richard L. Hall and Deardorff, "Lobbying as Legislative Subsidy," *American Political Science Review* 100(1) (February 2006).
15. Ibid.
16. McIver J. Weatherford, *Tribes on the Hill: The U.S. Congress Rituals and Realities*, Revised Edition (Massachusetts, MA: Bergin and Garvey Publishers, 1985), 119.
17. These estimates are from House Report 109–655, Providing for Earmarking Reform in the House of Representatives. September 13, 2006.
18. Morris P. Fiorina, *Congress: Keystone of the Washington Establishment* (New Haven: Yale University Press, 1977), 41.
19. Reported in the Arlington Sun, June 10, 2006.
20. See, for example, Barbara Sinclair, *Unorthodox Lawmaking*.
21. John Solomon and Jeffrey H. Birnbaum, "Pet Projects' Veil is only Partly Lifted," *The Washington Post* September 9, 2007. A1.
22. This point is consistent with one of the conclusions of Allan J. Cigler and Burdett A. Loomis, *Interest Group Politics*, 6th ed. (Washington, D.C.: CQ Press, 2002), 382.
23. Gary J. Andres, The Seven Secrets of Highly Successful PACs. National Association of Business Political Action Committees.
24. Matt Margolis, "Lobbyist Handling Senators' Finances," February 6, 2006. www.noagenda.org (accessed May 23, 2007).
25. Ibid.
26. Ibid.
27. For a good review of party involvement in campaigns in the 1970s and 1980s, see Herrnson, 1988. Also, see Herrnson, "Political Party and Interest Group Adverstising in the 2000 Congressional Elections," for a discussion of soft money in the 2000 election.
28. L. Paige Whitaker, CRS issue Brief for Congress. IB98025: *Campaign Finance: Constitutional and Legal Issues of Soft Money.* March 2, 2001.
29. Ibid. 2.
30. Ibid. 5.
31. "527" refers to the section of the tax code that regulates these new entities such as the conservative "Swift Boat Veterans" or the liberal "Media Fund." Contributions to these entities are not tax deductable, but their contributors are not widely known. Their ads, however, are similar in content to those done by party organizations during the 1990s and in the 2000 and 2002 cycles, before the passage of McCain-Feingold.
32. Morris Fiorina, *Divided Government*, 2nd ed. (Needham Heights, MA: Allyn and Bacon, 1996), 6, 7.
33. Examples of presidential/executive branch relations include James A. Thurber, *Rivals for Power: Presidential-Congressional Relations*, 2nd ed. (Lanham, MA: Rowman and Littlefield, 2002); Jon R. Bond and Richard Fleisher, *The President in the Legislative Arena* (Chicago, IL: The University of Chicago Press, 1990); and Paul Peterson, *Legislating Together: The White House and Capitol Hill from Eisenhower to Reagan* (Cambridge, MA: Harvard University Press, 1990).
34. Jim Snyder, "K Street Just Can't Get Enough Democrats," *The Hill*, May 2, 2007.
35. Jeffrey H. Birnbaum, "Lobbyists Profit From Power Shift in Congress," *Washington Post*, April 23, 2007, D01.
36. In the first few months of 2007, the Democrat majority passed legislation aimed at allowing the government to negotiate with the pharmaceutical industry for lower drug prices, a bill the industry successfully kept bottled up during the Republican majority. It began major investigations of the health insurance industry and threatened to remove the anti-trust immunity of the insurance industry enjoyed for decades. It also conducted investigations of defense contractors. Finally, it passed several bills making it

easier for unions to organize over the objections of business groups like the Chamber of Commerce.

37. Gary J. Andres, "Media Hypocrisy and Lobbying," *Washington Times*, Op/Ed page. May 17, 2007.
38. Ibid.
39. Hall and Deardorff, "Lobbying as Legislative Subsidy."

LOBBYING IN A HYPER MEDIA AGE

We used to call it a 'haymaker.' Get your client or issue on the Today show or Meet the Press and you were a made man. That's no longer the case. Now the whole process is a lot more incremental . . . you have to work on a lot more little parts in order to have success. One news show won't do it anymore . . . you have to build a whole new Gestalt—something bigger than the individual media pieces.

Greg Crist, Former Communications Director,
House Republican Conference

The last two chapters examined how a bigger, more activist federal government, and a near pandemic of partisanship in Washington continue to transform lobbying, creating a large electoral/advocacy complex. But another major change in the external environment of interest groups also deserves examination—the fragmentation of the old media world and the emergence of a new media age. Like the spreading government Leviathan and the pandemic of partisanship, the emergence of a hyper media age also has altered the structure, style, and substantive methods of lobbying. By "hyper media," I mean an environment where the size, fragmentation, delivery, and content of news have all changed, from a slower, structured, and generic framework to a faster, fragmented, and personalized model.

The revolution in media provides new challenges to which interest groups continue to adjust. It also provides fresh avenues to communicate with the public, identify and mobilize advocates, gauge support or opposition for policy ideas, help to shape public opinion—and more. This chapter investigates the impact of three changes in the media/technology environment of interest groups and their influence on lobbying:

- Media fragmentation.
- 24-hour news cycle.
- New media and the Internet.

Each of these changes is transforming the practice of lobbying. Understanding how and why will deepen our insights into the operation of the new advocacy world.

LOBBYING AND MEDIA FRAGMENTATION

A typical Washington lobbyist in the 1970s used to keep informed about national news and public policy by reading *The Washington Post*, maybe skimming *The New York Times*, and watching one of the three network news programs. Today's interest-group advocates can, and often do, monitor the news by doing none of the above, at least not in the same way.

Why are news consumption habits critical for lobbyists and interest groups to understand? Media watching shapes political attitudes and helps determine how to reach and mobilize citizens. Quite simply, media is a place where Americans congregate. Many citizens used to share the evening news with Walter Cronkite. Now these same audiences are dispersed over many mediums. Knowing these new congregation points allows one to listen, communicate, organize, and mobilize. How and where the media covers an issue also creates a "buzz" in Washington. Who is up, who is down? What issues are at the top of the agenda? Media coverage helps set the agenda. And in a fragmented world, the opportunities to shape these perceptions expand. Lobbyists and interest groups can't afford to ignore this new reality.

Twenty years ago, watching the evening news was much more of a societal common denominator. It was one universal thread in a tapestry of American life. In a more fragmented world, citizens no longer gather information the same way—a change with tremendous implications for politicians and those who seek to understand and influence them. In the old environment dominated by network news, elected officials and advocates could easily discern the main media messages of the day. Even when it was challenging to shape those themes, it was easy to glean the press's spin on particular issues. If an interest group or lobbyist sought to influence the media message—in order to shape elite or public opinion—the options for earned media were limited and the times of day when people focused on the media were more uniform.

In today's fragmented media world, both elected officials and lobbyists possess exponentially more earned and paid media options. If you can't get the networks to carry a story about why government negotiation of prescription drug prices will reduce consumer choices, no worries—pitch it to CNN or MSNBC. If you want to communicate with conservative voters about the need to curb lawsuit abuse, go to Fox News. If you are a labor interest group and you want to get out a story concerning poor treatment of union workers, try CNN. The one-size-fits-all of the network-news-dominated paradigm has been smashed, creating a much broader array of options and programmatic styles.

Fewer than 20 years ago, 60 percent of Americans reported regularly watching the national network news. By 2006, that number had been slashed by more than half.[1] Local television news has suffered a similar, but not quite as dramatic fate. The percent regularly watching that medium fell from 77 percent to 54 percent during the same period.[2] Instead of only tuning in to

CBS, NBC, or ABC, Americans now get their news from a wide variety of sources including cable outlets, such as CNN, FOX, MSNBC, C-SPAN, or CNBC, and many types of Internet news portals. They also receive information from newspapers, both print and online, as well as from a variety of online publications and blogs. In fact, studies show younger Americans get most of their political news now from a previously unlikely source—comedy shows. Comedians like Jon Stewart and Stephen Colbert are the new Walter Cronkites for many under 30 years old as the most popular sources of news.

And while it might be viewed as passé in the twenty-first century, given all the emphasis on Internet political applications talk radio also played a significant role in the fragmentation of media during the 1980s and 1990s. Conservative shows and conservative listeners still heavily dominate this medium, and advocates who work on issues that fall into this niche market can and do build talk radio into their strategies.

The explosion in the number of television channels available in the average household is one way to view fragmentation. Figure 6-1, developed by National Media, documents this change between 1970 and 2004.

Cable and satellite channels now have the largest share of the television audience. This represents another new factor affecting the advertising strategies of interest groups and advocates (Figure 6-2).

The market for specialized publications has also exploded. Capitol Hill now has three regular near-daily newspapers dedicated to the inside-the-Beltway policy and political world—*Roll Call*, *The Hill*, and *The Politico*. Add to that collection other niche publications such as *CQ Daily* from *Congressional Quarterly* and *Congress Daily* from *National Journal*. Then there is the ever-growing list of even more specialized publications dealing with energy, health, communications, or trade policy (to name a few). The sheer breadth and volume of

FIGURE 6-1 FRAGMENTATION OF TRADITIONAL MEDIA AUDIENCES DRIVEN BY INCREASE IN MEDIA CONSUMER CHOICES.

The number of channels available in the average television household has exploded over the past 35 years—from average of 7 to 100+.

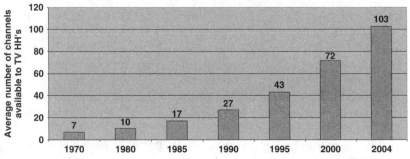

Source: National Media, Inc., Analysis of Scarborough Research 2002 Survey of U.S. Adults (*N* = 200, 500).

FIGURE 6-2 CABLE CHANNELS—HARD-WIRED AND SATELLITE—NOW HAVE THE
LARGEST SHARE OF THE TELEVISION AUDIENCE.

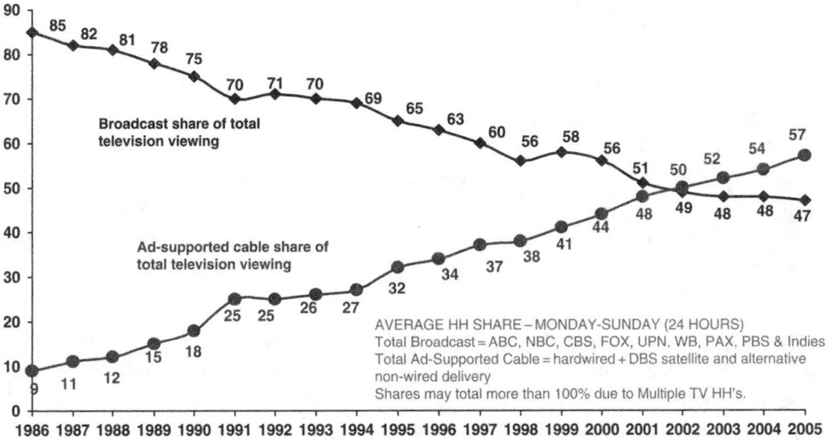

Source: National Media, Inc., Analysis of Scarborough Research 2002 Survey of U.S. Adults ($N = 200, 500$).

information potentially consumed daily by congressional staff, lobbyists, and other public policymakers is impressive and sometimes seemingly impossible to digest fully. Lobbyists and staff interested in energy policy, for example, don't want to miss any edition of *Inside FERC* (Federal Energy Regulatory Commission). The list of in-depth, policy-specific publications is near mind-numbing now in Washington. The insurance industry's Bob Rusbuldt has observed the proliferation of Washington publications and argues the market is now near saturation: "I'm not sure if anyone has time to read all these publications. The proliferation and fragmentation of the media has caused us to seriously rethink our advocacy advertising strategies." When interest groups engage in paid advertising campaigns, the series of options available to them to target messages is much broader. For example, a common tactic today includes interest groups attempting to shape opinion among inside-the-Beltway policymakers. In the fragmented media world, the number of options open to advocates has grown exponentially. It's not only cheaper, but more effective in shaping elite opinion to buy advertising in publications like *The Hill*, *Roll Call*, and *The Politico*, and to purchase ads on cable news stations than to purchase network advertising or full-page ads in *The Washington Post*. These targeted options did not exist in the paid media space 20 or 30 years ago.

Personalized media is also on the rise. Lobbyists can choose to receive e-mail alerts from media outlets on issues they deem important. They may also watch network news segments of interest, but it is now often in the form of video clips someone sends to them or a piece they find on YouTube. Interest groups and the voters they seek to mobilize, target, and influence all receive media content based on their personal preferences and schedules.

Lobbyists and advocates now build this "personalized media" dimension into their tactics. "Media used to be an afterthought," Greg Crist observes.

> Now it's a forethought. We were always looking to expand our audiences when I worked on the Hill to package information and create an echo chamber. That's why many congressional committees now have coalitions directors and outreach coordinators. It's to look for these new audiences. It's another form of advocacy. I remember a member of Congress who used to say, "I'm into the manufacturing of legislation, not the marketing." That's all shifted now.

All these changes significantly impact the lobbying world. Knowing where and how Americans in general and policymakers specifically consume news and gather information is critical for the advocacy industry. Gleaning this knowledge in the old world where 90 percent of Americans watched network television was challenging enough. Finding it in today's fragmented media world is an even more Herculean task.

Shaping and influencing earned media is one of the key items in the toolbox of successful lobbyists. Media fragmentation means these tools get deployed in a lot more places. The greater number of outlets also increases the overall need for content. This surge in supply and demand for earned media creates both challenges and opportunities for the advocacy world. It has created a cottage industry of communications specialists who help interest groups navigate through the fractured media world.

Fragmentation also impacts interest groups' paid media strategies. The progression of tactics in the issue advertising space follows a typical pattern. Creative advertising and buying ideas first get shaped on Madison Avenue for corporate and commercial clients. These private companies constantly review and adapt their approaches, developing what amounts to cutting edge, best practices for the advertising industry in general. Next, political campaigns adopt the most successful techniques and integrate them into electoral strategies. Finally, the tools used in the campaign context migrate to the lobbying industry. Following this sequence, media fragmentation has caused repercussions first in the advertising industry, then in the electoral realm, and now in the advocacy world. It creates what some communications specialists call a "cascade effect."[3]

Lobbyists using YouTube provides an illustration of this trend. A 2007 *Washington Post* story reports

> It was inevitable. In the Internet age, interest groups seeking influence in Washington are joining presidential candidates in discovering a new electronic tool to press their agenda: YouTube. "Send your underwear to the undersecretary," urges the actress in the Competitive Enterprise Institute's

stinging 66-second anti-regulatory video posted on YouTube, a free video-sharing site that is a subsidiary of Google. The video blames a 2001 Energy Department rule for an energy-efficiency standard that it says has made new models of washing machines more expensive while getting laundry less clean. The underwear video illustrates what other advocacy groups are finding out: YouTube is a cheap, creative way to get a message to a potentially vast audience. The slow migration is in addition to more traditional lobbying approaches, such as direct mail, Web sites and scripted phone calls to federal officials.[4]

A 2004 *Fortune* magazine headline captures the angst in the advertising industry about the splintering media world: *"Nightmare on Madison Avenue: Media Fragmentation, Recession, Fed-up Clients, TiVo—It's all trouble, and the ad business is caught up in the wake."*[5] The article notes that in a pre-fragmented world, "media planning was far from rocket science." Advertisers could reach 90 percent of the country by running prime-time television commercials. A typical campaign, according to the article, consisted of two television commercials and a few magazine ads. But that's all changed, causing Madison Avenue firms to scramble to find new pockets of viewers in this highly splintered world.

These same trends now affect political campaigns and advocacy efforts. Former Republican National Committee Chairman Ken Mehlman notes that while television ads still play a big role in election campaigns, fragmentation has caused them to lose some of their novelty. "In a world with a wealth of information there is a poverty of attention," he says.[6] Mehlman argues that ads work best when they are coordinated in some way to break through in a fragmented world where viewers have a variety of media competing for their attention. When the print and the TV spots say the same thing—and when a neighbor delivers the same message again on the doorstep and another friend sends a message via e-mail—the chances for people to notice go up.[7] Advertising is still important in electoral politics, but applying it successfully is a more daunting task.

Lobbyists face the same challenges. In a world with a wealth of public policy information, there is indeed a poverty of attention. How do you break through? How do you find the periodicals policymakers or voters are reading or the programs they are watching? In the old days, the networks served as that common denominator. Now viewership and readership are broken into many smaller pieces. How do you listen and how do you communicate in this highly segmented world?

One veteran media consultant summarizes the challenge in this way:

There are really three issues you have to deal with in today's paid advertising advocacy campaigns. First, there is the question of where to advertise given all the choices. There are some tools about who watches what, but it really comes down to a big tradeoff—choose the big networks, which hits a lot of people, some who will pay attention and others who will not, or more targeted communications like cable shows or targeted print or Internet. Second, you have to have good content in the ads so people really pay attention. Finally, in a campaign where an ad is supposed to illicit action, not just shape opinion, you have to make sure that it generates the desired behavior as well.

In other words, placement and message both matter. And persuading people to take action is part of the equation. In a fragmented media world, the challenges of accomplishing all three have grown exponentially. National Media, an Alexandria, Virginia-based media firm, has done extensive work on targeting political consumers and how voters now use media. By segmenting audiences into groups such as Democratic base voters, Democratic swing voters, Republican swing voters, Republican base voters, and nonvoters, the firm helps its clients more efficiently reach targeted populations in their advocacy-media buying efforts. Using techniques first pioneered by market research companies that then migrated to political campaigns, National Media is on the cutting edge of using targeting strategies to identify and reach key subpopulations for their clients with lobbying agendas.

For example, National Media demonstrates why it's harder to buy media targeting Republican audiences: Democratic voters watch more television.

> A careful study of syndicated media research shows that the television advertising playing field is clearly tilted in favor of Democratic candidates. Based on our analysis of hundreds of thousands of interviews with Americans from 2001 to 2006, we estimate that a traditional political television buy, on average will deliver 14% more impressions among high turnout Democrats than high turnout Republicans.

At first glance, this difference might seem small. However, if a Republican and Democrat each spends $2 million on television advertising, a 14 percent gross rating point (GRP) gap is a $280,000 bonus buy for the Democratic candidate. And the Republican cannot close the gap simply by spending more on television.[8] Understanding the impact of media fragmentation on the advocacy business is a critical part of the new world of lobbying. But there is more.

LOBBYING AND THE 24-HOUR NEWS CYCLE

The 24-hour news cycle is another component of the hyper media world affecting lobbying. Cable news programs web portals and other media run round-the-clock. And as a result, effective interest groups and lobbyists are never "off the clock". Regular vigilance and attention are required. The 24-hour news cycle needs constant content. And from an advocacy perspective, the insatiable need for information creates both opportunities and risks for those in the lobbying world. Feeding this beast has altered the menu of the advocacy industry.

The cable network CNBC, for example, runs regular segments on issues Congress might consider on a particular day. They interview House members, senators, administration and White House officials—and yes even lawyers and lobbyists. This type of round-the-clock programming allows advocates to get their point of view in the news cycle if they can plan creatively, recognize the opportunity, and communicate their point of view to the right people before they go on television. Greg Crist, former communications director to the House Republican Conference, explains the logic of lobbying in the 24-hour news world:

> Who is the last person to whisper in the ear of a congressman or senator before they go on to one of these many media outlets for radio or television— it's the press person or communications director. Who is lobbying them? Until recently no one, but one of the trends I see in the lobbying world is a growing need to lobby the press secretary or communications director to make sure our facts are in his or her mind.

So the proliferation of media—everything from more cable channels to an expanding number of talk radio shows and online media—provides numerous opportunities to lobby the individuals who appear on these shows or those who advise them and write their talking points. Appearing in these venues can help reinforce a particular interest group's message or sabotage an opponent's strategy. No matter what the particular tactic, successful advocates in today's fragmented media world and 24-hour news cycle exploit these opportunities.

This is just another example of why the advocacy industry is structurally larger and more tactically complex than conventional wisdom suggests. When most people think about "lobbying" they don't envision influencing a guest on Hardball or Colbert—but that's exactly where policy debates can take a sharp turn in an interest-group's favor or blow up in its face.

And the 24-hour news cycle has other implications for the way lobbying works. It's more than just the growing number of cable channels or publications, or an extended spin cycle. The shifting content of this programming is also a factor.

"In the old days they called it 'rip and read,'" Greg Crist says. The news people would just read content from the wire story or off a teleprompter. News used to be all about "hard news," according to Crist:

> Walter Cronkite (CBS) and John Chancellor (NBC) were the gold standards and the place where Americans congregated every night to watch hard news. As the news cycle expanded, news programming also included soft news, and finally opinion. It's all called "news," but it's very different. NBC Nightly News is different from CNN Day Break, which is different from Larry King. But they are all considered news now and can all shape the policy agenda. It is more provocative and it is all about viewership.

Each of the different kinds of programming is looking for a little special packaging on the message. "The smart people know how to pitch these different versions of the spin cycle," Crist argues.

> The better you know how to pitch your message to these various formats, the more chances you have to get your message delivered in these venues. *Larry King, 60 Minutes,* or the *NBC Nightly News* may all do stories about drug safety that might affect provisions in the FDA Reauthorization bill, but they will explore the topic from different perspectives and require different pitches by advocates attempting to shape the news narrative.

While media fragmentation and the 24-hour news cycle have both reshaped the challenges and opportunities for lobbyists and interest groups, another transformation is also changing the structure, style, and substantive methods of the advocacy industry: the Internet and the new media. "New media" is revolutionizing the interest-group world. The final section of this chapter analyzes the impact of this new technology on the lobbying world.

LOBBYING AND NEW MEDIA

It's hard to understate the impact of the Internet and the new media world on the advocacy industry, yet these influences are not widely understood. The technology is reconfiguring the practice of lobbying. It affects everything from advertising tactics, to grassroots organizing, to how interest groups gather information, promote and defend their causes, and communicate with government.

Pete Snyder, President and Founder of New Media Strategies, a firm dedicated to helping clients sort through the challenges and opportunities in the digital advocacy business, believes there are at least three key online applications in the public affairs environment. First, he argues that the Internet helps reveal Americans' thinking about salient issues. It's kind of a digital front porch, technological town square, or a virtual tavern—a place to listen and learn about citizen grievances, aspirations, fears, and hopes. All critical for message-savvy advocates. Mr. Snyder calls the Internet, "the world's largest focus group."[9] It is a place to glean information available nowhere else. Elected officials and those who hope to influence them need to understand and incorporate this information into their strategic and tactical planning.

Second, he says the Internet offers a new way to deliver advocacy messages, a critical tool for lobbyists and interest groups. You not only get a message out, but you can target it to various audiences much more effectively. If the military now uses computer-directed "smart bombs" to wage high-tech warfare, Internet technology provides advocates with the lobbying equivalent. You can canvass much larger populations, and in a more focused manner. It is to advocacy what campaigns and fund-raisers already do in direct mail appeals—only bigger, faster, and even more targeted.

Third, online technology is a great tool to protect brand names and defend policy ideas under attack from opponents—an effective way to play defense when needed. Mr. Snyder notes that if a company's brand or policy ideas are under attack, identifying the source and the exact nature of these criticisms is much easier to do now with cyber tools. The Internet also provides an early warning signal of sorts, identifying attacks in their very early stages, and allowing advocates to plan responses faster, smarter, and more effectively.

Due to the viral nature of the Internet, many stories that may start in a blog or a less widely read online publication can quickly spread to the mainstream media. Since most reporters for conventional media read blogs, the Internet pond becomes a fertile fishing ground for new story ideas in the old media. If Matt Drudge breaks a story about a White House policy shift in the yet-to-be-released Presidential budget, *The New York Times* will probably write about it the next day. "At the very least," Greg Crist argues, "when I used to work on the Hill, reporters would call me and say their editors were asking them to track down these Web stories. It's sort of mind warfare." These are all important considerations for lobbyists who need to know their opponents' arguments early and seek effective ways to promote their own message.

The Internet also is revolutionizing advocacy advertising, a critical component of the lobbying business. According to a 2007 Pew study, the number of Americans citing the Internet as the source of most of their political news and information doubled between 2004 and 2006.[10] And as the eyes of Americans moved online, so did advertising budgets. Indeed, online placements are the fastest growing portion of most interest groups' advocacy advertising budgets. Some estimates suggest growth as high as 25 percent to 35 percent per year—about two-to-three times as fast as growth in other media spending.[11] And more recent evidence suggests Internet ad sales are growing at an even more robust rate. While 2006 Internet ad sales soared to almost $17 billion, a 35 percent increase over the previous year, 2007 sales seem likely even to exceed that pace.[12] Interest groups have had to adapt to this new online world, determining where, when, and how to promote their messages in the new digital environment.

The Internet revolutionized the earned media space as well. Certain issues cascade through the cyber world and develop a life of their own and garnering far more noteriety than a traditional media story. A Republican media consultant recounted the 2007 ad posted on YouTube about Hillary Clinton—developed by a Barrack Obama supporter. The ad was a take-off of an Apple computer commercial and portrayed Hillary Clinton as the big brother watching the world from a large-screen TV. It wasn't part of any paid media campaign but had a tremendous impact. "I watched the ad one night, and it had 14,000 hits," he recalled. "The next morning it had over 100,000 views." The ad was so popular and interesting, even the network news covered the story of its then-anonymous creator and what it all meant to the campaign. Lobbyists will next try to harness that kind of energy and creativity in paid or earned media campaigns.

One communications director for a trade association underscores this point. "We don't have the money to do a national advertising campaign. We'll run our spots in a couple congressional districts. I will then take the spots, upload them to YouTube and hope for the best. Who knows, we might get lucky and get a lot of views." Everyone's looking for the next Harry and Louise ad.[13]

"This is obviously risky," Greg Crist warns. "And these tactics are often tempered by those who would rather spend the money and get a higher probability of viewership. It's all about risk, reward and money," he says.

But as mentioned above, professional advocacy campaigns now use the new media for a lot more than advertising. One issue advocacy specialist highlights the importance of new media stories driving the mainstream media and other thought leaders: "In the communications sphere, Internet publications clearly drive elite opinion." This statement is consistent with some scholars' view of why certain mediums like blogs yield large political impacts despite a small number of readers.[14] Harnessing this growing political clout is something on which the advocacy community is keeping close watch.

The applications of new media move well beyond alternative places to advertise. They also make identifying and organizing potential supporters that much easier. Like other aspects of the Internet, new media creates multiple opportunities for communication and modes of response, action, and follow-up. A veteran Republican media strategist involved in lobbying campaigns and electoral politics notes the transition the Internet has undergone even in its short history:

> We first applied the Internet principally as an advertising tool. It was a cheaper and more targeted way to reach people. But just in the past six months I'm seeing some new applications. The real impact is that it allows us to identify people and then encourage them to engage and take action in some way. People can engage how they want, when they want and to the level they want. The options for action are almost infinite. So it's no longer just an advertising tool—although we are getting better using it for that too. It's also a way to organize communities of people and encourage them to take action.

The Madison Avenue-to-political-to-advocacy cycle continues. The same process of identifying potential buyers of a product or supporters of a candidate is now being used to recruit and mobilize grassroots supporters for lobbying campaigns. The grassroots action might be people writing, calling, or e-mailing Congress, doing something in their neighborhoods to organize like-minded people, or showing up at a local meeting. The Internet can also track who is doing what and greatly improves the targeting of follow-up advocacy organizing. "Point and click used to be a term that applied only to advertising—now it means putting volunteers on the street or activists in the halls of Congress," a Republican communications consultant with experience on Capitol Hill and on presidential campaigns remarked.

Coalitions can now advertise on websites and Web publications where readers are of a known ideological persuasion. Potential activists can click on these ads and get more information about how to get involved: write letters, make phone calls, and send e-mails to policymakers. This method of building a grassroots lobbying campaign based on Internet solicitation is an advocacy cousin of microtargeting techniques used in political campaigns. Chris Meyers, a former Senate leadership aide and Bush/Cheney 2004 staffer who now works at the grassroots firm DCI in Washington puts it this way: "In terms of building a network of grassroots activists from scratch, there is no better lobbying tool than the Internet. We know the publications they read, and we give them a chance to respond and get involved in lobbying—it's all about targeting."

MICROTARGETING AS TACTICAL RESPONSE

A brief sidebar into how microtargeting can be used in lobbying campaigns is instructive. In the "outside" lobbying business, finding the right people willing to contact lawmakers, arming them with messages that resonate with policymakers, and motivating these citizens to act are critical to advocacy success. This is another example of the merging worlds of campaigns and public policy.[15] The concept of microtargeting emerged around the time of the 2000 presidential campaign and moved into full gear in the 2004 presidential campaign and 2006 congressional elections. Microtargeting blends survey data about consumer tastes and preferences with electoral information such as voting records, party affiliation, and place of residence. Using statistical techniques, this method allows campaign strategists to build profiles of citizens based on consumer and demographic information, which yield predictions about their likelihood to vote Democrat or Republican. For example, microtargeting might suggest that if you own a Volvo, are an unmarried woman, and don't regularly attend church, there is a 90 percent chance you always vote for Democrats. When this information is linked to registered voter files, it yields the names and addresses of people who meet particular profiles. Microtargeting helps strategists tailor mailings and other communications. They also can target "get out the vote" efforts to the subpopulations most likely to support their candidate or cause. So using the above example, every single female voter who drives a Volvo and doesn't attend church is a possible target for Democratic candidates and strategists.

National Media, one of the leading firms in creating microtargeting strategies for election and advocacy campaigns, has developed the graphic below, which became famous and widely used among Washington political consultants during recent election campaigns. It underscores what drives the microtargeting business—the relationship between consumer tastes and political preferences. Figure 6-3 reveals the nexus between automobile ownership and party affiliation. Porsche and Jaguar owners are disproportionately GOP, while those who prefer Volvos skew Democratic.

A clear pattern also emerges among alcohol drinkers, shown in Figure 6-4, with the Coors Light crowd affiliating with Republicans, while brandy and cognac drinkers prefer Democrats. On the surface these data may appear interesting, but only marginally relevant. Yet in an increasingly competitive, fragmented, and targeted world, knowing the relationship between these lifestyle choices and voting preferences can help direct advocacy campaigns more efficiently and effectively.

Will Feltus of National Media found some other patterns that help focus and target audiences for advocacy campaigns. For example, sports channels (ESPN), learning stations (Discovery, History Channel), and the Weather Channel all draw more Republicans. Pro football is a draw between the parties. CNN is the preferred station among Democrats, while Republicans watch Fox News and CNBC.[16] According to Feltus, why spend money trying

FIGURE 6-3 PARTY IDENTIFICATION OF U.S. AUTOMOBILE OWNERS.

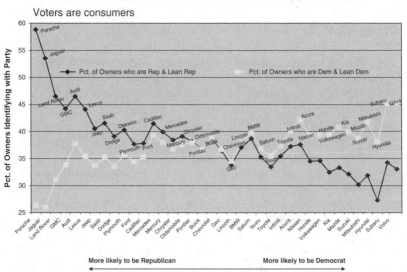

Source: National Media, Inc., Analysis of Scarborough Research 2002 Survey of U.S. adults ($N = 200, 500$).

FIGURE 6-4 POLITICAL BEVERAGE INDEX—ALCOHOLIC.

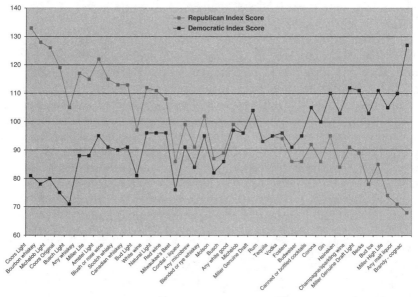

Source: National Media, Inc., Analysis of Scarborough Research 2002 Survey of U.S. Adults (*N* = 200, 500).

to persuade people who either already have made up their minds or don't vote? National Media's targeting tools are guiding the next generation of advocacy campaigns in much the same way these techniques helped revolutionize electoral politics.

A veteran Republican campaign operative familiar with the microtargeting techniques used by the Bush campaign in 2004 explains it this way:

> In the old days you would target voter turnout and mailings based on counties or some other geographic breakdown. You would focus "get out the vote" and do mailings in areas with higher concentrations of Republicans and avoid the ones with high percentages of Democrats. But this method was not very precise. You would just miss lots of people who lived in heavy Democratic districts and even turn out your opponents in areas where there might be majority Republicans, but a strong plurality of Democrats. Microtargeting changes all that. It allows you to reach into areas that we would traditionally write off and find pockets of supporters to communicate with and mobilize.

The technique was credited with helping George W. Bush win closely contested battleground states such as Ohio and Florida in the 2004 presidential campaign. Microtargeting helped Republicans offset the Democrats' historic advantage in turnout. In 2004, the 10 counties with the highest turnout in Ohio all went to Bush.[17] That was no accident. GOP strategists were able to "find" thousands of people who fit the profile of likely Republican voters through microtargeting, communicate with them on issues they cared about (guns, health care, abortion, education, etc.) and turn them out to vote on election day.

Microtargeting is a tactical political response to a fragmented media world. It allows campaigns to identify the specific periodicals or news programs their supporters read or watch and focus their paid advertisements and the substance of their communications in a more effective manner. These tools are now all migrating to lobbying campaigns. Finding the right people to join a coalition and contacting policy makers is easier than ever.

Another Republican political consultant reinforces the importance of microtargeting as a tactic in a splintered political communications environment: "We no longer have to send a mailing about a candidate's position on taxes to everyone. We only send it to the ones we know care about the issue. In the end, we may send out just as many mailings in total, but they will be targeted to different people who care about particular issues."

The Internet also adds the dimension of accountability and metrics to an advertising and advocacy campaign. Under the old model, political advertisers could only look to the places where many people likely would be watching. Now, in addition to maximizing the number of potential viewers, advocates can add another dimension: how many people actually viewed an advertisement and what they did about it. Chris Meyers of DCI agrees, "Successful Internet campaigns not only require knowledge about where to advertise, the nature of the content, and a call to action—but we now add a fourth dimension—measurement. Unlike other forms of advertising, we know how many people watch it and how mean people act on it. That's a whole new level of metrics we never had before."

The Internet dramatically expands the opportunities to build, organize, and activate communities of interest like never before. It gives these communities an unprecedented set of tools and options to use in the lobbying world. Political campaigns now include professional staff dedicated to Internet applications. Are lobbying firms, corporate Washington offices, or other interest groups going to create in-house e-advocacy positions next?

Applications of the Internet to lobbying grow every day and are changing the face of both political and advocacy campaigns. "During the last two cycles (2004 and 2006), a campaign was judged successful if it had a dedicated person to run the 'e-campaign,'" a Republican strategist working on a 2008 Republican presidential campaign recollected. "In 2008, the e-campaign is no longer a separate department but integrated into everything that we do. In the future, all campaigns will include Internet applications as a seamless part of their overall strategy," he said. The same will likely occur in advocacy campaigns. Right now, adding someone to monitor blogs, advise on online advertising, or use the Internet to mobilize grassroots is somewhat novel. In the near future, these tactics will become integrated into the normal practice of advocacy. They will be just as normal as a traditional direct lobbying contact with a congressional staffer or member of Congress.

Most discussions of lobbying fail to view the inside and outside components as an integrated whole and therefore fail to grasp the full implications of hyper media on the advocacy industry. Some reasons for this are discussed in the final chapter of this book. But one that should be raised now concerns the legal interpretation of these outside lobbying tactics such as grassroots advocacy and advertising. Unlike direct advocacy contacts, expenditures on grassroots and advertising are not even considered "lobbying" under current law passed by Congress in 1995. An Annenberg Public Policy Center study notes that these lobbying regulations do not include advertising (and grassroots initiatives) directed at members of Congress or their staffs.[18] Indeed, some corporations that list millions in direct lobbying activities actually spend *more* money on outside advocacy and issue ads, which is never reported. Expenditures on unreported advocacy advertising (and presumably grassroots and other indirect advocacy investments) represent a significant piece of their combined expenditures aimed at influencing the policy environment. This is not to suggest that these unreported activities are nefarious in any way. It only underscores one of the main points of this book—that the lobbying industry is structurally larger and more tactically complex than indicated by conventional wisdom.

SUMMARY

Lobbyists and interest groups ignore the new media world at their own peril. The advent of this hyper media environment, like other changes in the external environment of interests groups, is reshaping the structure, style, and substantive methods of the advocacy world. The fragmentation of the media world, including the growth of talk radio, the Internet, and the 24-hour news cycle, creates numerous risks, rewards, and tactical considerations for the advocacy industry.

Hyper media and rapid technological change influence both "outside" and "inside" lobbying tactics. But as several scholars suggest, they have led to particularly strong growth in the "outside" advocacy world. One political scientist noted the beginning of this trend over a decade ago: "The growth of the mass media has made it easier for representatives and constituents to communicate with each other, and technological advances have made it feasible for groups to generate, virtually instantaneously, thousands and even hundreds of thousands of letters, faxes, phone calls, and telegrams when an issue comes to a head."[19] Building on political theorist E.E. Shattschneider's observation that the flaw in the "pluralist heaven is that the heavenly chorus sings with a strong upper-class accent," two other scholars argue the "heavenly chorus has now gone high tech."[20] Indeed, the velocity and trajectory of change, and the centrality of hyper media to the lobbying world, have been revolutionary. And Internet applications to the lobbying world will continue to increase in influence and importance.

Reconsideration of lobbying requires this deeper understanding of how media fragmentation, the 24-hour news cycle, the Internet and new media are all reshaping the advocacy world. These changes also dramatically impact the new tools deployed by modern lobbyists. The application of these new advocacy tools is the next stop in this story.

NOTES

1. "Online Papers Modestly Boost Newspaper Readership," *Pew Research Center for the People & the Press*, July 30, 2006. 1.
2. Ibid. 1.
3. Greg Crist, Vice President of Dutko Worldwide and former communications director of the House Republican Conference, developed this term.
4. Cindy Skrzycki, "The Newest Lobbying Tool: Underwear," *Washington Post*, May 29, 2007, D1.
5. Devin Leonard, *Fortune Magazine*, June 28, 2004. Accessed on CNN.Money.com
6. Quoted in Mark Halperin and John F. Harris, *The Way to Win: Taking the White House in 2008* (New York, NY: Random House, 2006), 221.
7. Ibid.
8. Personal communication with Will Feltus and Robin Roberts, National Media, May 29, 2007.
9. Personal communication with Pete Snyder, President and Founder of New Media Strategies, February 2007.
10. Lee Rainie and John Horrigan, *Election 2006 Online*, Pew Internet and American Life Project, January 17, 2007.
11. Personal communication with Pete Snyder, President and Founder of New Media Strategies.
12. *USA Today*, Money Section B. May 25, 2007.
13. "Harry and Louise" was an ad sponsored by the health insurance industry to fight against the Clinton health care plan in 1993. The industry paid for some of the advertising, but most of the exposure occurred because media organizations like the three major networks did their own pieces about the ad, thereby exponentially expanding its reach and saturation.
14. Daniel Dressner, The Power and Influence of Blogs.
15. Allan J. Cigler and Burdett A. Loomis, *Interest Group Politics*, 6th ed. (Washington, D.C.: CQ Press, 2002), 382.
16. I am grateful to Robin Roberts and Will Feltus of National Media for sharing their data and insights with me. Some of National Media's findings are also reported in Douglas B. Sosnik, Matthew J. Dowd, and Ron Fournier, *Applebee's America: How Successful Political, Business, and Religious Leaders Connect with the New American Community* (New York, NY: Simon and Shuster, 2006), 45–50.
17. See Matt Bai, "Who Lost Ohio," *New York Times Magazine* (November 21, 2004).
18. Legislative Issue Advertising in the 108th Congress. The Annenberg Public Policy Center, March, 2005. 41.
19. Kenneth M. Goldstein, *Interest Groups, Lobbying and Participation in America* (Cambridge, UK: Cambridge University Press, 1999), 24.
20. Darrell M. West and Burdett A. Loomis, *The Sound of Money: How Political Interests Get What they Want* (New York, NY: Norton, 1999), 45–73.

THE NEW LOBBYING TOOLBOX

Congressional Staffer: *We need air cover to support the congressman's position if you want him to vote the right way. We need letters, phone calls, and visits from constituents.*

Texas Oil Lobbyist: *We can darken the sky over Washington with Lear jets tomorrow.*

It's 3:05 pm at the 116 Club, a musty old, private restaurant on the corner of 3rd and D Streets Northeast, only a short walk from the U.S. Capitol—even for long-winded lobbyists. Usually pretty empty by mid-afternoon, only a few old-timers with thinning hair and thickening girths remain, finishing up a few sips of a fourth Martini and the last drag on a Marlboro Light. Some say the upstairs maze of poorly lit private rooms replete with gaudy mismatched furniture used to serve as a bordello. But over the past 30 years, the 116 Club has garnered the reputation more as a place to solicit favors of the legislative variety. While much of what happened (or didn't) at the 116 Club may be urban myth, its stories are parables of old-school lobbying—and its late-afternoon emptiness an allegory of today's new world order of advocacy.

"Lobbyists used to sit and drink at the 116 Club until the senator's aide would come down from the Hill and get them," a veteran Washington representative recollects. "Then the aide would escort them to the Capitol, and they'd go have another libation with the senator and tell him what they needed. After they got all their business taken care of, they would all meet back at the 116 Club and drink some more. And lots of times, the senator would come down to join them."

While martinis and access-based advocacy will always play a role in lobbying, organized interests operate in Washington today as a fundamentally different trade. It's an increasingly complicated craft, requiring more sophisticated tools. As prominent Washington lobbyist and former senior White House aide David Hobbs puts it, navigating today's environment is a whole new game, "like the difference between checkers and three-dimensional chess."

This chapter outlines the specific methods organized interests use to compete in this more complicated setting and also details how and why the supply of these new tools has evolved. It demonstrates that these new tools are not only now routinely *expected, demanded, and integrated* in lobbying efforts by organized interests, but also that interests increasingly emulate the methods of political campaigns—forming the foundations of what was described earlier in this book as the electoral/advocacy complex. These changes follow the transformations in the external environment of interest groups outlined in the last three chapters. Reconsidering lobbying requires analyzing and understanding this new supply of tools. These new tactics include

- Research.
- Validators.
- Earned media.
- Paid media.
- Grass roots/grasstops.
- Specialized consultants.
- PACs.
- Independent expenditures.
- New media.

THE NEW TOOL BOX—PRELIMINARY OBSERVATIONS AND GENERALIZATIONS

The new toolbox didn't emerge all at once. It's been more evolution than revolution, episodic tremors rather than an abrupt earthquake. Nor have changes in the structure and number of interest groups—or their advocacy methods—occurred in a linear pattern. The modifications developed in waves, based on alterations in the interest environment. And sometimes, like in other American institutions, such as Congress, new tools get added while some of the old still remain, resulting in a system of advocacy that is sometimes disjointed, not completely rational, and certainly less politically omnipotent than suggested by the media. Arguments about institutional innovation in Congress and the policymaking process apply to lobbying as well. One legislative scholar puts it this way: "Congressional development is disjointed in that members incrementally add new institutional mechanisms, without dismantling preexisting and without rationalizing the structure as a whole."[1] Changes in the structures and tactics of advocacy lurch along in a similar fashion.

Indeed, lobbyists using multiple and creative tools is a strategy as old as Congress itself. Pennsylvania Senator William Maclay wrote in his journal on March 9, 1790, "I do not know that pecuniary influence has actually been used, but I am certain that every kind of management has been practiced and every tool at work that could be thought of. Officers of the Government, clergy, citizens (Order of) Cincinnati and every person under the influence of the Treasury worked for success of the bill."[2] So we might say the strategy is constant and the tactics change.

Multiple factors caused these changes in tactics. The emergence of a "permanent campaign" mentality in Washington; the growth and activism of legislative and executive branches of government; the proliferation of a fragmented, specialized news media; changing tactics by non-governmental competitors, opponents and allies; demands to participate in more venues; and the growing power of the Internet and "new media" like blogs—all have contributed to reshaping the lobbying industry. These new "demands" created a new "supply" of lobbying tools.

Organized interests alter their structures and advocacy methods based on changing external circumstances and as a way to manage uncertainty in a constantly evolving world. Yet in making these modifications, interests often destabilize the environment of their competitors or even government agents and policy, forcing even more changes in structure. Nothing happens in a vacuum. The pattern continues—changing environments force adaptation, which temporarily stabilizes some, while destabilizing others. My discussion of changes in the toolbox draws heavily on observations of Heinz, Laumann, Nelson, and Salisbury (1993). They argue that understanding the relationship between the structure and strategies of interest organizations and the uncertainty groups face is key to unraveling why change continually occurs. Interest groups often compete with each other and try to create countervailing power to offset the moves of competitors.[3]

In other words, changes in the structures and actions of one private interest can lead to other organizations taking actions in response. Wal-Mart's competitors begin a grassroots and paid media campaign, criticizing the practices of "big box" retailers. Wal-Mart responds with its own campaign and hires a new senior manager to monitor and strategize about how to fight back. One of the new manager's first suggestions is to deploy a paid media campaign on several influential weblogs and online publications. Wal-Mart's competitors respond by doing the same. So the beat goes on, resulting in a dynamic advocacy process and the deployment of new tools.

We also see examples of reciprocal effects with respect to government action. A former senior Republican House staffer now in the lobbying business uses this illustration:

> Sometimes the sheer number of lobbyists causes Congress to do things it otherwise would not have done. We did earmarks because a lobbyist asked. And then another organization saw how it was done and went out and hired their own lobbyist and we did another earmark. Sometimes we didn't have the money so we would put in some report language. But all this activity seemed to occur because the number of lobbyists increased.

In other words, lobbyists facilitate government action, which creates the demand for more lobbyists, leading to even more government action. That government expansion and size of advocacy grow in tandem is no accident.

Today's new toolbox also reflects the continued blurring of the lines between the politics of public policy and the politics of elections, consistent with recent scholarship emphasizing the conflation of the two.[4] Most likely a symptom of the partisan polarization that has infected Washington in the past decade, permanent campaign fever now runs rampant in other elements of the body politic—especially in lobbying. Indeed, most of the tactics highlighted in this chapter, such as research, paid media, grass roots, and Internet organizing, were first introduced in electoral politics. One prominent Republican lobbyist who previously worked on Capitol Hill and with a number of political campaigns puts it this way: "It's almost as if lobbying practices lag slightly behind campaigns. Political campaigns introduce new tactics and technologies, and then these practices ultimately get adopted into lobbying."

Partisan boutique lobbying firms employing lobbyists of only one political party—either Republicans or Democrats—or one institution, like interest representatives who exclusively lobby the White House and executive branch, also grew over the past decade. This trend, and how government relations managers at corporations and trade associations must now manage this new breed of partisan advocate, is explored in more detail later in this chapter.

Finally, in a more fractured, hyper-pluralist, hyper-media, and hyper-partisan world, just getting an issue on the agenda of policymakers requires more "influence" than ever. Too often scholars and journalists focus on a single, late-stage point where advocates try to impact the process. However, analyzing influence this late in the game masks important dimensions of lobbying—like how the issue moved on to the agenda in the first place.[5] The tools outlined in this chapter do more than just shape roll call votes and final regulatory decisions. They help gather information, reduce uncertainty, and form the initial agenda of policymakers.

Anecdotes abound showing that many public affairs firms grasp these changes in the political, competitive, and technological environments. Their marketing materials reflect new structures to address the uncertainties of a changing world. The Glover Park Group, a Washington-based public affairs firm, sums up the new battlefield well on its Website:

> Clients rarely want strategy without tactical execution, or communications plans without strategic guidance. In looking at the communications industry, we noticed a gap: strategic consultants lacked the ability to implement their own plans, and public relations firms who could implement those plans lacked the necessary strategic experience. But by bringing both strategic thinkers and advertising and public relations professionals together, The Glover Park Group has bridged the divide—offering comprehensive client

service from the earliest strategic planning to the final execution of advocacy and image advertising campaigns.

DC Navigators, another full-service public affairs/lobbying firm takes a similar approach and talks about the changing nature of its services and the contents of its toolbox this way:

> Navigators is an elite team of lobbyists, political strategists and public relations experts that offers integrated campaigns to solve difficult public policy problems. From the trenches of political campaigns to the height of corporate crises, we've navigated the toughest terrain. Whatever your challenge is, we can guide you to victory.

Note in both cases the absence of language about how "well connected" or how much "access in Washington" they possess. These firms grasp the new, integrated, highly public nature of advocacy. When it comes to advertising their wares, successful advocates must offer more than "access" to a subcommittee chair or to a member of the congressional leadership.

Today's most leading-edge lobbying firms, like those mentioned above, routinely market a wide array of public affairs tools and bristle at being characterized as "access-only" organizations. Steve Perry, veteran lobbyist and vice chairman of Dutko Worldwide, agrees, "In pitches to potential clients we routinely say, 'If you're just looking for door openers, don't come to us. We do a lot more.' "

The public affairs firm Berman and Company in DC captures this new mind-set well in its literature. Its toolbox is fully loaded. The company, according to its marketing brochure, offers more than access; it possesses "the power to change the debate." It goes on to boast: "PR firms offer access to the media. Law firms pledge to defend their clients. Lobbying firms promise meetings with legislators. At Berman and Company, *we do all of this* (emphasis added). But we go further. We change the debate. If necessary, we start the debate."

The examples above demonstrate how lobbyists today are blazing a new trail compared to access-only advocates—their supply of practices and tactics go well beyond "who you know." Lobbying is changing its structures, making investments to better manage uncertainty by getting more involved at different levels of a broader public policy environment. But what are the new tools and why have these particular ones been adopted?

Each of the tactics outlined in this chapter could serve as the topic of a separate monograph. One scholar, for example, devotes an entire book to how organized interests mobilize one tool in the toolbox, grassroots lobbying.[6] My purpose here is not to present an exhaustive review of each lobbying tactic. Instead, I offer a description of each as part of a collage of advocacy, a mosaic of the current state of an always-changing and evolving set of tools. Each section includes contemporary examples of how organized interests use these tools.

RESEARCH—INFORMATION AS POWER

Scholars argue that interest groups attempt to reduce uncertainty in their environments by expanding their capacity to participate in policy deliberations and by increasing the amount of policy-relevant information they possess. The level of information is critical for both the interests' internal decisions and the effectiveness of influencing the policymaking process.[8]

"Research renders all opinions unequal," one long-time public affairs consultant with an extensive background in polling and political campaigns says. In today's environment, facts matter. "The days of the back slapping, 'You help me, I help you,' quid pro quo lobbying are long gone" the late Dan Dutko, founder of Dutko Worldwide, used to say. There are now too many staff, too many policy experts, too many competitors, too many reporters, and too much accountability to just get by on friendships and relationships. You've got to have good facts and arguments to succeed in this environment. Information is power. And the best lobbyists today often include some kind of research in their advocacy toolbox.

The Glover Park Group says this about the interrelationship between lobbying and research:

> We believe that successful communications strategies are predicated on finding and leveraging target insights among key constituencies. Research tells you where you are and how to get to where you want to be. Whether your audience is internal or external, the smart, strategic research we offer will help you develop, execute and track (measure) the effectiveness of a winning communications campaign.

We offer a full-service research operation, including

- National, regional, and local polling.
- Web-based online survey research.
- Focus groups.
- Highly targeted in-depth interviews with key decision-makers.
- Dial/keypad testing/mall intercepts.

Research can be critical in message development. When health care companies began advocating for the Medicare Modernization Act in 2003, several did substantial research into the best way to talk about adding a prescription drug benefit for senior citizens. They found that while many conservative lawmakers were inclined to laud "Medicare reform," that term did not test well with elderly voters. Many viewed it as a way "Washington would 'experiment on us' by changing a popular entitlement program," according to one strategist who conducted focus groups on the issue. Research showed that using words like "strengthening," "preserving," and "protecting" Medicare resonated much better with voters. Possessing this kind of strategic information provided a major advantage in the lobbying debate. Congressmen and senators not only wanted to hear about this research—which created access and credibility—but they used it in talking to their constituents and wanted more.

Rich Thau, president of Presentation Testing, a New York-based business consulting firm, who regularly talks to members of Congress and has advised the White House on a variety of entitlement reform issues, puts it this way:

> Lawmakers are comfortable with this data in a policy context because they are used to seeing polling and focus group data for their campaigns. They are becoming increasingly familiar with it and in some ways almost expect it. Polling and focus groups are like "crack cocaine" for political junkies on the Hill. Once they try it they always want more. It's like "milk." It gets stale when it's old and you have to keep it fresh.

Research is utilized in a variety of ways. Message development as discussed above is just one example. "Rendering all opinions unequal" can also apply to the political impact of supporting or opposing a particular initiative on Capitol Hill. A company in the transportation industry knew that its employees in several key states were subject to adverse implications from a particular tax policy. Instead of just approaching the lobbying challenge in the traditional way—informing senators and congressmen that the company employees, who were the lawmakers' constituents, supported a particular piece of legislation changing the policy—these companies chose a new approach, taking their advocacy to another level of sophistication.

They commissioned a poll of their employees and members of their company's union in selected states. The poll analyzed the level of knowledge about the tax proposal and its political salience. Would these company employees and union members be more likely to vote for someone who supported this change in tax policy? Would the lawmakers' position on this legislation trump other considerations? These were all significant questions and the poll provided answers. Adding this type of research to the advocacy campaign did indeed "render all opinions unequal."

Could some say the poll was self-serving, or perhaps even one-sided? Sure. But no one had any competing information, so the poll became part of the advocacy equation. It quantified constituent salience on this issue. It was not a silver bullet in the heart of a lobbyist's opponent, but it became a useful data point and a creative use of research in an advocacy campaign.

Political scientists Darrell M. West and Burdett A. Loomis demonstrate the value of research such as polling and the use of think tanks in their book, *The Color of Money: How Political Interests Get What They Want*. They note that this research is important not only to help frame the debate but also to advance a convincing narrative, a tactic we have already seen as critical in communicating in a world with a wealth of information and a poverty of attention.[9]

A prominent Republican polling firm—Public Opinion Strategies—recognizes the power of research in advocacy campaigns. The firm's motto on its Website is "Turning Questions into Answers." Indeed, lobbying campaigns overflow with questions and uncertainty. What is the political impact of supporting versus opposing a particular bill? What's the best language to use in advocating a particular position? Will policymakers listen more if research supports a particular position? In modern advocacy campaigns, research may not guarantee winning the debate, but it's part of the uniform needed to get on the field of play.

Well-respected Republican pollster Whit Ayres underscored the growing importance of polling in a recent interview with *Roll Call*. According to the publication, "Ten years ago, three-quarters of his business was polling for political candidates, with one quarter for corporate and trade association clients. Now, that ratio has flipped: 75 percent of his business is issue advocacy polling."[10]

In 2007 the pharmaceutical industry turned to polling, research, and paid media as a way to bolster its advocacy efforts. House and Senate Democrats sought to pass legislation allowing the government to negotiate directly with pharmaceutical companies over drug prices. The industry opposed this measure, preferring to keep the government out of the negotiating business so they could bargain with private health plans and insurers. Early in 2007, the Democrats touted a series of public polls demonstrating strong support for the concept of "the government negotiating lower drug prices." The pharmaceutical industry argued the question was somewhat biased because "government negotiations" would also lead to fewer choices for consumers and stricter formularies. "The only way for the government to achieve lower prices is to limit the number of drugs they pay for," a pharmaceutical industry lobbyist argued.

The industry quickly commissioned its own polls, asking citizens the follow-up question, "What if you knew government negotiations would lead to fewer choices?" With that additional information, opposition rose sharply. Figure 7-1 is an example of a full-page ad the pharmaceutical industry ran the week of a key Senate vote on the negotiating provision. The industry position narrowly prevailed. Many believed the polling information, demonstrating strong swings in public opinion once citizens learned more about the impact of government negotiations, contributed to the industry victory.

Polling is also used in a targeted manner. Recently a trade group facing cuts in federal funding for a program most of its member companies cared deeply about commissioned a poll in a single congressional district of a vulnerable member of Congress. The survey investigated the political impact of the lawmaker voting for these cuts among likely voters and other key constituencies in his district. The results showed a dramatic impact, and the association planned private briefings with the lawmaker conducted by pollsters he knew and trusted. The association planned to replicate the technique and conduct similar briefings in about a dozen other swing

FIGURE 7-1 CHALLENGING RESEARCH WITH RESEARCH.

89% of Voters Oppose
Government Negotiation of Medicare Drug Prices.

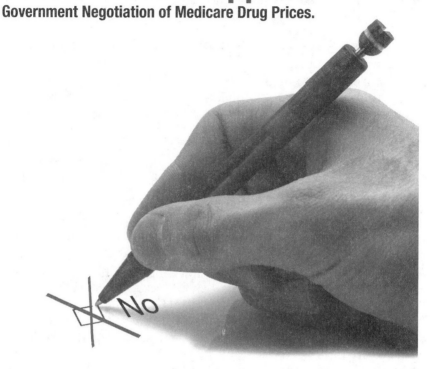

Majorities of Democratic, Republican and Independent voters *do not* want the government negotiating prescription drug prices under Medicare. In fact, 89 percent oppose government negotiation if it could limit access to new prescription medications.

Those are the results from a recent bipartisan survey conducted by two leading Democratic and Republican polling firms. Other findings include:

• 78% agree that government negotiation would *limit access* to prescription drugs

• 75% agree that the *market should set prescription drug prices*, not the government

• 66% agree that government negotiation gives the federal government too much authority and is *a dangerous precedent*

Americans have reason to fear that allowing the federal government to negotiate prices for drugs in Medicare will limit their access to medicines. A recent letter from the Congressional Budget Office (CBO) stated: "...without the authority to establish a formulary, we believe the Secretary would not be able to encourage the use of particular drugs by Part D beneficiaries, and as a result would lack the leverage to obtain significant discounts in his negotiations with manufacturers."

In case you missed it, that's bureaucratic speak for "restricted access to medicines."

Call (202) 224-3121. Tell Congress to protect today's Medicare.

PhRMA
New Medicines. New Hope.

www.PhRMA.org

Source: www.PhRMA.org

districts. The information was fresh, powerful, and starkly demonstrated the impact of voting for the budget cuts. It "rendered all opinions unequal" and represented a powerful advocacy tool. This illustration underscores the growing importance of research in the arsenal of advocates.

VALIDATORS: THINK TANKS AND ISSUE EXPERTS

Another aspect of research involves the identification, recruitment, and engagement of "validators"—think tanks or other issue experts who can "independently" bolster a particular interest's views. Again, Berman and Company's marketing brochure speaks to this point. "We commission more than a dozen research projects each year from independent academics at leading universities. The credibility of the material produced by these independent academics is unparalleled among trade associations, law firms, or consultants active in the public policy arena."[11]

The use of "formers" is another popular validating strategy. Op/eds written by "former cabinet members," whether former Health and Human Services Secretary Joe Califano arguing for tougher anti-smoking laws or former Secretaries of State joining forces to say why the United States should pay its U.N. dues, are now employed to bolster advocacy campaigns.

Utilizing think tanks is a little trickier. Institutions like Brookings, the American Enterprise Institute (AEI), and The Heritage Foundation are obviously independent organizations, and paying them to support a position they would otherwise not advocate is both inappropriate and unethical. Nevertheless, researchers and institutions do have ideological predispositions. And when their point of view aligns with an advocacy campaign, utilizing these scholarly resources can be an effective advocacy tool.

"Having the power of a think tank behind you really helps," Greg Crist, former communications director for the House Republican Conference, remarks. "I think that increasingly, having a think tank on your side and rolling their research into your overall strategy is going to give those who use the research a real competitive advantage." As long ago as 1978, conservatives such as Irving Kristol began urging corporations to invest in think tanks to help preserve a strong private sector, wrote David Callahan in a 1999 *Washington Monthly* piece "The Think Tank as Flack." Many corporations are expanding their investments in this area, particularly with conservative think tanks like AEI, CATO, and The Heritage Foundation. While labor unions or other liberal interest groups rely on left-leaning think tanks like the Economic Policy Institute or the Joint Center for Political and Economic Studies.

Business interests concerned with issues related to tort reform, product liability, medical malpractice, and frivolous lawsuits could support AEI and utilize information from its Liability Project as an advocacy tool. The think tank describes the project on its Website as follows:

> In 2003, AEI established a project to conduct and publicize research on the ever-expanding liability litigation crisis in the United States and abroad. The AEI Liability Project devotes its energies and resources to examining the institutions, procedures, and political economy of contemporary liability law, as distinct from substantive tort doctrines. The project's output consists principally of short monographs and papers on selected liability problems and reform options.

AEI doesn't manipulate its research or its scholars' opinions to fit with sponsors' goals. However, its free-market approach to issues dovetails with the concerns of the business community about a broken tort system, dominated by their political opponents in the trial bar. "When we believe a free-market solution fits our problem, we go to a free market-oriented think tank," the vice president of government affairs for AT&T says. "By hiring them we don't change their views, but it does get them focused on our issues, questions and problems. It gives us a credible piece of research, by a credible scholar that comes down on the same side of the issue as us—and we use it and distribute it all over the Hill," he argues.

Rich Thau puts it this way: "We want our clients to know more than their competitors—have better, newer, fresher information. Not only for themselves, but for their external audience." Think tank research provides this tool.

The use of think tanks also escalates because of the imitation principle, a practice repeated with many of the utensils in the toolbox. Adoption by some destabilizes the environment for others, which normally leads competitors and opponents to adopt a similar tactic. Once one side in an advocacy campaign chooses to engage a think tank, its opponents do the same. Sally Murphy of the Wine Institute says she has seen many "wars of studies," where each side presents favorable research from either a think tank or university to bolster or validate its case. "Nature abhors a vacuum," she remarked. "And the same is true when it comes to convincing studies. If one side does one you can bet their opponents will do it too."

EARNED MEDIA—SHAPING THE PLAYING FIELD

Expert information, think tank reports, and university research are among the tools organized interests use today to convince the media to report favorable stories. Packaging information and pitching the media on a particular argument is an increasingly utilized utensil referred to as "earned media." And like other new tactics, organized interests invest in these activities as a way to reduce uncertainty and as a response to the growing use of the practice by their competitors. How consumers benefit from public policy decisions related to telecommunications deregulation, or demonstrating the benefits of the new prescription drug coverage are just two examples of stories the communications industry and the pharmaceutical industry used to shape a more positive environment through earned media strategies. Their opponents, typically representing so-called consumer organizations, would try to promote stories on the other side, arguing that corporate coffers, not consumers, stood to gain the most.

Experts note a growing activism among organized interests promoting earned media stories and integrating this tactic into their overall advocacy strategies. "Most of the stories you read in *Roll Call, The Hill,* or *Congress Daily* were promoted specifically by someone trying to get a favorable process story about an issue gaining momentum or broader support, or trying to frame the debate a particular way. These reports don't happen by accident. They are usually part of a spinning process," Greg Crist argues.

A narrative—telling a story about an issue—is an increasingly critical component of lobbying. "It's not only a way to get noticed," Crist observed. "But it's also the way members of Congress think about the issue. They view these policy questions more holistically. Your narrative is just as important as the legislative language. And it's this story that grabs the media and public attention and helps you break through on arcane issues."[12]

Crist cites an illustration from the health care field. "No one understands the details of a Medicare payment issue. But a hundred doctors in white lab coats standing on the steps of the Capitol talking about how they won't be able to provide medical services anymore will get a story and your issue on the front page of publications like *Roll Call* or *The Hill* that members and staff read."

Reflecting further about earned media he says, "Lobbyists have to do more now than just care about legislative language. Earned media stories are the 'punctuation' at the end of your message. It completes the picture. Or maybe a better way of saying it is, 'It adds color to a black and white picture.' But without it, your message often gets lost."

Political scientists who study modern advocacy agree, "The politics of influence has never been cheap, but as increasing numbers of interests enter the fray and as the stakes of decisions reach historic proportions . . . the need to make clear and convincing arguments has never been greater." In their words, it's important to "always tell a story."[13]

A public affairs executive with a major corporation commenting on getting earned media stories puts it this way: "There are many doors to go through to be successful in advocacy. Most people try to go through the front door. They don't realize there also are backdoors, side doors and even basement doors. We want to be able to go through them all. Getting earned media about our issue or our efforts helps us do that."

Shaping comments to the particular media outlet is another important component of earned media. "I am a regular on TV," the insurance industry's

Rusbuldt notes. "Whether I am talking about terrorism insurance, natural disaster legislation, flood insurance, tax issues or regulatory reform, it's absolutely essential to frame issues for consumers and to talk about what is important to the viewers of that network."

Of all the utensils in the toolbox, earned media strategies may represent some of the newest and most innovative, yet also the most unpredictable and under-utilized, tactics adopted by advocates. Many interest groups "back into or stumble upon" the importance of earned media, Greg Crist notes. "Right now people who do this are more artisans than scientists," he says. "But for those looking to what gives them an edge over their competitors, getting this kind of 'pull through' on their story really gives them a leg up." It's another tool to break through the clutter in the fragmented new world.

PAID MEDIA—AIR COVER

If sophisticated research, including the use of think tanks and earned media, is kindling to heat up advocacy campaigns, paid media is an accelerant to start and spread the fire. The permanent campaign mind-set that influences the demand for research also stimulates the desire for paid media as part of modern advocacy campaigns. Former Majority Leader Tom DeLay (R-TX) used to tell lobbyists that if they wanted support on a controversial issue, they should invest in a paid media campaign in lawmakers' districts. "It's not enough to just lobby in Washington," one of DeLay's staff argued. "These members need air cover in the media."

Paid media is the admission ticket to enter the big-time Washington stage. Without deploying this type of capital, a public affairs/lobbying campaign isn't considered serious these days.

"Investing in a paid media campaign is what I call meeting the legitimacy factor," one veteran media consultant opines. It sends a message to people on the Hill and others on the policy playing field that your issue or group is a force with which to be reckoned. "It shows your seriousness of intent," he says. And that's one of the first steps to getting people in policy-making positions to pay attention.

Expenditures on paid media are hard to track. Unlike lobbying disclosure and campaign finance, these activities are not regulated. But just because they are difficult to track does not diminish their power as a lobbying tool. Many observers don't even include paid media in their definition of lobbying. Part of our reconsideration of advocacy, however, demands that we integrate this tool to more fully understand the scope of advocacy.

The Annenberg School at the University of Pennsylvania conducted several studies that take this broader view and provide some useful insights. First, their research demonstrates dramatic growth in paid media over the past several years.[14] It estimates that inside-the-Beltway expenditure on paid media quadrupled in four years. Annenberg finds that interest-group spending on paid media ballooned from approximately $105 million during the 107th Congress (2001–2002) to over $404 million during the 108th Congress (2003–2004). Interestingly, most of this spending is concentrated among a small group of sponsors with "the top 1% of organizations account[ing] for 57% of the spending."[15] Corporate interests outspent citizen causes, the study notes, by a five-to-one margin.[16] And six out of the top 10 issue advertising spenders reported more expenditures on paid media than on lobbying expenses overall. Yet it should be clear by now that distinctions between "lobbying expenditures" and "issue advertising," while interesting, are also artificial. Both kinds of expenditures fit into the new strategies and tactics of advocacy and are integral to lobbying success.

It's one way that advocates "go public."[17] As one interest-group scholar notes, "Just as elected officials in Washington feel the need to monitor and assuage public opinion through polls and public relations, modern lobbying increasingly requires sophisticated methods of public mobilization. Lobbying in Washington is not just a game among well-paid lawyers, ideological activists, and legislators in the Capitol. The outside public is increasingly involved."[18]

And in some ways, it's the gift that keeps on giving. As with other lobbying tools, a "me too" phenomenon also applies to paid media. When one side of a debate invests in paid media, it raises the ante and opponents normally have to respond. "We invest in paid media because we know our opponents have and will," one vice president for government relations at a major DC trade association says.

This practice was on full display in 2006 when advocates from the high-tech industry, representing companies such as Yahoo, Google, and Amazon, ran the advertising campaign for "net neutrality"—seeking new regulations to ensure lower costs and equal treatment from telephone and cable networks for Internet access. Not long after these ads began gaining political attention, the cable and telephone companies began running their own ads—creating a paid media arms race of sorts.

Then, there is the issue of trying to shape the media's reporting by investing in a paid advertising campaign. "We couldn't get the issue framed the right way or even get a lot of reporters to pay attention to us," one media consultant recalls. "We decided that a paid media campaign, framing the issue the way we wanted it, would get reporters to write stories about the legislative battle. It worked."

Net neutrality was a highly technical issue that meant a lot to Internet providers, but no one initially paid attention. The advertising campaign helped frame the legislative debate as "all about access" to the Web. Would the telephone and cable companies discriminate? Once the specter of some being kept off the Internet was raised, telephone and cable companies had to fire back. Net neutrality—they said through paid media—was tantamount to "reregulation." Each side attempted to use paid media to frame the debate on its terms. A highly arcane regulatory issue was reframed in more politically salient terms like "access" versus "reregulation."

And while it may seem ironic in today's dog-eat-dog partisan world, paid advertising is also a tactic to express good manners. "We use it to say 'thank you' a lot these days," one knowledgeable advisor notes. "If members of Congress cast a tough vote we try to run some type of ad either in print, TV or radio thanking them from constituents back home. It makes a big difference the next time you're asking for their support."

A large public health association in Washington DC routinely runs "thank you" ads in lawmakers' local newspapers—as well as in inside-the-Beltway publications like *National Journal, Congressional Quarterly, The Politico, Roll Call,* or *The Hill* —after these members of the House or Senate cast a vote consistent with the organization's grassroots and Washington advocacy positions. These campaigns send a subtle message to legislative staff and members of Congress: "We're watching you and your vote has a consequence." "It's one side of 'spanks and thanks,' " a trade association executive says. "You can't always run ads that criticize people for not voting with you, but then not say 'thank you' when they do."

But "spanks" are also used. On a budget vote to raise the tobacco tax, a move supported by a number of public health organizations, some groups ran ads in lawmakers' districts chastising them for voting against the levy increase. This is obviously a riskier tactic, but it also gets politicians' attention.

Changes in technology contribute to the growth of paid media in advocacy campaigns. "I see the growth and popularity of cable contributing to this trend," one media strategist remarks. "It used to be that you could reach your target demographic goal by just advertising on broadcast TV and radio. No more. People are busier now, and their viewing patterns are different. Media markets are more segmented due to the growth of cable. We may now do separate, targeted spots for the Golf Channel, the Weather Channel or the Food Network. Today it's not uncommon to spend 25 percent of our media budget on an issues campaign on targeted cable buys."

More sophisticated technology also improves targeting. And as lobbying campaigns continue to take on more of the characteristics of political campaigns, targeting becomes even more important. It's not uncommon for lobbying campaigns to target inside-the-Beltway opinion leaders as part of their media strategy. Full-page ads in *Roll Call, The Hill,* or *Congress Daily,* or advertising on Sunday talk shows or drive radio in DC are now commonly used techniques by lobbying organizations. "Going public" tactics like these are not normally intended to change or persuade public opinion about the substance of an issue. Rather, the intent is to communicate a message of seriousness, frame the debate in a favorable manner, or even just say thank you to supporters.

This tool, like others, however, has its limits. "Paid media is sometimes the knee-jerk solution for the public relations firm," Crist argues. "But in the din of messages and ads, sometimes it's hard to break through and get people to notice." A political consultant with a senior position in a 2008 Republican presidential campaign says the same thing. "Sometimes you can have the best ad, placed in the right medium, but if no one is paying attention or it doesn't result in any action, what's the point?" This gets back to the point former RNC chairman Ken Mehlman likes to make about the new world of politics. "In a world with a surplus of information, there is a deficit of attention."[19]

Paid media is also one of the best examples of the "campaign-infused" advocacy world. "Look, no one likes to admit it, but negative campaigns work in elections. There is no reason why these same techniques shouldn't be used in lobbying—and they are. We need to break through the clutter and get noticed. Paid advertising—especially if it has an 'edge' to it—works," a vice president for government affairs of a DC trade association argues. "Just imagine a political world without ads," he says. "Someday people will say that about lobbying. In fact, it's already the case." Paid media is now a core discipline in the school of campaign-infused advocacy.

But if air cover in the form of earned and paid media in modern advocacy campaigns is now demanded, targeted, and integrated, the ground cavalry can't be far behind. That's the role of grass roots/grasstops.

GRASS ROOTS—GROUND COVER

During debate in Congress concerning the Central American Free Trade Agreement (CAFTA), an undecided lawmaker told a representative of a pro-free trade organization, "I don't need to see any more CEOs or lobbyists, I need to start hearing from employees and constituents in favor of free trade agreements. That's what will make a difference with me." In other words, no more arguments from elites or those paid to advocate. He wanted to hear from the folks back home about why free trade helps them.

This type of sentiment is probably not new in Congress, but new communications technologies and the power of targeting provide advocates with the ability to fulfill that Congressman's request. Insurance association president Bob Rusbuldt has witnessed the power of mobilizing people in lobbying campaigns. "There are some lobbyists who deliver checks and others who can deliver people. Usually people are more important than money, so grassroots advocacy matters."

Systematic accounts of how grassroots lobbying influences the legislative process are sparse. One notable exception is Goldstein (1999), who focuses on how and why grassroots advocacy is used in legislative campaigns. Goldstein also shows how grassroots lobbying has grown in recent years.

Illuminating the role of elites (e.g. interest-group leaders and lobbyists) in recruiting, motivating, and directing mass participation in advocacy campaigns (e.g. employees, union members, etc.) is one of the major contributions of Goldstein's work. In other words, decisions to mobilize and participate in grassroots activities are not spontaneous, citizen-led efforts. Grassroots participation is usually encouraged and organized by organized interests and lobbyists. These activities have expansive impact.

Elites, like lawmakers in Congress, signal the intensity of citizens toward a particular issue. They help frame the arguments in the debate. And, as Goldstein notes, they even indicate the potential electoral consequences of policy decisions. But these actions do not happen spontaneously. Normally, grassroots contacts occur because someone first educated the voters about an issue and then asked them to take specific actions.

A former member of the House Republican leadership recounts a story about a meeting with senior citizens to discuss Medicare issues. "I thought I was going to meet with a bunch of seniors and hear them complain about their Medicare plan. Instead I met with a group of 200 seniors who said they were happy with their Medicare. (These seniors were part of what's now called Medicare Advantage—a managed care version of Medicare administered by private health plans). That really impressed me. I expected complaints and all I heard was praise. It made me think, 'I need to support what these people have.' "

And while the lawmaker didn't know it, these seniors were actually mobilized and recruited by a managed care plan as part of its grassroots lobbying campaign. Their message was simple: "Don't pass any federal policies that would take away this form of Medicare I enjoy and value." That message came through loud and clear. This particular member of the House Republican leadership was one of the most outspoken supporters of Medicare Advantage years after his grassroots encounter. And this particular meeting seemed to have a major impact on his thinking as he mentioned it repeatedly to the company's lobbyists in Washington for the next several years.

Better targeting through technology has also increased the size of the grassroots industry. In an ironic twist of "less is more," one grassroots consultant explains how targeting and technology have been a boon to his business.

> In both electoral and issue campaigns, we used to traditionally do one or more generic mailings, trying to raise awareness about an issue or mobilize support, but all aimed at our general target audience. With better techniques like microtargeting we can refine our message and focus six or seven different grassroots mailings/appeals to different segments of the population. We may want to mobilize seniors with one message, women with another, and conservative men with still another. From a business standpoint, instead of doing one mailing, I now do six.

Others agree with the major impact of technology on grass roots. "I think the biggest change in the lobbying world I've seen over the past 20 years is how technology has improved grass roots," Nelson Litterst, now a lobbyist with the C2 Group in Washington, remarks. Litterst formerly worked with the National Federation of Independent Business and then served as a senior White House lobbyist in the Bush administration in 2001. "It used to be the biggest and most effective tool was shoe-leather lobbying and personal connections," he says. "Now it's grass roots. Groups have taken it to a whole new level using technology." He also notes that while business groups first deployed grass roots, public interest and consumer groups now have the advantage. "I think it went to a whole new level when business fought the Clinton health care plan in 1993. But since that time it seems like the opponents of business are using grass roots and technology most effectively."

Grassroots lobbying, however, must be deployed with care. "It can really anger people," one Democratic Washington lobbyist warns. "You have to be careful how you use it." The technique can annoy lawmakers and staff, particularly if they believe it's not genuine. "Many times grassroots lobbying looks and feels like a lot of trumped up crap," lobbyist Michael Boland argued. "If that's the case, it usually doesn't work."

"I've only used it once in my career," the Democratic lobbyist recalled. "And I was pretty sure I was going to win before I even used it." Using grassroots as part of the advocacy toolbox is growing in importance and sophistication. Mobilizing citizens and stakeholders from the "outside" represents a stark contrast to the conventional view of "inside" lobbying conducted by well-connected influence peddlers.

SPECIALIZED CONSULTANTS

Organized interests, particularly institutionalized interests with a high level of resources and multiple potential problems and opportunities, will also invest in numerous, specialized Washington representatives to advocate for them.[20] Political scientist Ronald G. Schaiko includes the growth of specialized lobbying firms as one of the dominant new trends in the practice of advocacy by organized interests over the past decade.[21]

A brief review of *Washington Representatives*, a compilation of lobbyists and lobbying firms, confirms this point. Pfizer, for example, is a large, complex organization that uses its own in-house government relations employees as well as multiple and specialized consultants as part of its toolbox to control uncertainty and gather information. It employs nine individuals in its in-house Washington office and 28 lobbying firms. Other major corporations follow a similar pattern. Intel's Washington office includes nine employees and four outside firms. Goldman Sachs employs five government relations staff in DC and 10 outside lobbying firms. And UPS's Washington operation lists 13 company employee lobbyists and 10 lobbying firms. In many cases, the outside lobbying firms focus on niche advocacy, such as relationships with Republican or Democratic leaders, or specific committee or subcommittee liaisons.

The supply of these specialized advocates, such as so-called "sole practitioners" (a lobbying firm built around one individual with a highly specialized background and contacts) or partisan boutique lobbying shops, has grown dramatically in the past two decades and described in more detail in Chapter 5. The emergence of specialized partisan, institutional or issue-based consultants is a direct response to the growing polarization and proliferation of staff and other public policy experts in Washington. In the past, particularly "Republican only" or "Democrat only" firms were rare, but now they play an important niche role in the overall advocacy equation, especially given the increased frequency of mixed party control in Washington.

Managing these specialists is a new skill senior leaders of organized interests in Washington must now marshal. "A consultant is only as good as you manage them," Nick Franklin of PacifiCare Health Systems explains. "You need to lay out your expectations, brief them on strategy, talk about the other process drivers and program goals. You need to get them to buy in to what you are doing. And after all that, you need to keep in regular communication with them," he says.

LOBBYING THE WHITE HOUSE WITH SPECIALIZED CONSULTANTS

The practice of representing interests at the White House represents one of the best uses of specialized consultants in today's lobbying world. Surprisingly, political scientists know little about lobbying this branch of government,[22] an unfortunate gap given the major role of the Executive Office of the President in the lawmaking process. And the importance of the White House grows during periods of divided government when practices such as vetoing bills become more relevant factors in tracking legislation.

The president is a key actor in everything from setting funding priorities in the budget, to issuing Statements of Administration Policy (SAPs) on legislation, to adding legislative lobbying muscle trying to pass or oppose measures in Congress, and ultimately to signing or vetoing bills.

In today's more specialized and partisan policymaking process (see Chapter 5), using consultants who not only know the process inside the White House but also garner the trust of the president's staff is critical. Few interest-group representatives would say they have the resources to hire a consultant just to lobby the White House (although depending on the specific nature of the issue and the level of resources the interest possesses, some do), but most sophisticated organizations today recognize the need to include someone on their team who knows the White House staff and processes.

As I argue in Chapter 5, little academic research has been done on "lobbying the White House." Some have described lobbying for the president.[23] But how interest groups lobby the White House remains largely unexplored terrain. I begin to fill in some of these gaps below.

Lobbying the White House is not fundamentally different from a tactical perspective than representing interests before the legislature. But to lobby the White House effectively, an advocate must understand the complexities of the policymaking process inside the executive branch. The president's staff is more layered and multifaceted than a typical congressional staff. For example, say the president is formulating a position on legislation related to global climate change. Lobbying the White House on this matter might include visits to Karl Rove or his assistants in Political Affairs, Strategic Initiatives, or Intergovernmental Affairs; the Domestic Policy Council (which handles energy policy); the Economic Policy Counsel; the Office of Legislative Affairs; and the chief of staff or his deputy. It might also involve visits to the appropriate staff member at the Office of Management and Budget (which will craft the SAP on any climate change legislation). Finally, it could include contacts with the Council of Economic Advisors or the Council on Environmental Quality.

Effective lobbying of the White House recognizes the intricacies of the policymaking process and appreciates the different constituencies represented by the dozen or so staff mentioned above. Like Congress, the Executive Office of the President now has many more specialized offices and staff that lobbyists need to contact and influence, and from whom intelligence and information is needed.[24] For example, the Office of Legislative Affairs will want to make sure the president's position is not out of sync with his party leaders' in Congress. The Domestic Policy Council representative will be particularly sensitive to how a new White House position on climate change squares with previous statements. The Economic Policy Council and the Council of Economic Advisors will care about the impact of the legislation on the economy. The Offices of Political Affairs and Intergovernmental Affairs will want to know the electoral implications of supporting or opposing legislation and the view of state and local elected officials.

Many of the tools outlined in this chapter aimed at influencing the legislative branch are equally as effective and needed in lobbying the White House. Research, advertising, grass roots, and grasstops influence the president's staff in many of the same ways a lawmaker is influenced.

Moreover, sophisticated lobbyists recognize that mobilizing congressmen and senators to push the president in one direction or another is a particularly effective lobbying strategy. Some of the most valuable advice a specialized consultant can provide helps interest groups connect these legislative/executive branch dots, showing how the White House can affect Congress and vice versa.

The partisan pedigree of the advocate lobbying the White House is just as important as understanding the intricacies of the process. Sending in a well-known Democrat to lobby the Bush administration is a mistake. A friendly face that maybe worked side by side with a current White House staffer earlier in the administration or on the campaign can immediately establish trust and credibility when lobbying the president's staff. And in today's specialized and more partisan environment, lobbyists have built entire practices around representing interest groups before the White House. Ron Kaufman of Dutko Worldwide highlights this point: "I know one lobbyist with close ties to the White House who never goes to Capitol Hill. His whole practice is centered on helping clients lobby the right power centers in the White House. They (White House staff) know him and trust him. And he knows where the decisions are made. He has built a successful practice of lobbying around his knowledge of the White House."

Lobbying the White House is an important tool in the lobbyist's toolbox. It has become even more important due to changes such as more specialization, the growth of the Executive Office of the President,[25] partisanship, and the increasing frequency of mixed party control of government. Advocates must build this piece of the government policymaking process into their strategic and tactical calculus.

MONEY TOOLS—ACCESS AND CHANGE

Campaign dollars are no stranger to the neighborhood of lobbying. So arguing money is a "new tool" in the advocacy arsenal is a bit of a misnomer. The influence of money in politics is as old as the republic.[26] Moreover, one section from Chapter 1 could not adequately cover the many dimensions of money in the public policy process. But my purpose here is more targeted. Consistent with the broader theme of this book, this section demonstrates how organized interests adjust to changes in their external environment by altering the structures and methods of their advocacy strategies. As with other tools in the toolbox, participating in campaign finance is expected of organized interests, often as a response to competitors or opponents and integrated into broader advocacy efforts. In Chapter 5, I outline how growing partisanship over the past two decades led to increased use of leadership PACs by elected officials. I also demonstrate how soft money and issue ads created a closer relationship between political parties and lawmakers during the 1990s—and then shifted again after the Bipartisan Campaign Reform Act (McCain-Feingold) passed in 2002. But political tactics, as suggested earlier, are viral in nature—once one side adopts successful tactics, others quickly follow.

There is no better illustration of the viral nature of political tactics than PAC growth among business interest groups during the 1970s and 1980s. How and why PACs proliferated during this period offers a microcosm of the changing world of lobbying.[27]

The second illustration concerns the use of "independent expenditures" (IEs). While PACs typically help friendly incumbents and allow lobbyists to gain access, IEs are a more sophisticated form of electoral-based advocacy aimed at managing uncertainty, where interest groups try to help their friends or defeat their opponents. IEs involve much more than just giving a campaign contribution. They include polling, advertising, or paying for grassroots operations, all completely separate from the formal campaign organization. Both of these money hammers are part of the new toolbox.

PACS: THE INSTITUTIONALIZATION OF CAMPAIGN FINANCE

The early 1970s were a tumultuous time for interest groups and the campaign finance system. Congress sought to bring some order to the changing money world by passing the Federal Election Campaign Act of 1971 (FECA) and followed up with FECA amendments in 1974 and 1976.[28] These broad changes were motivated by corporate scandals involving Gulf Oil and ITT, as well as the entire Watergate affair.

But as we've seen before, change begets a response. Prior to the 1970s, many businesses found themselves reluctant to get involved systematically in campaign finance—their senior managers contributed individually in an ad hoc manner, but contributions from corporate treasury funds had been outlawed since the Tillman Act passed in 1907. Businesses avoided forming PACs until FECA and its amendments clarified several matters, including whether business and labor PACs could use their own treasury funds to administer these new entities. Once Congress clarified the legal environment, many businesses looking for new, systematic ways to participate in campaign finance decided to institutionalize their political participation by forming PACs. The adoption of PACs exploded during the 1970s and 1980s, especially among larger firms. The Fortune 500, for example, went from nearly zero firms with PACs in the early 1970s to well over half forming PACs by the beginning of the next decade.[29] And the trend has continued over the past 20 years. Today, 72 percent of the Fortune 500 and 85 percent of the Fortune 200 have PACs.

Not surprisingly, companies with the most at stake in their regulatory environments or with multiple policy exposures due to their size—those with the greatest need to manage uncertainty—were among the first to adopt a PAC as part of their advocacy toolbox.

A PAC manager from a large business underscores this point: "Highly regulated businesses were among the first to become involved in PACs because they had the most at stake. Their employees were aware of the firm's exposure and could easily make the connection between the impact of government and how it affected them."[30] These companies were motivated by external circumstance and new demands. The new "demands" produced a new "supply" of advocacy tools, including PACs.

Copying or responding to the actions of competitors or political opponents was also a factor in adopting a PAC. "Once our CEO found out one of our main competitors formed a PAC, our decision was made," a corporate government relations manager recalls.

Today, only outliers in the business community do not have a PAC. "Not having a PAC is like unilaterally disarming yourself," Katie Maness, who previously ran the PAC for Union Pacific Corporation, argues. "And not having one also gives your competitors a major advantage," she says.

PACs also took an ad hoc process of campaign giving by organized interests and institutionalized it inside the company, allowing the firm to integrate political contributions into larger lobbying strategies. "If you are going to do it, do it right," Nick Franklin observes. "You have to educate your employees and executives about how the PAC fits into your overall strategic plan," he says.

Most government affairs managers reject the idea that PAC contributions buy votes. "First of all, money buying votes is a myth," Nick Franklin adds.

> It's much more complicated and nuanced than that. We attend fundraisers using our PAC to gain visibility for our company, to gather information, to generally be part of the Washington scene. It's like buying a ticket for admission. It just gets you to the event with everyone else—competitors and allies. You still have to tell a convincing story. But it's just a first step. An acquaintance at a cocktail party recently joked that since I was a lobbyist I knew about "delivering bags of money." I got kind of mad because that's just such a false stereotype. In all my years of lobbying, I have never seen money buy someone's vote. The system just doesn't work that way.

Katie Maness agrees. "It's only one tool," she says. We use it to defeat people who do not agree with us and elect those who do. I wish we could just 'buy' votes, but we can't. That's not the way it works in the real world."

This type of commentary is common today among government relations professionals. PACs, like many other lobbying tools, help organized interests to learn, interact, and position themselves to gather intelligence and minimize uncertainty about the public policy environment. They certainly don't buy votes. But they do help interests get to know incumbents if strategically utilized.

The PAC process also wastes a lot of money, many lobbyists say. One source of waste, according to some, is contributions to large, impersonal events. "We try not to do that," Sally Murphy of the Wine Institute notes. "We try to attend smaller events, maybe ones focused on just our industry. The difference between spending $1000 on a large 'cattle call' and going to a small industry dinner, in terms of the member knowing my issues and me, are like night and day. I knew a lobbyist that used to boast about attending seven events in a night. He would almost literally knock people down to shake a congressman's hand."

And PACs, like other tools, themselves change and adapt: "I know more and more people who host events now in their homes. It's much more personal and people are more relaxed in those settings. You just get to know people better that way. I try to get to know the congressman or senator's fundraiser and also ask them to look for smaller events I can attend," Murphy says. "The big, impersonal events, you know what they call them— gang bang—that says it all."

Electoral reform, like many political reforms also produce unintended consequences (See Chapter 5). Ironically, instead of driving interest groups out of the process, the confluence of well intentioned reforms in the law empowered PACs and lobbyists in the minds of most elected officials. Due to changes in Congress and partisanship, PACs created a national fund-raising platform for elected officials at a time when money demands were rising, individual contributors were cut back, and the congressional seniority system was fragmenting. This meant PACs became an indispensable utensil in the lobbying toolbox.

INDEPENDENT EXPENDITURES: SHAPING THE ENVIRONMENT

If PACs are an institutionalized mechanism to do what is expected and to stay visible, remain active, and manage uncertainty in Washington, IEs are a way to tilt the battlefield and shape inside-the-Beltway policymaking structures in one direction or another. From distributing voter guides to members of interest groups, to producing videos about issues, to involvement in local party caucuses and national conventions, interest groups are now heavily involved in electioneering as part of the overall advocacy equation.[31] IEs are one way organized interests exercise this involvement.

IEs are one of the least transparent utensils in the toolbox. Little is known about the size and scope of IEs. Groups as wide-ranging as Realtors, Independent Insurance Agents & Brokers of America, the Chamber of Commerce, the National Federation of Independent Business, labor unions, environmental organizations, and the pharmaceutical industry all engage in the practice.

Interest-group involvement in IEs in political campaigns often parallels the campaigns of politicians and includes tools such as polling, get-out-the-vote efforts, campaign communications, and issue ads.[32] Most publicity and debate surrounding IEs focuses on so-called "issue ads," discussed in more detail below. However, it's important to note that this very public form of advocacy is just a subset of the broader category of IEs. Some conflate the two terms, concluding issue ads and IEs are synonymous. It's more accurate to think of issue ads as just one part of the broader arsenal that some interest groups use to shape the complexion of Congress and win friends with lawmakers through participating in electoral and public policy campaigns.[33]

Groups that do IEs usually receive major kudos from lawmakers on the side supported by this advocacy tool. For example, pharmaceuticals invested heavily in IEs during the late-1990s, and lawmakers noticed. "No group is more responsible for the Republicans retaining the majority in the House during the 1998 and 2000 election cycles than the drug industry," a member of the House Republican leadership notes. "We very much appreciate their efforts."

However, this type of political involvement is not for the faint hearted. It's highly partisan and can just as easily make enemies as friends. In my experience as a lobbyist I've often heard my colleagues say things like, "It's one of those cases where 'If you're going to shoot the king, you better kill him.' " This adage is well known among Washington lobbyists when it comes to money in politics. Trying to help your friends or defeat your enemies can be a very effective advocacy strategy, but experts warn this tool is not for novices.

Lawmakers do not place high expectations on interest groups when it comes to IEs. They tend to be expensive and thus are not as widely adopted as are some other tools. Increasingly, though, organized interests are investing because they see their competitors and opponents doing so. Interest groups integrate IEs into some of the most sophisticated advocacy campaigns, utilizing new technology, and providing an example of the new campaign-infected world of advocacy.

In recent years, organizations known as 527s have emerged as major players in the IE arena. Most 527s have focused heavily on electoral politics. Organizations such as MoveOn.org and Swift Boat Veterans for Truth received considerable attention for their aggressive involvement in electoral politics in the 2004 presidential campaign. 527 organizations are beginning to focus more attention on public policy issues as well. Progress for American Foundation, for example, is a Republican 527 organization heavily involved in advocacy on behalf of President George W. Bush's judicial nominations and his Social Security reform proposals. Interest groups and lobbyists will use 527s to achieve their policy objectives and to win favor with elected officials who support their particular causes. When it comes to lobbyists and interest groups investing in these organizations as a tool, however, they are more likely to participate through funding existing 527s than creating one. Under current law, donations to 527s do not have to be disclosed to the Federal Election Commission.

In June of 2007, the independent expenditure world took another strange twist. Recall the Bipartisan Campaign Finance Reform Act of 2002 (McCain-Feingold) banned the use of issue ads paid for by corporate or union treasury funds 60 days before the general election (30 days before a primary). A group called Wisconsin Right to Life (WRL), however, sued the Federal Election Commission (FEC), arguing the McCain-Feingold law violated their First Amendment rights. WRL had sought to run ads urging their two senators, Herb Kohl and Russ Feingold, to oppose filibusters on President George W. Bush's federal court nominees. WRL believed its ads were not electioneering, but aimed at legitimate public policy lobbying. "Incumbent politicians should not be able to shield themselves from lobbying about upcoming votes in Congress through campaign finance regulations," the group's attorney argued.

In a 5–4 decision on June 25, 2007, the Supreme Court ruled that communications that lacked electoral content were not subject to the McCain-Feingold 60- and 30-day blackout periods. Writing for the majority, Chief Justice John Roberts ruled, "Where the First Amendment is implicated, the tie goes to the speaker, not the censor."[34]

The decision opens the door for renewed focus on issue ads moving into the 2008 election cycle. If history is any guide, the Supreme Court's decision could open a floodgate of new advertising on a host of issues by the advocacy community. It also provides another example of how the changing regulatory and legal landscape continues to reshape a dynamic lobbying world.

NEW MEDIA/INTERNET/BLOGS—LEVERAGING A FRAGMENTED WORLD

President George W. Bush in 2006 signed a bill creating a new database of federal spending. But the Rose Garden guest list included more than the usual suspects of congressmen, administration officials, lobbyists, and association executives. This signing ceremony included bloggers.

As Stephen Dinan wrote in *The Washington Times*, "President Bush has invited bloggers to join him today as he signs into law a bill creating a database of federal spending—a recognition of their role in forcing the bill through Congress over the objections of senior senators and an indication of how much bloggers are changing the political process."[35]

As outlined in more detail in Chapter 6, new media and weblogs are an increasingly important part of the advocacy world. They represent a new way to learn what Americans are saying and a valuable communications tool to "talk back" to a more fragmented audience.

Pete Snyder, founder and CEO of New Media Strategies, a communications and consulting firm that helps clients navigate public affairs applications on the Internet, told *Washingtonian* magazine recently, "To reach people you can't just put a sign on the side of a bus or buy a half-minute ad during the Super Bowl. You have to take your message to where they live on the Internet."[36]

If Americans used to meet at local taverns, town squares, or share common experiences through reading the local newspaper and watching network television, now they congregate on the Internet. Yet the gatherings are more splintered and fragmented—a phenomenon that offers both problems and opportunities for public policy and political applications. "The rumor mill used to be school cafeterias. Now it's online." Snyder says.[37]

Audiences are smaller and diffused, presenting a challenge in reaching large numbers. But it's an opportunity because it allows those using new media to better target their information sources to a specific audience. Sorting through these problems and opportunities will clearly define the future applications of the Internet and blogs as part of the new advocacy tool kit.

Integration of new media applications in the public affairs field is small but growing dramatically. In 2003, the Bankruptcy Reform Coalition, a loose-knit group of financial services firms and retailers all advocating passage of bankruptcy reform legislation, coordinated its strategy through a weekly conference call. In the last few months before passage of the legislation, the coalition's efforts included a new tactic—a weekly report from a vendor analyzing the content of blogs and other Web-based publications discussing the pros and cons of legislation's prospects.

Advocates for weakening or defeating the legislation were using the Internet to promote arguments against the bill. Opponents of the legislation on Capitol Hill were routinely using this information as fodder for floor debate in the Congress. Proponents needed to capture this information, dissect the arguments, and develop rebuttals.

Not only has the Internet created an online community of opinion that requires monitoring and influencing, it also has opened up an entire new mode of paid advertising. Issue advertising on online publications has skyrocketed as organized interests attempt to capture this new medium for their advocacy purposes. This trend mirrors skyrocketing growth in general online advertising, which sets new records every year and grew again at about a 40 percent rate between the first half of 2005 and the same period in 2006, according to the Interactive Advertising Bureau.[38]

Advocates also increasingly use technology such as cell phones and text messaging. The Personal Democracy Forum recently highlighted a campaign aimed at getting students involved in lobbying for legislation to make college more affordable.[39] The campaign, sponsored by a group called Campus Progress, asks students to text message the word "debt" to a short code on their cell phones. A student then receives a text message reply prompting the student to send his or her e-mail address and zip code. The student then is contacted with instructions about how to contact his or her congressman and senators. These examples illustrate the growing links between technology, organization, and lobbying.

Again, as we have seen with the other new utensils in the toolbox, using the Internet as an advocacy tool allows interests to gather information, manage uncertainty, gain advantage over competitors, and better target a lobbying message to the right audience.

SUMMARY

This chapter began with an anecdote about an old club and the old way of lobbying. The influence business today is bigger, faster, more organized, increasingly complicated, and difficult to define. When Republican National Committee Chairman Ken Mehlman was profiled by *The New York Times*, he used an anecdote from the book *Moneyball* that sums up his campaign philosophy, but also describes the new world of advocacy:

> When Mehlman talks about politics, he doesn't talk about Machiavelli; he talks about *"Moneyball,"* Michael Lewis's book about how the Oakland Athletics employed statistical modeling to assemble a powerhouse baseball team, sending to pasture the old-line scouts with their years of calling it from their guts. "We are the party of *Moneyball*!" Mehlman proclaimed, practically shouting and bouncing on the balls of his feet, talking to a room of slightly bewildered Republicans in California last year. "They measured everything. We are doing the same thing in politics."

The new world of advocacy is like *Moneyball* politics[40]—it's all about better information, knowing more than your competitors, and working faster and smarter. Now *Moneyball* has rolled into the advocacy field—and this new style of advocacy is about a lot more than cash and martinis. The new world of lobbying is technologically driven, partisan-infused, and dynamic. And as in *Moneyball*, these changes mean lobbyists can't just be "calling things from their guts." Here are a few generalizations.

First, expectations among policymakers and advocates concerning adopting new structures and new advocacy techniques have increased. Deploying many of these tools is now almost demanded as a sign of seriousness, as a way to provide political cover and support for political allies, as a way to say "thank you," and as a method to frame the debate.

Second, as in electoral politics, the new advocacy techniques are highly targeted. Changes in technology and tactics borrowed from political campaigns bolster modern lobbyists' ability to target audiences for mobilization and communication purposes. Our fragmented new world of voters, policy specialists, media, and the Internet demands it.

Third, it's integrated. "Inside lobbying" of members of Congress or other policymakers is now closely coordinated with research, media campaigns, grassroots mobilization, and political contributions, all aimed at influencing the constituents of these decision-makers or the policymakers themselves. This integration between the "outside" and "inside" tools created demand for a new breed of public affairs advocate, who understands the interrelationships of media, technology, advertising, and the lawmaking process—another sign pointing to the advent of the new "electoral/advocacy complex." It also led to a new supply of lobbyists with specialties such as knowing how to represent clients with the White House.

Fourth, interests often adopt the latest and most effective tactics and organizational structures of their competitors. Once one side introduces a new tool or institutional arrangement (e.g. forming a PAC, designating an internal grassroots manager, or hiring a highly specialized consultant) into the advocacy game, their competitors are not far behind. Scholars in organizational behavior call this a "typified response."[41] In the absence of clear methods for evaluating performance, organizations make "typified responses" that derive from accepting a particular social construction of the situation rather than from a means-end calculus. Typified responses often mimic the approaches of similar or leading groups in an organizational field. "Just as most large corporations develop relatively standardized personnel departments in response to government mandates and the rise of professionalized personnel management, it is apparent that the business organizations in our sample have developed similar structures to organize the government affairs function."[42] This observation applies to the organizational structure of interest groups as well as the tactics they deploy. It also drives institutional change in the advocacy business.

Fifth, these new structures and tactics are all intended to reduce uncertainty and gain information about organized interests' external environment. But these attempts to improve future clarity don't guarantee "influence." In other words, despite these investments, interest-group power remains limited. Contrary to conventional wisdom, lobbying is better understood as "information gathering" than "influence peddling." Just because organized interests adopt new structures and methods doesn't promise success. Indeed, one of the greatest myths about lobbying and interest groups, explored in more detail in the final chapter, is their omnipotence. Sophisticated advocacy tools do not always translate into lobbying success. Competition among groups, the ability of lawmakers and policymakers to play one off the other, and other factors outlined next, often mean lobbyists get a lot less than they ask for or than the media suggest they receive. And seeking influence is not always even organized interests' primary goal.

Sixth, applications of the new utensils in the toolbox are reciprocal. In other words, interest groups adopt new structures, styles, and substantive methods based on changes in their external environment, but their advocacy also reshapes the public policy environment. Government growth demanded changing lobbying practices, but the enlargement of the advocacy world also facilitated more government activity.

This interaction suggests a seventh generalization about the toolbox: it is dynamic. The interplay among organized interests—their desire for better, faster, more successful tactics and information; responses to their competitors, policymakers, and technological change—means the toolbox is always evolving.

Finally, these tools and their applications emulate the style and methods of political campaigns. Partisan polarization cuts a wide swath in Washington, and the advocacy industry is not exempted. This new campaign-infused form of lobbying and its limits are explored in more detail in the next chapter.

The 116 Club still exists in Washington, but much of what used to go on there has left the building. The new structures, styles, and substantive methods outlined in this chapter provide ample fodder to reconsider the world of lobbying. Yet despite the availability of all these new tools—and a fresh set of tactics beyond "button-holing and direct access"—not all lobbyists use them, or at least not in the same way. Why? Advocacy also involves strategic choices. Deciding when and how to deploy these tools is another critical part of the lobbying puzzle. The next phase of our reconsideration of lobbying looks at the complicated maze of decisions that professional advocates face and make everyday.

NOTES

1. Eric Schickler, *Disjointed Pluralism: Institutional Innovation and the Development of the U.S. Congress* (Princeton, NJ: Princeton University Press, 2001). For a discussion of how the policymaking process generally changes, see Frank R. Baumgartner and Bryan D. Jones, *Agendas and Instability in American Politics* (Chicago: University of Chicago Press, 1993).
2. Quoted from Pendleton Herring, *Group Representation Before Congress* (Baltimore, MD: Johns Hopkins University Press, 1929), 32.
3. This concept of "countervailing power" was first developed by John Kenneth Galbraith as a way to explain competition in the U.S. economy. He argued that even if competition doesn't work to reach optimal price levels, organizations develop countervailing powers. Unions organizing to help employees maintain fair salaries from corporations is one example. Government regulation of monopolies is another.
4. Allan J. Cigler and Burdett A. Loomis, *Interest Group Politics*, 6th ed. (Washington, D.C.: CQ Press, 2002).
5. See, for example, Frank R. Baumgartner and Beth L. Leech, Basic Interests: The Importance of Groups in Politics and in Political Science (Princeton, NJ: Princeton University Press, 1998), Chapter 9.
6. K. Kollman, *Outside Lobbying: Public Opinion and Interest Group Strategies* (Princeton, NJ: Princeton University Press, 1998).
7. Robert H. Salisbury. "The Paradox of Interest Groups in Washington: More Groups, Less Clout," In Anthony King, ed. *The New American Political System*. 2nd version (Washington, D.C.: The American Enterprise Institute, 1990), 203–230.
8. John P. Heinz, Edward O. Laumann, Robert L. Nelson, and Robert H. Salisbury, *The Hollow Core: Private Interests in National Policy Making* (Cambridge, MA: Harvard University Press, 1993).
9. Darrell M. West and Burdett A. Loomis, *The Sound of Money: How Political Interests Get What They Want* (New York, NY: Norton, 1999), 156–164.
10. Kate Ackley "Pollsters: Lobbying's Next Frontier," *Roll Call*, September 25, 2007.
11. This quote is from a marketing brochure Berman and Company provides to potential clients.

12. The importance of narrative in public policy and lobbying is explored in great detail in West and Loomis, *The Sound of Money*.
13. Ibid. 15.
14. Legislative Issues Advertising in the 108th Congress. The Annenberg Public Policy Center of the University of Pennsylvania, March 2005.
15. Ibid. 3.
16. Ibid.
17. See Sam Kernell, "Going Public", for a description of how presidents use public arguments and media strategies to shape voters opinion.
18. K. Kollman, *Outside Lobbying*, 3.
19. Get citation Ron Fournier, Douglas B. Sosnick, Matthew J. Dowd, *Applebees America: How Successful Political, Business and Religious Leaders Connect with the New American Community* (New York: Simon and Shuster, 2006).
20. Robert H. Salisbury. "Interest Groups: Toward a New Understanding," In Allan J. Ciglar and Burdett A. Loomis, eds. *Interest Group Politics*, 1st ed. (Washington D.C.: CQ Press, 1983).
21. Ronald G. Shaiko, "Making the Connection: Organized Interests, Political Representation, and the Changing Rules of the Game in Washington Politics," In Paul S. Herrnson, Ronald G. Shaiko, and Clyde Wilcox, eds. *The Interest Group Connection: Electioneering, Lobbying and Policymaking in Washington* (Washington D.C.: CQ Press, 2005).
22. I am indebted to Burdett Loomis of the University of Kansas for pointing out this gap in the scholarly literature and suggesting I discuss lobbying the White House in more detail in this book.
23. Gary J. Andres "Lobbying for the President: Influencing Congress from the White House," In Paul S. Herrnson, Ronald G. Shaiko, and Clyde Wilcox, eds. *The Interest Group Connection* (Chatham, NJ: Chatham House Publishers, 1997), 224–337.
24. For a good description of the expansion of the White House staff, see Kathryn Dunn Tenpas, "Lobbying the Executive Branch: Outside-In and Inside Out," In Paul S. Herrnson, Ronald G. Shaiko, and Clyde Wilcox, eds. *The Interest Group Connection*, 2nd ed. (Washington D.C.: CQ Press, 2005), 249–257.
25. The Executive Office of the President includes not only the White House staff itself, but also the Office of Management and Budget, the Special Trade Representative, the Council on Environmental Quality and other smaller sub agencies that shape the Administration's policies on issues.
26. Scott H. Ainsworth, *Analyzing Interest Groups: Group Influence on People and Policies* (New York, NY: W.W. Norton, 2002); Mark J. Rozell, Clyde Wilcox, and David Madland, *Interest Groups in American Campaigns: The New Face of Electioneering* (Washington, D.C.: CQ Press, 2006).
27. For a good description of the legal and regulatory changes leading to the growth of PACs, see Paul S. Herrnson, *Congressional Elections: Campaigning at Home and in Washington* (Washington, D.C.: CQ Press, 2004), Chapter 5.
28. Edwin Epstein, "Business and Labor under the Federal Election Campaign Act," In Michael Malbin, ed. *Interest Groups and Campaign Finance Laws* (Washington, D.C.: The American Enterprise Institute, 1980).
29. Gary J. Andres, "Business Involvement in Campaign Finance: Factors Influencing the Decision to Form a Corporate PAC," *PS. Spring,* Vol. XVIII, No 2 (Washington, D.C.: The American Political Science Association, 1985).
30. Gary J. Andres, "Business Involvement in Campaign Finance: Factors Influencing the Decision to Form a Corporate PAC," *PS. Spring,* Vol. XVIII, No 2 (Washington, D.C.: The American Political Science Association, 1986).
31. Rozell, Wilcox and Madland, *Interest Groups in American Campaigns*.
32. Herrnson, *Congressional Elections*, Chapters 4 and 5.
33. I am grateful to Paul Herrnson for suggesting the need to make the distinction between IEs and issue ads. His book, *Congressional Elections: Campaigning at Home and in Washington*, outlines in more detail how interest groups use the IE tool, including issue ads, in electoral campaigns.
34. *Federal Election Commission v. Wisconsin Right to Life*. Docket 04–158, June 25, 2007.
35. Stephen Dinan, "Bloggers Will Join Bush in Bill-Signing Ceremony," *Washington Times,* September 25, 2006.

36. Ken Adleman, "Interview with Pete Snyder, CEO New Media Strategies," *Washingtonian*, July 2006.
37. Ibid.
38. Interactive Advertising Bureau Press Release, September 25, 2006.
39. Debt Hits Hard, www.personaldemocracy.com/blog, October 18, 2006.
40. Michael Lewis, *Moneyball: The Art of Winning an Unfair Game* (New York, NY: Norton, 2003).
41. Heinz, Laumann, Nelson, and Salisbury, *The Hollow Core.*
42. John W. Meyer and Brian Rowan, "Institutionalized Organizations: Formal Structure as Myth and Ceremony," *American Journal of Sociology* 83 (1977) 340–363.

8

LOBBYING AND STRATEGIC CHOICES

Lots of people say they want "visibility" in this town. They want to get their issue on the agenda or become better known. But strategically sometimes it's better to keep your head down; because when you raise it up, there is a good chance it can get chopped off.

Jeff Becker, President, The Beer Institute

The last chapter outlines the new tactics in the advocacy toolbox and how representatives of interest groups utilize them. But "getting under the influence" requires us to identify another missing piece of the advocacy puzzle. Despite the availability of these new and more sophisticated tools, not all advocates or interest groups use them. Why? Even more troubling, sometimes interest groups deploy the same mix of tactics yet experience vastly different results. How can that be? This chapter fills in some of these gaps in understanding, explaining the practical and strategic choices underlying lobbying decisions.

Strategic decisions in lobbying are somewhat idiosyncratic—based on the judgments of individual interest-group representatives—but they are far from random. Drawing from discussions with lobbyists and my own personal observations, it is possible to put some structure around these advocacy choices. This chapter develops such a framework and concludes with a recent case study of how all these pieces fit together.

Strategic choices in lobbying vary based on several considerations, including

- Resources
- Competitive pressures
- Air cover/ground cover demands
- Visibility of the issue
- Relation and role of allies
- Early adapters
- Time of season
- Offense versus defense
- Institutional context (lobbying the White House, lobbying the Senate, lobbying the leadership).

RESOURCES

The first piece of the puzzle is straightforward and somewhat obvious—the level of resources available. Size matters in the lobbying world; but not always in the way you might think. Larger corporations, trade associations, the bigger unions, and a growing number of public interest groups have resources sufficient to use more of the utensils in the tool box. "We have a lot of resources," Tim McKone, who runs AT&T's Washington office, asserts. "And we use them. We have a large PAC, we have a big footprint of employees. When the time is right we advertise. We don't have to use these tools all the time, but when we need them we're not afraid to use them, and we have the money to do so." But not every interest is like AT&T.

The lobbying "have-nots" sometimes feel intimidated by their lack of resources. "We don't have a very big PAC," says Sally Murphy, vice president of government affairs for the Wine Institute. "So we can't do all the things that some others can do. We can't participate in all the events; we can't give all those $5000 contributions to congressional leadership PACs. So we are a little less visible because we don't have the kind of money that others do."

Those with more resources are almost expected to use a more robust set of tactics. Interest groups never want to get into the position—particularly in the midst of a major lobbying campaign—where their allies in Congress can say they haven't "done enough" to promote a particular cause. Organizations with a high level of resources are particularly sensitive to this. The head of a major health care organization reinforces this point: "I always ask if there is something else we should be doing that we're not. I never want to get to the end of a lobbying campaign and have someone say, 'Well, you should have done this or that.' " These groups are open to using more tools. They often are looking for directions and ideas about how to deploy their resources. They are not resource constrained; they will fund creative tactics.

So just as we saw a positive correlation between interest-group size and the probability that they institutionalize their government relations function, so too do those with more resources tend to use more tools in the advocacy toolbox.

But every rule has its exceptions. Sometimes size matters in the other direction. Smaller interests often look for ways to compensate for their lack of resources by utilizing creative new approaches. They may not have the money to hire the best-known lobbying firm, pay for media campaigns, or hire Internet strategists, but they may, for example, focus on mobilizing their own grass roots. One well-respected Republican lobbyist, who has worked in the Senate, at the White House and for a major trade association, says this:

> We have a client that doesn't have the resources of the big guys, but they compensate for it in other ways. They have what I call "real grass roots." Their members answer the call. It's not manufactured, and I think members

of Congress get that. This is not corporate America's version of grass roots where they say in an almost clinical way: "Tell me what it costs, and how many calls it will produce, and I'll write the check." These people are invested in their businesses, their communities, and they really care. It makes a big difference and can help offset the big guys' money advantage.

Another veteran Washington lobbyist recounts a fascinating anecdote about resources:

> In the late 1980s and early 1990s the music industry was undergoing a major battle over royalties. The Recording Industry Association of America (RIAA), which had all the resources of the music companies behind them, had a proposal that they sold very quickly to some key lawmakers on the Hill. The proposal, however, was great for the companies, but bad for the artists. And because the RIAA got out there so quickly, had lots of resources, and had powerful supporters, the side representing the artists really had to scramble. Our side was not funded very well, but we compensated by bringing in a lot of well-known musicians that did the lobbying for us. In the end, we scuttled the original bill and got a new one moving that was much fairer to the artists and musicians we represented.

In this case, resources made a difference, but they were not financial resources. Smart tactics on the part of this lobbyist and his client recognized the impact of "star power" on the Hill. They compensated for a lack of finances by using other tools at their disposal.

So in the end, size and resources do have an impact on which lobbying tools get deployed. In many cases, bigger interests possess the luxury of using more of these advocacy utensils. However, as the examples above demonstrate, smaller actors sometimes find ways to compensate, using tools that fit their budgets and the other unique assets at their disposal.

COMPETITIVE PRESSURES

Interest groups' public policy adversaries also shape strategic choices. As mentioned earlier, some advocacy battles take on the characteristics of a public policy arms race—one side initiates an action and the other responds in kind or even escalates the effort. Shaping perceptions and opinions in Washington, particularly in the midst of a legislative battle on Capitol Hill, is key. "You can't unilaterally disarm," is a well-worn phrase in the lexicon of veteran lobbyists in Washington.

Referring back to the battles over rewriting telecommunications laws in the early 1990s, lobbyist Michael Boland, who previously worked for the House Energy and Commerce Committee and later as floor assistant to then-House Minority Whip Trent Lott, recounts a poignant anecdote about the impact of competitive pressures on lobbying strategies. During the early 1990s, Boland was a lobbyist for Verizon Corporation, a holding company that included several of the local telephone companies spun off as part of the AT&T divestiture. The Bell company lobbyists had strong allies in the House Energy and Commerce Committee leaders such as former Rep. Billy Tauzin (R-LA) and Rep. John Dingell (D-MI), but they lacked robust support in the Senate. "We knew Senator Hollings (a former chairman and ranking member of the Senate Commerce Committee) would never allow Tauzin/Dingell (a bill that lifted restrictions imposed on the Bell Companies from offering long distance and other information services by the AT&T consent decree) to pass the Senate." Due to heavy spending on grass roots and paid advertising by Bell company competitors such as AT&T and MCI, the local telephone companies had to shift from offense to defense. "We had to spend a lot of money just to hold our own because of what our competitors were doing," Boland recalled.

A more recent example occurred in 2007. Enmeshed in a pitched battle with the biotech firm Amgen, which has utilized a sizable lobbying team in Washington, Swiss pharmaceutical company F. Hoffman-LaRoche responded vigorously to its competitor.[1] According to published reports, with the clock running down on the congressional session in 2005:

> Roche tried to slip language into a Senate appropriations bill that would have changed patent law and help the company to import a new drug into the United States (that would compete with an Amgen anemia drug). Amgen got wind of Roche's gambit and quickly assembled a multi-industry coalition that successfully countered it. Roche not only ended up looking sneaky but it also galvanized Amgen's vigorous defense of its lucrative anemia-drug franchise.[2]

Due to competitive pressures, ". . . the dueling firms have ramped up their influence operations and campaign donations dramatically in the past two years . . . and although Amgen and Roche lobby on multiple issues inside the Beltway, they have unquestionably expanded their efforts since the anemia drug issue took off at the end of 2005."[3] Both companies, according to informed sources, increased investments in lobbying, public relations, and other advocacy tools. It is the law of lobbying physics: every action usually causes a reaction.

The proposed merger in 2007 between XM Satellite Radio and Sirius Satellite Radio generated another major lobbying campaign between these two companies and the National Association of Broadcasters (NAB). According to news reports, "few other industries have put together as much firepower for a single issue. Their effort (both sides) includes a dozen law and public relations firms. Advertising and investment banking assistance is layered on top of that."[5] And as the two satellite companies geared up, using more tools in the toolbox, so did the NAB. *The Washington Post* noted,

"The broadcasters are orchestrating an equally outsize response. 'Being effective in D.C. means having high visibility, enlisting allies and using all the tools at your disposal to neutralize adversaries,'" said Dennis Wharton, executive vice president of the NAB. Both sides, responding to their legislative adversaries, geared up, mimicking the tactics of their opponents—one of the best illustrations of a modern-day lobbying arms race. Figure 8-1 demonstrates the balance of resources between the two sides.

FIGURE 8-1 WASHINGTON POST LINE-UP OF ADVOCATES IN LOBBYING OVER SATELLITE MERGER.

Fighting to Be Heard

National Association of Broadcasters Team

IN-HOUSE STAFF

Government Relations:

➤ Laurie Knight, executive vice president
➤ Mildred Webber, senior vice president
➤ Michael S. Hershey, senior vice president
➤ Kelly Cole, vice president
➤ James Gillespie, director
➤ Mike Mullen, director

FCC Relations

➤ Douglas S. Wiley, executive vice president of administration and agencies
➤ Marsha J. MacBride, executive vice president of legal and regulatory affairs
➤ Lawrence A. Walke, associate general counsel

Public Relations

➤ Dennis Wharton
➤ Kris Jones

CONSULTANTS

Lobbyists

➤ Bluewater Strategies
➤ David Leach
➤ Daniel Mattoon
➤ Tony Podesta
➤ Max Sandlin
➤ Cormac Group
➤ Loeffler Group
➤ Ashcroft Group

Lawyers

➤ Wilkinson Barker and Knauer
➤ Willimas Mullen

Public Affairs

➤ Blattner Brunner
➤ Carmel Group

Economist

➤ James C. Miller III

XM-Sirius Team

Lawyers

➤ Wiley Rein (Sirius) (also lobbying)
➤ Simpson Thacher & Bartlett (Sirius)
➤ Latham & Watkins (XM)
➤ Jones Day (XM)
➤ Skadden, Arps, Slate, Meagher & Flom (SM)

Public Relations

➤ Joele Frank, Wilkinson Brimmer Katcher (Sirius)
➤ Brunswick Group (XM)

Public Affairs

➤ TSD Communications (XM)
➤ Chlopak, Leonard, Schechter and Associates (Sirius)

Lobbyists

➤ Paul Laxalt Group (Sirius)
➤ Riccetti Inc. (Sirius)
➤ Quinn Gillespie & Associates (Sirius/XM)
➤ Mehlman Capitol Strategies (XM)
➤ McBee Strategic (XM)
➤ Palmetto Group (XM)
➤ McGuiness LLC (XM)
➤ Patton Boggs (XM)
➤ Raben Group (XM)
➤ Monument Policy (XM)
➤ Wexler & Walker (XM)

Advertising

➤ National Media (XM)
➤ McCarthy Marcus Hennings (Sirius)
➤ Della Femina/Rothschild/Jeary Partners (Sirius)

Source: Adapted by the author from a graphic in *The Washington Post*, July 25, 2007, D-1.

Examples of tit-for-tat deployment of various tools occur every day in Washington. If the telephone industry decides to mount a paid advertising campaign in Capitol Hill publications, the cable industry will usually follow suit. When the generic drug industry mounts a grassroots campaign from patients, major pharmaceutical companies respond in kind. Competitors do not always dictate interest-group strategies, but they regularly affect them. It is impossible to evaluate the strategic choices of interest groups in a vacuum. Lobbyists usually watch and evaluate their competitors' behavior, and then respond accordingly. Understanding these intricacies of the game is critical. They explain a lot about the nuances of contemporary lobbying and why the advocacy industry is as large, structurally complex, and dynamic as it is today.

AIR COVER/GROUND COVER DEMANDS

Lawmakers often demand a show of political support from constituents or other stakeholders before taking action. Interest groups will sometimes invest in tools such as paid advertising or grassroots mobilization in response to those requests.

I once attended a meeting where a lobbyist asked a member of the congressional leadership why the House had yet to take action on a bill. "Because you're the first person who talked to me about that piece of legislation," the congressman said. This particular advocate learned a painful lesson that day: vocal public support reinforces congressional action. Building air and ground support through advertising and grassroots efforts is a way to generate that attention. Without that kind of positive environment, convincing lawmakers to invest time and energy in passing legislation becomes more challenging.

Congressional leaders also often demand air and ground cover as political protection for their members and themselves. "I can't ask my members to walk the plank on an issue that lacks political support," a Republican member of the leadership argues. Doing so endangers the rank-and-file member of Congress politically, as well as the leader's reputation and support from other lawmakers. Congressional leaders who ask their followers to vote for controversial measures without a sufficient amount of air and ground cover may lose their rank and file to electoral defeat, as well as their own leadership posts at the hands of angry colleagues, rather quickly. A growing number of interest groups recognize this new demand, which fuels the growth of media and grass roots oriented lobbying.

Congressional committee chairs face the same pressures from their colleagues. They take steps to ensure the environment is right so their members don't have to cast votes without requisite political support. It's common in the lobbying world to have committee chairs ask interest groups to invest money to reshape the public environment. Winning the issue for the chairman often means partnering with advocates who invest resources. One Democratic lobbyist tells this anecdote.

> I took some clients in to see a particular committee chairman, and he told them they would probably have to spend $15 to $20 million in advertising to reshape the public environment. Without that kind of investment, they could not win the issue. Their jaws almost dropped when they heard that number. But in the end they ended up doing it because of the chairman's advice.

In 1993, when the Clinton administration pushed a controversial budget measure through the House that included something known as the BTU tax, Washington developed a new verb—getting "BTUed." This referred to voting for a bill that couldn't make it through the other body of Congress due to lack of political support. The Clinton budget plan was an important political priority for the White House, but many rank-and-file members complained it lacked air and ground support in their districts. This meant many congressmen were nervous about bringing up the bill, and it made legislative leaders nervous about pushing it. In the end, the White House prevailed and won House passage by a narrow margin. However, many lawmakers believed their vote for the budget measure put them in electoral jeopardy. Today, any time legislative leaders ask their members to walk the plank on something that lacks political support—often because it doesn't have enough air or ground cover—lawmakers say they "got BTUed." Generating enough support so rank-and-file members and their legislative leaders feel comfortable addressing issues often calls for new and creative advocacy tools.

And sometimes "support" means reframing the issue using tools and creative tactics. A lobbyist I worked closely with captures this point:

> We normally think of air cover or ground cover as "boots on the ground" and lots of volume of messages. But it can also mean changing the message. We worked for a death penalty reform coalition for many years and ultimately passed a significant reform measure, making greater use of DNA evidence to prove innocence. For years the anti-death penalty movement was made up of liberal abolitionists. We needed to reframe the debate and make it more about "protecting the innocent" than overturning the death penalty. Through some research, message testing, polling, paid and earned media, we were able to reframe the question and bring people together from the left and the right, death penalty supporters and those opposed to it, around the issue of using DNA evidence to prove innocence.

In 2002, the lobbyist's strategy paid off. After reframing the debate, and giving supporters from the left and right the requisite amount of political cover and support, Congress passed and the president signed the Innocence Protection Act.[6]

A former Senate staffer turned lobbyist who helped manage a lobbying campaign for the accounting industry offers this reframing example concerning Securities Litigation Reform, one of only two bills vetoed by President Clinton that Congress successfully overrode.

> Congress received political cover on the Securities Litigation Reform bill because we reshaped the debate. For years the issue was framed as a fight between the trial lawyers and deep-pocketed accounting firms. The deep pockets usually lost. This time we brought in some key entrepreneurs and innovators. The debate shifted to "how do we protect entrepreneurs and risk takers"—people who generate economic growth. Once we broadened and reframed the debate away from protecting accounting firms with a lot of money, to people who produce something, we generated a lot more support and overrode a presidential veto, which is a very difficult undertaking.

VISIBILITY OF THE ISSUE

The visibility and attention lobbyists' want drawn to an issue or an interest group also determines which tools get deployed. For example, some measures require shaping attitudes at a variety of levels—the public, Congress, regulators, and so on. Other initiatives demand less visibility, such as including an earmark in an appropriations bill. Advocates often want to keep legislative proposals like earmarks under the radar lest a program get labeled as the latest "bridge to nowhere."[7] The visibility lobbyists want drawn to an issue is an example of what E.E. Schattschneider calls "the scope of conflict."[8] Schattschneider observes that politics is about those directly involved in a battle, *as well as those watching*. And often the observers play a significant role in shaping the outcome. "If a fight starts," he writes, "watch the crowd, because the crowd plays a decisive role."[9] The size of the crowd, what they do, and with whom they side are all critical factors in determining who wins and who loses public policy battles.

In some cases, lobbyists work hard to limit the visibility of a conflict. "We are not involved in the earmark game," AT&T's McKone remarks, "but if we were, I would not take out a full-page ad announcing what we were doing." On the other hand, building public support by raising the visibility of an issue is often a critical component of successful advocacy campaigns.

In 2005, the Bush administration—supported by a host of business allies—engaged in an ultimately failed effort to reform Social Security.

Raising the visibility of the issue was a key part of the White House's strategy. But, they quickly found out, their opponents also knew how to bring more people into the fight. And just as Mr. Schattschneider predicted, the visibility of the fight and who was involved dramatically shaped the outcome. Unfortunately for Mr. Bush and the White House, the crowd grew hostile.

The White House and its allies in the lobbying community sought to convince the public Social Security's future was at risk without reform. Raising the visibility of the issue was the best way to accomplish this task. The president talked about the issue in detail in his State of the Union address and then barnstormed the country trying to draw attention to the looming crisis. Many business groups—such as the Business Roundtable, the Chamber of Commerce, and a handful of individual financial institutions—committed to a Social Security overhaul and also tried to educate the public about the need for change through high-visibility advertising campaigns.

The opponents of reform engaged in similarly visible campaigns, but communicating an opposite message: the real risk was President Bush's Social Security "privatization" plan, opponents charged. The American Association of Retired Persons (AARP), a group opposed to President Bush's Social Security reform proposal, ran a very effective advertising campaign, communicating the theme that the Bush proposal was the policy equivalent of taking a wrecking ball to your house. The ad showed family members in a house while it was literally destroyed around them. "It was one of the most effective ads in the debate," Rich Thau, president of Presentation Testing, a New York-based research firm, remembers. It raised the visibility of the issue in a negative way, communicating the idea that President Bush was not protecting Social Security, and, in fact, was endangering it. "While President Bush wanted to convince people he was helping the solvency of the system, the AARP suggested he was taking billions of dollars out of it," Thau says. "The ad was powerful because it transformed President Bush from being the 'protector-in-chief' of this entitlement program for seniors to being the 'imperiler-in-chief.' " The president successfully raised the visibility of the issue, but failed to make a convincing argument. The AARP and others then also raised the visibility of the Social Security issue—and convinced Americans that the White House plan put their retirement security in great jeopardy.

The Medicare Modernization Act (MMA) provides another example of two sides in a debate raising the visibility of an issue. The legislation was passed in 2003 but was not implemented until 2005. During that two-year period, both the proponents and the opponents of the legislation worked hard to raise the visibility of and either support or attack the new prescription drug benefit. Both sides used many tools in the toolbox, including research, paid media, grass roots, and engaging think tanks to make their points. Some in the Bush administration described the ramp-up to implementation as the largest public health education effort in 50 years. Opponents argued the legislation would "force seniors into HMOs" or cause them to "loose their retirement coverage."

With high-visibility campaigns on both sides, as the drug benefit was phased in, seniors became increasingly comfortable and positive about the legislation. In this case, the visibility campaign mounted by the White House and supported by others in the advocacy world paid off. Opponents were largely foiled in their attempts to change or scuttle the MMA before it was implemented.

As the 2004 and 2006 elections unfolded, the issue became less salient in the minds of voters. Democrats and allied groups like Families USA wanted to convince seniors the drug benefit was not generous enough or created too many complicated choices. By effectively raising the visibility of the issue— reminding voters that they now had at least some drug coverage and that the predicted negative outcomes never occurred —the pharmaceutical industry fended off these attacks.

Legislation in 2008 on the issue of climate change offers another good example. Automakers, energy companies, environmental activists, consumer groups, and labor unions each had a major stake in the legislation and attempted to shape the public debate by raising visibility. Oil companies, for example, underwrote a major paid media campaign urging Congress to avoid punitive policies like raising the windfall profits tax. They argued that they used their profits to explore for new sources of production, thereby helping to keep prices down. The auto industry used grassroots resources to urge lawmakers to eliminate tough fuel economy standards, while unions argued the government policies could cost them their jobs. How the government restructured rules on emissions, energy production, and land use policy all would impact companies, jobs, and lifestyles. Interest groups in all these areas tried to shape public opinion and motivate actions by impacted constituencies.

But not all public policy issues or interest-group advocates require this degree of visibility. In fact, sometimes lobbyists deliberately eschew public notoriety, opting instead for a more low-key approach. Narrowly defined public policies, such as earmarks, were mentioned earlier as one type of policy where expanding the scope of conflict and making the issue more visible is usually not advantageous. But other broader considerations exist.

"The decision about how visible you want to get, and which of these tools you want to deploy, is all very strategic," Jeff Becker, president of the Beer Institute argues.

> Sometimes people think we *don't* get attention because we *can't* get attention. That's not the case at all. You have to evaluate what's the best strategy for success. And sometimes the best thing to do is get your ego out of it and just say, "I'm not going to get noticed or mentioned, but that's not all bad either." Sometimes the most thoughtful, strategic and effective thing to do is stay out of the spotlight and not try to use too many of these advocacy tools. Often that's the best way to win in this town. And I'm happiest—not when my ego gets stroked—but when my companies are happy.

RELATIONS TO ALLIES

How an interest group interacts with its allies also affects strategic choices. The relationship between corporations and their trade associations, or individual unions and broader umbrella groups like the AFL-CIO, can impact decisions. Nick Franklin of PacifiCare underscores this point:

> The first motivation is to realize there is strength in numbers. That's one of the strategic reasons why we sometimes rely on coalitions or trade associations. Certain people or companies might also have strength in particular regions or with key lawmakers. That's another consideration. It's also not advantageous to put a target on your back. Sometimes you want to be part of a bigger group. Joining a larger group also helps create critical mass that you would not have on your own. But sometimes because of the nature of the issue, you have no choice but to go it alone. These are all important strategic decisions, and they affect how and where we spend our money.

So from the standpoint of individual interest groups, strategic choices are driven by what other allies might be doing or how the issue impacts the group. In 2007, for example, most unions worked together in Washington to persuade the Democratic majority to pass a piece of legislation known as the "card check" bill. It allowed unions to conduct elections by having employees fill out forms declaring by name their support for forming a union, rather than having secret-ballot elections. Business-oriented trade groups such as the Chamber of Commerce, the National Association of Manufacturers, and the Business Roundtable all worked vigorously to defeat the legislation.

Both sides used many utensils in the advocacy toolbox, including grass roots, paid media and earned media, as well as polling and other research. Yet because broader organizations such as the AFL-CIO and the various business groups engaged in these debates, few individual corporations or specific unions expended their own resources directly. And while individual businesses or unions with a large presence in Washington cared about this issue, their tactical choices were influenced by how their allies engaged in the process.

Sometimes trade associations face internal conflicts that mean they can no longer represent all of their members; and they then leave the lobbying to their individual member companies. A lobbyist who formerly represented the insurance industry underscores this point:

> The industry had a major split when I represented them on the issue of state versus federal regulation of insurance (the McCarran-Ferguson Act). Some of their companies wanted it repealed while others wanted it unchanged. This meant all the individual companies could not rely on their trade group to lobby for them and had to make more investments in various lobbying tools on their own.

Divisions among allies usually lead to another outcome in Congress—legislative stalemate. In the case of the specific legislative change facing the insurance industry, the split between those who wanted state regulation and those who sought federal preemption meant years of congressional gridlock on the topic. Congress has yet to significantly modify the McCarran-Ferguson law.

EARLY ADAPTORS

Some interest-group representatives possess the resources and the interest to incorporate new tools. They are constantly looking for new and innovative applications of lobbying techniques and use them with alacrity.

"We have some clients who see the value of new and sophisticated strategies. More sophisticated clients use more sophisticated strategies," well-respected Washington lobbyist David Bockorny, president and founder of the Bockorny Group, says. "Some want us to help produce numbers and see the value of economic studies, others don't. Some just say when we talk about doing a study: 'Are you nuts? We hired you to set up meetings.' "

"Early adaptors" are the pioneers of lobbying. Once some advocates try a new technique or tool and find it successful, others quickly follow suit. One of the most innovative techniques in 2007 was organized by lobbyists in the health care industry and involved the use of recorded messages left after hours in congressional offices. They recruited volunteers willing to give their names, phone numbers, and addresses, and these individuals recorded personal messages to selected members of Congress. The grassroots vendor then compiled and reviewed these recorded messages for accuracy and "called them in" to lawmakers' offices after hours, leaving personalized messages on a congressman's or senator's voicemail. The next morning staff might retrieve 40 or 50 personalized messages, all from constituents and all including call-back information. These voicemails expressed more intensity, focus, and personal concern than typical letters that often seem manufactured by a grassroots vendor.

The jury is still out on this particular approach. The House ended up passing legislation making the budget cuts this particular group opposed, but the impact of this particular tactic is impossible to isolate. At the same time this health care interest group was organizing calls, interests on the other side were urging passage of the same bill.

My point here is not to focus on effectiveness of the tool. It is more significant to note that this new and innovative technique was first adopted by a few creative advocates. But if lobbying strategists deem it effective (especially within the context of a major media and grassroots campaign advocating on the other side of the issue), it will likely get broader application soon, until it is replaced by a new technique, pioneered again by the early adapters.

Innovative applications of Internet technology and new media strategies rank among the most interesting tools embraced by early adapters. Monitoring blogs, for example, discussed in more detail in Chapter 7, is a growing tactic in lobbying. Many do not use it yet, but as early adapters realize success, others will quickly follow suit. These are all a part of the continuing narrative of lobbying, a story that changes based on experimentation, risk taking, and adjustment.

TIME OF SEASON

Lobbying has a rhythm—and the best advocates know how to keep the beat. Sometimes an interest-group's agenda and its timing don't coincide with the policymaking process timeframe. When that happens, advocates must adjust. The smart ones know there are other activities in which to engage, even when an interest group's issue is not on the front burner of, say, the congressional agenda. During those times, advocates make investments in educating policymakers that they hope will pay off later.

Ron Kaufman, a former senior White House aide and now a lobbyist with Dutko Worldwide, puts it this way: "We advise our clients to make investments in political capital all the time, knowing someday that capital will have to be deployed." Most smart Washington operatives know this instinctively.

Talking about the strategic choices his company deploys when its issues are not front and center in Congress, AT&T's McKone sums it up well: "We want to be ready when we need it. We don't know when that will be. So we constantly talk about our employees, the taxes we pay, many things related to our economic footprint. We want them to think about us as good corporate citizens during these times when we're not asking for anything."

This is a key observation. What interest groups do during "downtimes" is important to study as well. For example, they may use different tools but they are still heavily engaged. Most major interest groups maintain a constant presence in Washington, even though their issues are not always high on the policy agenda.

Nick Franklin underscores this point: "We're not always asking for votes. We are trying to develop a context or mosaic about the company. Who we are, what we are, and what we are doing, are all critical components of building our brand and reputation. It takes time to build that." How and why interest groups engage the process—even when policymakers are focused on other issues—is an important part of better understanding the lobbying process.

CONTEXT—PLAYING OFFENSE OR DEFENSE AND TYPE OF POLICY

Whether interests are playing offense or defense also affects lobbyists' strategic choices and the tools they deploy. Accomplishing proactive change in public policy is normally a Herculean task given the institutional constraints built into the American system. Creating the Medicare prescription drug benefit, rewriting existing laws governing air and water pollution, and altering telecommunications and labor laws are just a few examples of the changes advocates have tried to enact in the past several years. Pushing these reforms through the House and the Senate and securing a presidential signature is a daunting challenge that includes numerous substantive and procedural challenges. Research, media strategies, grass roots, and specialized consultants are just a few of the tools advocates promoting a positive agenda often must use to navigate through these waters.

Playing defense, on the other hand, is much easier. "Blocking things in the Senate is the oldest trick in the book," a veteran Democratic lobbyist said. "It doesn't take a lot of investment. Lining up a cadre of Senators to be against something is not that hard."

That playing defense is easier and less expensive than offense is a well-known truism among veteran lobbyists and Washington observers. Most experts realize that enduring institutional structures such as bicameralism and separation of powers give the upper hand to those who support the status quo. Self-styled public interest lobbyist Fred Werthheimer underscores this point: "In this town, defense has always been easier, and the diffusion of power in Congress has made it all the more so."[10] Werthheimer believes business had success blocking some of the more egregious examples of increased government regulation and then tried to go on offense after Ronald Reagan was elected president in 1980. The shift in strategy from defense to offense was both more costly and increasingly difficult. ". . . As they've gone on offense, the yardage has gotten a lot tougher," he said.[11] A veteran Democrat lobbyist says this: "We built an entire practice during the 1990s when Republicans were in the majority in the Senate around lobbying a handful of Democrats to either keep them (the GOP) from getting 60 votes (to break a filibuster) or help them reach that number."

Interest-group preferences and circumstances also determine whether advocates choose offensive or defensive strategies. "Some clients consciously choose to play offense, and that dictates a certain set of tactics," Greg Crist, vice president of communications for Dutko Worldwide, remarks. "They want to shape public or elite opinion, frame a message a certain way, so that when the ground troop lobbyists come in they have an easier sales job. But it's consciously offense, trying to shape the playing field."

Other interest groups take a different tact. They just want to be left alone. These advocates are happy *not* being mentioned in the press or the subject of congressional hearings. These interest groups usually never play offense; their view of advocacy tends to focus only on defense. "Most of our clients consciously try to stay out of the press. Or if they are in the press, we're helping them manage stories they didn't generate," a Washington-based public relations executive notes. "It's all defense and that's the way they want it," he says. Again, interest groups that approach the public policy environment with this more defensive posture will make different tactical choices than those who play offense. "I normally approach these questions only from an offensive posture," Crist observes. "But I suppose if a client came to me and said, 'Look, we have this problem, we didn't want to be here, but here we are,' it would dictate a different set of tools."

The type of policy also shapes the strategic choices of lobbyists. Political scientist James A. Thurber argues, "The type of policy being considered affects the politics of the decision-making system handling it."[12] Thurber developed a typology of policymaking subsystems, categorizing policymaking processes based on the visibility of the decision, the scope of the conflict, the level of conflict, and the number of participants. His typology then categorizes policymaking for various policy subsystems (macro, regular, and micro subsystems)." He defines macro policy subsystems as those decisions with "major political effects involving broad public interests, visibility, divisiveness, extensive media coverage and many participants."[13] Micro policy subsystems are defined as involving very small, narrowly focused decisions. He then predicts what kinds of decisions, conflicts, and participants each policymaking system produces. This is a valuable contribution to understanding the policymaking process. And it also has implications for lobbying. The tactics and strategies used in various policy subsystems also vary. The type of lobbying that occurs in a "micro policy" subsystem differs from the advocacy required in a "macro policy" subsystem. Understanding the different tactics used and required in different policy subsystems is important to developing a deeper understanding of lobbying.

CONTEXT CONTINUED—VENUE SHOPPING

Venue shopping in lobbying is another critical implication of a fragmented, decentralized policymaking process. For example, some interest groups may secure the policy change they want or block a prospective modification by lobbying only the White House. This strategic decision becomes particularly relevant during periods of divided government.

When Democrats took over the congressional majority in January of 2007, many business-oriented lobbyists immediately saw the increased value of advocates who knew how to lobby the White House and argue for vetoes. President George W. Bush only vetoed one bill during his first six years in office (2001–2006), because the Republican congressional leadership essentially had said, "We won't send you any bills we know you won't approve." That all changed after the 2006 elections. The veto strategy became an important way to venue shop. If lobbyists could not change or block legislation in the Democratic Congress, getting the president to veto the bill became another tool in the advocacy arsenal.

This increased the demand for partisan lobbying firms that understood how the White House decision-making process worked, were well-trusted by the president's staff, and could persuasively argue why a measure should be rejected. Of course, this type of venue shopping was purely a defensive strategy. Yet helping interest groups avoid new taxes or regulations potentially imposed by Congress was worth the investment.

Legislative signaling from the White House is another part of venue shopping. One of the most effective ways to shape policy in Congress is to get the president to signal what legislation he would approve and what he would not. By lobbying the White House, advocates can help shape and send messages through Statements of Administration Policy (SAPs), letters from the president or informal communication from the Office of Legislative Affairs or other senior staff, about the changes required to win White House support (or at least avoid a veto). The pharmaceutical industry wanted to stop a major Democratic push to mandate the government negotiate directly with drug firms for lower prices. Industry lobbyists secured a strong veto signal from the White House early in the process. When the House passed the legislation with far fewer votes than required to override a veto, the measure languished and died.

Venue shopping takes other forms as well. The Senate's supermajority rules create another excellent venue to stop legislation. "Majority or minority status haven't mattered much to me in my career," a lobbyist who specializes in the Senate says. "As long as my party can either help or stop the other party from getting sixty votes, I'm relevant," he says. Knowing how to manage the "pivotal politics" of getting enough votes to achieve or overcome a filibuster is another key tool in the lobbying world.[14] "41 votes in the Senate IS a majority in many circumstances," a veteran lobbyist with many years of Senate experience said.

Lobbying multiple congressional committees also has become a way to shop venues in a more fragmented legislative environment. Local telephone companies have built strong allies in the House Energy and Commerce Committee and the Senate Commerce Committee. Their competitors (cable firms and others seeking to win advantage over the monopoly control of local telephone networks) routinely "venue shop" by taking grievances to the House and Senate Judiciary Committees, historically a forum more averse to local telephone monopolies because of these panels' interest in anti-trust issues.

A host of factors drive the strategic choices of lobbyists when it comes to the tools deployed and resources invested. And while there are always exceptions to the rule, some of the variables can be organized more systematically. Table 8-1 summarizes these choices and the impact they have on the level of resources deployed (few or many "tools"). This chart helps organize our thinking about how and why lobbyists choose to use different tools under various circumstances.

TABLE 8-1   STRATEGIC CHOICES AND LOBBYING: UTILIZING THE TOOLBOX

ADVOCACY CONDITION	ADVOCACY TACTIC	
	Few Tools	Many Tools
Scope of policy Change		
Narrow	√	
Broad		√
Level of Partisanship		
High		√
Low	√	
Mobilization of Opponents		
High		√
Low	√	
Type of Advocacy		
Offense		√
Defense	√*	√
Lobbying venue		
Narrow (small # of decision makers)	√	
Broad (large # of decision makers)		√

Note: *While playing defense sometimes requires fewer resources and tools, stopping a policy change where advocates have a lot of momentum and support can also require major investments.

PUTTING IT ALL TOGETHER—LOBBYING
ON HEALTH CARE

Health care lobbying represents a valuable prism through which to view strategic choices in advocacy. This sector of the U.S. economy is not only critical to voters and elected officials, but it often generates large levels of conflict both politically and among industry players. For these reasons, many of the strategic choices discussed above play out regularly in this field, providing a useful case study to observe the new lobbying world.

For example, the 110th Congress devoted a great deal of energy to legislation previously mentioned, reauthorizing the SCHIP. But it wasn't expanding SCHIP that caused segments of the health care industry to mount a ferocious intramural lobbying campaign. It was how to pay for it. The Senate sought a more modest expansion of the program costing about $30 billion over five years, while the House measure would have cost $50 billion during the same time period. Who would get stuck paying the bill for expanding a popular kids health care initiative was the lobbying equivalent of musical chairs—and whoever was left without a chair when the music stopped would incur a huge financial hit.

The Senate considered several financing options, including reducing payments to health care providers, cutting the Medicare Advantage program, and raising the tobacco tax (a popular option among lobbyists in the public health community). Senate Finance Committee Chair Max Baucus (D-MT) recognized he not only needed the votes to pass a bill in his committee and on the floor, but most likely needed to overcome a possible Republican filibuster. He worked hard to secure support from Republican senators on the Finance Committee as a way to improve the bill's chances of winning the necessary votes to overcome a filibuster. By keeping the total cost of the bill near $30 billion and by avoiding cuts in Medicare and Medicare Advantage, Baucus secured the support of both ranking Finance Committee member Charles Grassley (R-IA) and another key GOP member, Orrin Hatch (R-UT).

Baucus, Grassley, and Hatch were all subjected to massive lobbying campaigns from hospitals, managed care companies, and the public health industry. All of these interest groups utilized significant resources from the advocacy tool box, including specialized consultants, research, traditional grass roots, and earned and paid media, along with a host of new media techniques.

On the House side, the $50 billion expansion required even more offsets. House leaders focused on reducing payments to managed care companies involved in the Medicare Advantage program. The CBO estimated these private plans were "overpaid" on average 12 percent more than traditional Medicare. Cutting Medicare Advantage payments back to traditional Medicare rates would save the government $50 billion over five years, exactly the number needed to expand the SCHIP program. But House Democratic health care leaders such as Pete Stark (D-CA) and John Dingell (D-MI) also had another agenda. They had long opposed the Medicare Advantage program because, like many other liberal health care advocates, they viewed the program as a first step toward privatization of the Medicare program. They also viewed it as largely a Republican initiative, one promoted by a GOP Congress working in lockstep with the Bush administration.

With the stage now set, the various lobbying organizations kicked into high gear. In an example of "reverse lobbying," hospital trade groups, the American Medical Association (AMA), and AARP all agreed to requests from Democratic leaders on the Hill to engage in paid advertising campaigns supporting the House version of the legislation. Public health groups also undertook their own paid advertising campaigns supporting the tobacco tax increase in the Senate version of the legislation.

The health insurance industry, however, engaged in one of the most intense lobbying campaigns. Deconstructing their tactics and strategic choices fits with the calculus laid out above. For example, lobbyists for America's Health Insurance Plans (AHIP) worked hard on inside advocacy, using its own staff and paid consultants and coordinating closely with the lobbyists from its member companies.

AHIP hired the Dewey Square group to conduct grass roots and grasstops activities in more than 25 congressional districts, principally those with members facing tough reelection prospects and high concentrations of seniors. AHIP also invested in a paid advertising campaign of its own, focusing on many of the same lawmakers as well as inside-the-Beltway publications and national cable television buys.

The inside lobbying, grass roots, and media campaigns were all coordinated and conveyed the same message—cutting Medicare Advantage was tantamount to cutting Medicare benefits for seniors, a narrative long known as one of the third rails of American politics. This message was reinforced with poll results from Republican and Democratic firms demonstrating the negative reaction among seniors to the prospects of cutting Medicare Advantage—which as of 2008 will cover about 20 percent of seniors.

AHIP also recognized the nuances of the venues it was lobbying. While many Democrats—particularly in the House—likely were going to vote to cut Medicare Advantage (primarily because of their political commitment to expand SCHIP and their ideological opposition to private sector participation in Medicare), the White House and Republicans were allies and required cultivation. The trade group and its member companies dispatched its specialized consultants to work with the White House and Republicans on Capitol Hill, providing critical information about the number of seniors who would have their benefits cut due to proposed changes in the Medicare Advantage program. They also shared polling and focus group information, showing voter reaction to these reductions in Medicare benefits.

Combined, the effort used many of the utensils in the toolbox. It integrated inside lobbying of key congressional leaders and other legislative stakeholders (recognizing the fragmentation of decision making). It also recognized the partisan nature of the debate, supporting key Republican allies on the Hill and in the White House. The insurance industry also knew their lobbying required a compelling "narrative" (seniors support Medicare Advantage and do not want to see any cuts in Medicare) as well as calibration between venues (arming allies in the White House, while trying to persuade undecided lawmakers). It utilized earned and paid media tools, as well as sophisticated research by pollsters and policy experts who could "validate" the claims of harm to seniors. It also used new technology such as recorded messages from seniors to congressional offices and ads on Web-based publications. Some involved in the campaign considered filming angry seniors at Democratic town hall meetings and then posting those videos on YouTube.

The strategic decisions used in the campaign to avoid cuts to Medicare Advantage followed the schematic outlined in Table 8-1. The scope of the change was broad (cutting the Medicare program). The level of partisanship was high (Democrats supported the cuts, while Republicans opposed). Competitors such as the hospitals AMA and AARP were all mobilized and highly engaged. The insurers were playing high stakes defense. Finally, the venue was broad (lobbying was needed in the House, the Senate, and the White House).

Together, these conditions drove the health insurance industry to make tactical choices that led to major investments in and utilization of the toolbox. Their actions followed the predicted path outlined above because of the conditions they faced. But as with so many other examples provided in this book, the link between lobbying investments, tactics, strategies, and *outcomes* is unclear. It all depends on the metric of success. Did all of the interest-group activity provide valuable information, reduce uncertainty, and help make better-informed tactical decisions? No doubt. But the question of changing hearts and minds of lawmakers through influence is much murkier. The House ended up passing legislation that made deep cuts in Medicare, an outcome the health insurance industry wanted to avoid. Using the metric of influence only, in the House the efforts were not successful. On the other hand, the Senate took a different route and the president promised to veto the legislation if it included the Medicare changes. These two outcomes look like industry wins. But a broader view of lobbying suggests investments and tactics paid dividends along the way that helped reduce uncertainty and gathered significant intelligence for the advocacy organization. Viewed in this way, even though the health care insurance industry "lost" a particular battle in the House, the investments were necessary and worthwhile as the debate went on to its next iteration.

This point is critical in developing a more accurate picture of lobbying. Too often scholars and journalists focus on one particular "play" and assume it's a good depiction of the entire game. But they need to examine the larger picture.[15] As one leading scholar of interest groups notes, "As the saga unfolds, individual episodes may be singled out for separate treatment, but unless they are seen in their larger historical/developmental context, any particular story, however melodramatic it seems to be, is likely to generate more misunderstanding than insight . . . it is not that influence is irrelevant, it is simply not the best way to frame the central questions."[16]

SUMMARY

Much of the research on interest groups focuses on how and why they try to influence the public policy process. Yet we know a lot less about the strategic choices behind the decisions to use different tools and their effectiveness. These are important factors for several reasons.

First, understanding how, when, and why interest organizations deploy various arrows from the advocacy quiver provides a richer understanding of the lobbying world. As I have argued throughout this book, the inordinate amount of attention on the stereotypical "influence peddler" engaged in direct lobbying of lawmakers misses much of the complexity, richness, and tactical diversity that now pervades the new advocacy world. Comprehending the full range of tools, and when and why they get used, helps improve public understanding.

Second, detailing the menu of strategic advocacy choices helps better to evaluate lobbying effectiveness—not only the efficacy of various tactics, but also the conditions under which some work and others do not. Is paid advertising a better persuasive technique than grass roots? Is it better to communicate a message through targeted Internet ads or television? Is hiring a lobbyist with close personal ties to lawmakers a better strategy than bringing in constituents? Do some techniques work more effectively when an interest group is playing offense versus defense? How does "venue shopping" fit into the lobbying equation? Why do two different interest groups use the same tools and yet one "wins" and the other "loses?" These are not merely interesting academic questions. They represent the concerns and issues raised on a daily basis by practitioners in the real world of lobbying. Answering all of these questions stretches outside the scope of this book. Yet too often those trying to understand the role of lobbying in American public policymaking ignore these queries. Comprehending which tools work best, in what settings, and why represents another important dimension of deepening our understanding of lobbying.

Finally, how—and with what degree of effectiveness—interest groups apply various tools poses enormous questions about political equity and democratic theory. If it is the case that "the more you do, the more you get," or "the more you spend, the more you persuade," those with the most resources should dominate the public policymaking process. According to this view, if an interest group can invest in many tools—deploying grass roots, hiring well-connected lobbying firms, investing in media, developing studies, and conducting message research—they should be able to accomplish most of their objectives in the government relations arena. Some, like those who believe in the "military/industrial complex," might think that's how Washington works. But the real world is more complicated. Resource deployment on advocacy makes some difference, but so does the effective use of the tools, as does selecting the right techniques for the given conditions.

Finding the right mix of tools and how to apply them effectively is very difficult—if not impossible—to quantify. Tactics that might work and produce a successful outcome under some conditions might not work during other times. Social scientists genuinely want to develop a quantitative model for lobbying success, but it's probably impossible to construct. Still, strategic choices in lobbying are not entirely random. As seen throughout this chapter, we can begin to develop a framework outlining the conditions under which different tools get used.

Advocates for new military weapons systems face a different set of challenges and use a different set of tools than those who lobby for increased school lunch funding. Those who represent alcohol or tobacco companies seeking lower taxes confront different conditions than do technology companies interested in anti-trust issues. Furthermore, sometimes using the same tactics produces wildly different results.

Part of the reason for this latter point goes back to the inordinate amount of attention in the study of lobbying on the question of "influence." If we step back for a moment and analyze interest groups from a broader perspective—and think about advocacy beyond "just persuasion"—some of their investments in various advocacy tools make more sense. Viewing interest-group behavior in a broader context as we have throughout this book—focusing on variables like information gathering, public education, and reducing uncertainty—explains some of these mysteries.

Getting "under the influence" means reconsidering the myths, preconceptions, and complexities of the advocacy industry—many of which are outlined in the first eight chapters of this book. In the final chapter, I catalogue a series of points about lobbying that deserve reconsideration. It is my hope that understanding some of these complexities in the lobbying world will deepen our understanding of how it really works and change a host of misconceptions about the role of interest groups and advocates in the American public policymaking process.

NOTES

1. Lisa Caruso, "Lobbying Drug War," *National Journal*, May 19, 2007.
2. Ibid. 1.
3. Ibid. 1–2.
4. John Godfrey, "Liberal Groups Campaign Against Medicare Insurance Subsidy," *Dow Jones Newswire, MarketWatch*, June 8, 2007.
5. Jeffrey H. Birnbaum. "Bit Players XM, Sirius Hold a High Stakes Merger Game," *Washington Post*, July 25, 2007, D3.
6. The Innocence Protection Act became Public Law, 108–405.
7. In 2006, the disclosure of an earmarked federal project in Alaska linking an airport to a smaller populated island became the poster child for wasteful pork barrel spending. The project became known as "the bridge to nowhere."
8. E.E. Schattschneider, *The Semi-Sovereign People: A Realists View of Democracy in America* (Singpore, Wadsworth: Thompson Learning, 1975). (Not sure how to cite this the book says Wadsworth: Thompson Learning: Asia, Canada, Singamore and then the Wadsworth division just says Singapore.)
9. Ibid. 3.
10. Paul Taylor, "Lobbyists Lose the Game, Not the Guccis," *Washington Post*, July 31, 1983, A12.
11. Ibid.
12. James A. Thurber, "Political Power and Policy Subsystems in American Politics," In Peters, Guy B. and Bert ARockman. *An Agenda for Excellence 2: Administering the State* (New Jersey: Chatham House, 1996), 76–104.
13. Ibid. 77.
14. See Keith Kreihbel, Pivotal Politics for the importance of getting 60 votes to overcome a filibuster or 67 votes to override a veto.
15. See, for example, Frank R. Baumgartner and Beth L. Leech, *Basic Interests: The Importance of Groups in Politics and in Political Science.* (Princeton, NJ: Princeton University Press, 1998), 60–61, who incorporate some of Robert Salisbury's thinking here.
16. Ibid. 61.

9

LOBBYING RECONSIDERED

When we refer to interest groups as "stakeholders" they are legitimate; when we refer to the same people as "lobbyists" they grow horns.
Patrick Griffin, former White House aide and Washington strategist

This book weaves a new narrative about the web we call lobbying in America. By integrating new threads and storylines, it reconsiders the way we think about organized advocacy and interest groups. It looks "under the influence," peering below the hood of conventional wisdom and many biases about the role and impact of the advocacy industry in American politics and policymaking. It tells a story of change, one that I hope is both provocative and enlightening. It began with a caricature, a familiar plot acted out every few years, just substituting different actors. Jack Abramoff was an archetype—nothing new, just an extension of an enduring misconception. He represents a classic current meandering through the history of American politics and carved deeply into the public psyche. And, like some veteran lobbyists, old myths die hard. Yet lobbying deserves reconsideration.

A generation ago, reporters wrote narratives similar to those seen as the Jack Abramoff affair unfolded. "The storied tools of the trade have been booze, broads and black bags," according to a 1983 article from *The Washington Post*.[1] But the allegories of corruption began even earlier. Nearly 80 years ago, scholar Pendleton Herring also recognized the advocacy industry's image problem. Writing words that apply as much today as in the 1920s, he said, "The lobby has always been and still is a much maligned institution. There is nothing that will so arouse the ire of a congressman as an accusation that he is or ever has been influenced through the machinations of the lobby."[2] Herring also clearly believed lobbyists' reputation problems were not without merit. "The record of the lobby in years gone by provides ample evidence to justify the connotations that it still arouses in the minds of many people. The pages of American history show not a few blots left there by the stains of political corruption; and the lobby is responsible for many of them."[3]

With the media and academics all spinning in a vortex of conventional wisdom, the public only hears the echo chamber of sleazy tales. I argue in this book that this view of lobbying is too narrow at several levels. This constricted view hampers our ability to comprehend the important changes that have unfolded in the past 40 years and the true role of lobbying in American public policymaking.

Bob Rusbuldt, President of the Independent Insurance Agents and Brokers of America, offers this insight:

> The lobbying profession is often misunderstood and maligned, but if you want a simple explanation of this profession it is this: we are educators. We educate our members or clients, members of Congress, the media, our foes and allies in the private sector and the public. We never stop educating.

Another scholar observing the Washington scene says this:

> . . . lobbyists are by no means just outsiders trying to influence the system of legislative processes. Rather, they are the internal conduits by which the process operates—the communications links among members of Congress. Lobbyists act as the foot soldiers fighting the political battles of the Congressional Big Men; without them, the practice of politics would grind to a halt.[4]

Some political scientists who study lobbying also take a broader view:

> . . . traditional textbook notions of inside lobbying are incomplete. Groups simply have more options of influence available to them. Moreover, the actions of large numbers of organized interests have contributed to a growing level of uncertainty over each group's ability to influence important policies . . . [5]

These experts remind us lobbying is less nefarious and more structurally diverse, tactically varied, and even politically limited than suggested by conventional wisdom. My experiences as participant and observer and the evidence presented in this volume all support those conclusions. Indeed, the real world of advocacy is so different from conventional wisdom, the way we think about it requires almost complete reconsideration. I end by offering some suggestions about how we might reassess the role of lobbying, suggesting we think of it as more than *just* influence; and, that we take a more expansive view of influence itself. Like any parable, this one also concludes with some lessons—observations I hope will challenge and enlighten our thinking about lobbying and interest groups. These final observations fall into three main categories:

- Reconsidering the impact of lobbying on public policy and advocacy's broader strategic goals;
- Reconsidering the structure and dynamism of lobbying;
- Reconsidering the unintended consequences of reforms in the advocacy world.

IMPACT ON THE PROCESS AND STRATEGIC GOALS

LOBBYISTS AND INTEREST GROUPS ARE NOT OMNIPOTENT

Most accounts of lobbying growth predict ominous consequences for American democracy. This is because most journalists and even academics adopt many of the assumptions and conclusions of the critics of pluralism.[6] If politics is all about "who gets what, when and how," to paraphrase political scientist Harold Lasswell, critics of pluralism assumes private interests get *whatever* they want, *whenever* they want it, and usually through some type of sleazy means, like pouring money into the coffers of politicians in return for particular benefits and policy favors.[7]

But evidence from the real lobbying world does not support this menacing conclusion. Employing lobbyists doesn't necessarily guarantee more power for special interests. Numerous factors check their influence. For example, as the advocacy industry has grew during the last 40 years, the buildup often occurred in competing industries or policy areas, often creating new constraints on the power of interest groups. As business interests institutionalized their advocacy efforts, so did consumer groups, environmental advocates, labor unions, and others who oppose the corporate policy agenda in Washington. As Berry and Wilcox note, "With the growing number of interest groups came a greater variety of interests. The new groups were not just carbon copies of those that already existed."[8] They go on to quote a real estate interest-group representative who describes the ferocity of this competition.

> If you go back a few years ago, you would have to say that if the National Association of Realtors and the (National Association of) Home Builders spoke, that was the whole industry speaking. Now there are more groups, such as low income housing groups, real estate developers, residential real estate developers, etc. . . . Members of Congress have to listen to all these groups.[9]

These kinds of checks and balances exist in virtually every policy area.

Telecommunications giants such as AT&T face scrutiny from consumer groups and labor unions. Energy companies such as Shell or Exxon-Mobil must combat the efforts of environmental groups. Insurance interests such as Allstate often do battle with the trial bar. Nearly every interest faces organized opponents that often check or deter them from achieving their goals in the policy arena without some kind of a fight. We might call these checks on the power of interest groups "inter-interest group" battles.

But another constraint on the power of advocacy groups—especially the business lobby—is what I describe as "intra-industry" checks and balances. Interest-group scholars agree, "The greatest restraint on business may not be its critics, but, rather, the divisions within and between industries" (Berry and Wilcox).

One veteran Republican lobbyist, Bruce Gates, with the prestigious bipartisan lobbying firm Washington Counsel, Ernst and Young, puts it this way: "There definitely is a lot more intramural competition among businesses today that didn't exist 20 or 30 years ago. Before the mid 1980s it was rare to have companies fighting each other in the legislative process. Now it happens all the time."

Gates believes a confluence of events has caused this new level of business bickering. "Everything is just more complex now. Government rules, technology, globalization, as well as business itself." This creates new niche opportunities and risks for businesses that might often pit one against the other, he observes.

But Gates raises an even more interesting point that suggests the unintended consequences of government policy also have played a role:

> Beginning with the 1986 tax bill (which pitted some industries against others in terms of whose taxes were raised) and then again in 1990, when Congress instituted the "pay-as-you-go" rules (PAYGO), the business community became increasingly competitive with each other in Washington. Now, if someone else's taxes can be raised or government payments shaved, you can avoid getting hit. I don't remember as much intramural fighting before the days of PAYGO.

His point also helps underscore why more companies have chosen a more individualized approach to lobbying over the past two decades. Tighter budgets and increasing demands for spending, within the context of zero-sum PAYGO rules, have created a host of new risks and rewards for individual interest groups—and a host of new competitive pressures, as well as checks and balances. Political scientists Darrell M. West and Burdett A. Loomis agree, "More and more decisions are perceived as redistributive (or zero-sum) in an era of budget deficits and reductions in spending."[10]

More individual participation in lobbying—as opposed to reliance on trade groups—also has contributed to this phenomenon of intra-industry checks and balances. It was obviously a lot more difficult for trade associations to take firm stands on issues with member firms on both sides. Now with more heightened individual involvement, more conflict occurs.

Democratic lobbyist Bert Carp sees another check on unbridled power of interests, particularly business interests: "One of the reasons business lobbying grew so much during the 1970s and 1980s was because of the large influx of public interest groups at the same time. Business didn't come to Washington because they were civic-minded—it was because a lot of other groups came here with ideas that might put them out of business."

There are other checks and balances on the advocacy industry. One former senior Republican congressional aide-turned-lobbyist gives this example:

> One of the great ironies that most people don't realize is that the more a lobbyist or interest group helps you financially, the less you feel like you can do for them. I'm not sure everybody realizes that. For example, in the days of soft money, if someone gave you $100,000, you really didn't want to do anything in return if they asked because it just looked bad.

So much for quid pro quo politics! Lawmakers do not simply bend to the wishes of Washington lobbyists or interest groups. constituents matter a great deal. Donald Mathews in his famous book about U.S. senators quotes a lobbyist who says, "In the last analysis, a senator won't go along with us because of friendship, or persuasiveness on our part, or even logic. The real argument is that the bill will do something worthwhile for his state. That's why someone from his state is often the best person to approach him."[11] This type of thinking led to the growth of the grassroots and then "grasstops" movements outlined in Chapter 7. Yet as is the case in so many areas of lobbying, once one side of an issue chose grassroots tactics, their opponents usually followed suit. Like an advocacy arms race, once one side uses new tools, their competitors try to catch up—which often leads to advocacy escalation (a reason why the lobbying industry is growing) and standoff (a reason why the lobbying industry is not omnipotent).

Another political scientist reinforces this line of reasoning. "The descent on Washington of so many hundreds of associations, institutions, and their agents does not mean that these private interests have acquired greater sway or even a more articulate voice in shaping of national policy. In many ways the opposite is true."[12]

Then there is the old argument: *Everything has been said, just not all the lobbyists have spoken yet.* Jerry Jasinowski, former head of the National Association of Manufacturers, makes this point: "More lobbyists doesn't equal more influence," he told *The Washington Post.* "You get to the point where you start tripping over each other. You reach a point of diminishing returns."[13]

Given these checks and balances—competing industries in the business case, the sheer number of organized groups (businesses versus labor versus public interest groups, etc.), a more open process because of the press and new media, and even the growth and decentralization of Congress–are we to conclude pluralism is working perfectly? Not at all. The inequality of resources deployed raises some intriguing questions that also deserve consideration.

No doubt asymmetries in resources among interest groups exist. And these differences are not insignificant.

. . . moneyed interests will be able to construct narratives more clearly and effectively than other groups or organizations. To be sure, political parties, populist voices, and public interest groups all work to convey their perspectives. All continue to have some real success in shaping the policy agenda. In the end, however, none of these voices can sing with the specificity, direction and forcefulness of private interests that can purchase a clear, coherent, and often repeated message."[14]

This is true—up to a point. But lobbying power is also more nuanced. Telecommunications giants such as AT&T have bigger budgets for advocacy, more internal lobbyists, larger PACs, more ability to hire outside consultants than, say, a fledgling competitor. As a result, AT&T is well known in Washington among policymakers, probably gathers better legislative intelligence, and has a good chance of stopping policy changes directly averse to its interests. For example, when its competitors tried to pass legislation mandating access to AT&T facilities under conditions extremely favorable to these competitors, the measure stalled. AT&T was able to use its political power and influence to block legislation it did not like—despite the pro-consumer arguments advanced by its competitors.

Yet several years later, when AT&T attempted to move legislation making it easier for the company to enter the video-to-the-home business and compete directly with cable and satellite providers, its offensive federal efforts languished.

Grasping this insight improves our understanding of the advocacy world. Lobbying power is not *guaranteed* based on size or resources. These factors play a major role in helping interest groups play defense, but they are no assurance of dominating the policy process or even getting offensive legislation or regulatory change enacted. Advocacy success is more conditional, changing based on several factors. It varies depending on all the circumstances outlined in Chapter 8.

The experience in 2007 of major lenders in the student loan business provides a case in point. Large financial institutions such as Bank of America, Citigroup, and Sallie Mae are the beneficiaries of a government subsidy aimed at making college loans more affordable. They created large government relations practices, spend millions on lobbying, and organized well-financed PACs and charitable giving programs. They possess all the resources that some believe would help them master the lobbying game and achieve favorable policy outcomes.

Yet early in 2007, these companies experienced a major defeat as Congress advanced legislation reducing the subsidy, meaning a direct hit to the banks' bottom line. "The new Democrat majority pushed student loan reform to the forefront of the national agenda within the first 100 hours of the 110th congressional session by passing the College Student Relief Act; this would reduce interest rates under both the Federal Family Education Loan Program (FFELP) and Direct Loan program."[15]

A recent comment by an official from the American Association of Collegiate Registrars sums up the attitude about the lobbying largess of the lenders: "(The loan industry is) so lucrative that even the Bush administration, which has been their patron saint, has put them on the chopping block. . . . They are a lobbying operation that happens to conduct lending."[16] The "lobbying operation that happens to conduct lending" had suffered a major reversal of fortune.

How could well-funded, well-organized interest groups such as these major financial institutions experience such a dramatic setback? Under the conventional wisdom model, powerful interest groups dominate the process and are not supposed to lose. But as these lenders learned, success in the advocacy process is not always guaranteed. Spending more money, having a bigger government relations organization, or hiring more lobbyists doesn't always translate to policy success. Instead of gushing with influence, Gucci Gulch can sometimes run dry. And for these lenders, it did.

The takeaway for students of interest groups is that there are limits to lobby success. Power is often more nuanced, limited, and conditional than suggested by conventional wisdom. Advocates and lobbyists often *fail*— even large, well-funded, highly-skilled ones. The implicit presumption among many who study or report on lobbying is that if you just throw enough resources or money at an issue, you can accomplish your policy objectives—in other words, that the process is always malleable to private interests. But as these lenders and others learn in Washington everyday, that view is incorrect. The real world of lobbying includes a lot more uncertainty, unpredictability and, quite frankly, legislative and policy "losses." There are limits to lobbying. For every lobbyist who uses money, power, and influence to win legislative favor, there are many others who use the same tools and lose. Recall the "dirty little secret" from Chapter 2—lobbyists lose a lot too. Understanding these limits, and appreciating where constraints exist and why, is an important part of getting under the influence.

Success in lobbying and the "power" of interest groups is based on a number of factors beyond size, resource deployment, or advocacy tactics. Unlike an assembly line, where investing more time and money produces additional outputs, pouring increased resources into lobbying doesn't always translate to legislative or regulatory success. Size, resources, or clever tactics can sometimes be *necessary* conditions for advocacy success, but they are definitely not ever *sufficient*.

Another twist on the "lobbyists are not omnipotent" theme concerns why some pressure groups succeed with particular tactics, while others using the same techniques fail. In 2007, an example of this unfolded when Congress considered energy legislation. Two powerful interest groups, the auto industry and the oil industry, each engaged in heated legislative battles related to this bill. The auto industry sought relief from higher fuel economy standards and lost; oil companies fought against higher taxes and won. Both industries used many of the same utensils from the lobbying toolbox. In many cases, they even employed the same lobbyists. For example, both industries retain major bipartisan and well-respected lobbying firms such as Timmons and Company and the Duberstein Group.[17] Both industries also invested resources in mobilizing grass roots and paid advertising. But when the U.S. Senate passed an energy bill in 2007, it produced contradictory results for students of lobbying. On the same day, in the same story *The New York Times* reported, "The vote . . . was a major defeat for car manufacturers, which had fought for a much smaller increase in fuel economy standards . . ." Yet the next paragraph continued, "In a victory for the oil industry, Republican lawmakers successfully block a crucial component of the Democratic plan that would have raised taxes on oil companies by about $32 billion and used the money on tax breaks for wind power, solar power, ethanol and other renewable fuels."[18] Like many other corners of American life, competition is alive and well in the advocacy world, and lobbyists feel its impact everyday.

DEBUNKING THE MYTH OF COMMODITIZATION

Lobbying influence is not a commodity—it can't be purchased like martinis. Nevertheless, many observers of the advocacy business think it can. This myth, often conceived and perpetuated by journalists writing salacious tales about unscrupulous lobbyists trying to bribe and buy their way to successful influence, is more titillating than accurate. This myth suggests just spending enough money or hiring the most "connected" lobbyist creates a magic policy antidote. A potential client once called a major lobbying firm in Washington because the World Bank stopped making loans to his businesses. The bank curtailed the loans because the businessman was using the money to invest in projects that had a high default rate. Instead of fixing the problem through better business practices, he sought resolution in the policy and political process. He looked to hire a well-connected lobbying firm in Washington, make a couple of phone calls to the White House, and "fix" his problem. In the end, other lobbyists gave this individual the same advice – better business practices will "fix" the problem, not a lobbyist. While the narrative of "hired guns fixing political problems" is attractive—buy a lobbyist, get a "solution"—it is just not accurate. Ironically, journalists tend to perpetuate the myth but also help make it false. With so much press scrutiny of public officials' behavior, it would be difficult for such inside deals ever to develop. Government officials and lobbyists who do behave in this way are more likely to buy a ticket to prison than influence a policy decision.

Still, the myth of commoditization persists and will no doubt endure. Government will always shape rules that create winners and losers. Fed by stories about lobbyists and interest groups manipulating the process, Washington will always attract a steady stream of supplicants, thinking they can buy influence like ordering a steak dinner. Real-life outcomes, as well as the lessons outlined in this book, should modulate this myth. But over 200 years of experience in this country suggests it will persist in the public psyche and the body politic.

LOBBYING ABOUT MORE THAN INFLUENCE

We also need to broaden our lens concerning the strategic goals of lobbyists. Interest groups care about more than just influence. Granted, influence is important. But a fuller understanding of advocacy suggests there are other factors at play. If "success" is not guaranteed, why do interest groups invest money in lobbying in the first place? Interest groups invest in lobbying and government affairs to reduce uncertainty and gather information about their external environments.

"Influence is just part of what we do," says Tim McKone from AT&T. "We try to monitor trends and developments on policy and issues. We help our senior management know what is on the horizon so we can prepare." Communications consultant Rich Thau concurs, "I always tell my clients you want to have more information than your opponents. It takes money and work to get that information." Other interest group scholars agree that focusing just on "influence" is too narrow of an emphasis. Salisbury, for example, argues, "I contend that a great many interest group representatives seek information more than influence...."[19]

Could the student loan industry just "invest" enough in the process to produce the outcome it wanted? Many think so. But not in the real world. These companies still "invest" time, money, and personnel in trying to manage the public policy process, because their lobbyists and government relations personnel can help figure out the contours and nuances of potential actions. They cannot "produce" outcomes, but they can minimize uncertainty and help company leaders ascertain the art of the possible and provide better information. In other words, lobbying is not a linear exercise. You do not "purchase" legislative outcomes or policy decisions in the same way you acquire raw materials or financial assets. There is a lot of uncertainty in the public policy environment. Favorable outcomes are not guaranteed by better data, access, or messages.

This conclusion supports the argument that gathering "information" as opposed to seeking influence may be a better way to think about what lobbyists really do.

> Washington is, after all, the main source of information about what government officials are doing or planning to do. To get that information in a timely way, a continuous and alert presence in the capital is vital. Moreover, in this quest for information the interest representatives are often in a position of profound dependence. They need access to the officials not so much to apply pressure or even to advocate policy as to be told when something important to them is about to happen.[20]

Washington Counsel Ernst and Young partner Bruce Gates underscores this point:

> I had a three-hour meeting the other day with a client talking about the future of subsidies for energy. It was all aimed at making sure they were positioned well in the future. We try to make sure our clients don't have their heads in the sand. We help them watch for things coming down the pike. It's the modern day equivalent of someone telling the buggy whip industry that the automobile was just created.

And some put a higher premium on this information than others. Interest-group leaders—corporate CEOs, trade association executives, public interest advocates, or labor union officials—estimate the value of managing uncertainty through lobbying or the value of trying to influence policy decisions in very different ways. How leaders calculate the results of these investments determines how they approach the lobbying world. Differences in how inter-est-group leaders view the advocacy world are important because they shape their behavior in the public policy process.

An example from the corporate world is instructive. Nick Franklin of PacifiCare Health Systems, a large managed care company, makes this point:

> Some CEOs view Washington and lobbying as a necessary evil. They make minimal investments and they hope their problems just go away. They rarely see the public policy process as providing any business opportunities. The person they put in to run their lobbying operation has few tools, usually reports to the CEO through several layers of corporate bureaucracy, and is not integral to the firm's strategic business planning.

Other CEOs take a completely different view. They coordinate government affairs under a senior executive who reports directly to the CEO. The lobbying operation is integral to managing uncertainty, avoiding potential costs and creating business opportunities. Persons who run the Washington office or government affairs for companies like this are very involved in creating and executing the overall strategic plan. For these companies, government affairs is not a necessary evil, but an integral part of the compa-nies' future. It is part of their strategic business plan and gets executed in a coordinated, holistic way. These firms usually invest more in government affairs and use more tools in the toolbox.

Getting under the influence means recognizing these differences exist. One size does not fit all when it comes to how interest-group leaders view the role, value, and necessity of lobbying. These differences in attitude and perspective concerning lobbying lead to dramatic variations in the style, structure, and substantive methods adopted by interest groups in the advocacy world. And these differences in approach also lead to variations in outcomes and account for the many inconsistencies and disparities we see in the way interest groups practice public affairs.

Students of lobbying also pay too much attention to the late stage in the process—for example only looking for interest-group impact on roll call votes. But a critical part of influence occurs much earlier in the process as interests try to shape the agenda. Many tools used today are just as important in this initial stage of public policy as in the end. For example, interest groups will use many of the tools in the advocacy toolbox just to get an item on the legislative agenda. Cultivating lawmakers as champions of an issue assisting lawmakers in making the case for moving an item to the top of the list (or taking it off) are important forms of "influence" that deserve more attention.

Finally, the care and feeding of allies is an important part of the advocacy game. Too much emphasis on persuasion of the undecided policymaker misses another major component of lobbying—arming allies with information, political cover, and other types of support. In the real world of lobbying, interest-group representatives probably meet a lot more with allies than opponents. Keeping friends and supporters armed with the necessary policy and political weapons to fight policy battles is an important part of the advocacy game. The notion of lobbying as a *legislative subsidy* is consistent with many examples of real-world experience described in this volume.[21]

Students of lobbying need to move beyond just looking for evidence of persuasion. Focusing more on the information gathering/uncertainty-reducing behaviors and agenda-setting of lobbyists helps develop a much clearer and realistic understanding of what interest groups and their advocates actually do.

Context also matters when it comes to understanding the advocacy world. Lobbying investments and tactics change based on a variety of factors, including the resources an interest group possesses, the competitive pressures it faces, the air cover/ground cover demands, the visibility of the issue, the role of allies, willingness to adapt new tools, the level of conflict, whether they are playing offense or defense, and the partisan atmosphere. Moreover, the type of policy under consideration also affects lobbying. Just as the politics of the decision-making systems vary based on factors such as the visibility of the decision, the scope of the conflict, and the number of participants, these changing contexts also influence the lobbying tactics deployed.[22]

Partisan context deserves a special note. As I argue in this book, partisanship is one of the defining characteristics of politics in Washington in the first part of the twenty-first century. Yet its impact on lobbying remains largely unexplored. For example, after the 2000 election, a more conservative, pro-business environment existed in Washington due to unified control of Congress and the White House by Republicans for the first time in almost a half century. Did business back off after 2001 because of lack of risk? Did labor and environmental groups ramp-up their activities because they had to play defense? And how did business and labor respond to the new context in 2007? Did labor rest on its laurels or view the new Democrat Congress as a place to play offense for the first time in over a decade? Similarly, did business beef up its lobbying presence because of the new challenges in DC?

The interaction between lobbying and presidential/congressional relations raised in Chapter 5 is also instructive here. Is a president less influential in a mixed party government? President George W. Bush, for example, may have looked more successful and persuasive when his party controlled the Congress more because of the GOP majority than the White House's legislative prowess. The same can be said for lobbying. Labor is accomplishing more of its agenda in 2007 and 2008 with a Democratic majority in Congress. Have unions improved their lobbying skill or has the context changed? I would argue the latter is a better explanation.

The important conclusion here is that context matters in the advocacy world. And it's vital to appreciate how changing lobbying contexts alter styles, strategies, and outcomes of interest groups and their representatives.

STRUCTURE AND DYNAMISM

LOBBYING MORE STRUCTURALLY AND TACTICALLY DIVERSE THAN SUGGESTED BY CONVENTIONAL WISDOM

The typical portrait of lobbyists paints them as influence peddlers engaged in direct advocacy, buttonholing lawmakers wherever possible. As Chapter 2 outlines in great detail, this caricature meanders throughout American history, carving deep impressions on the body politic. But this view is also deeply flawed. Conventional wisdom characterizes lobbying as a small, specialized, niche business. But in reality, the advocacy industry today is more like a multinational corporation, with its many divisions. The lobbying world exhibits structural complexity and tactical diversity—grassroots firms, media specialists, pollsters, researchers, and more all play significant roles in the advocacy industry, which is an important part of the new Washington Establishment, as outlined in Chapter 4.

A journalist who closely covers the Hill and lobbying sums up the new structural diversity and tactical complexity well:

> A highball and a handshake don't go as far as they used to in this town. Washington's sophisticated influence industry has become increasingly reliant on grassroots message campaigns to swing votes in Congress, forcing lobbyists and other influence peddlers to trade steaks at The Capital Grille for phone banks in Cape Girardeau, Mo.[23]

LOBBYING NOT STATIC—CONSTANTLY ADAPTING

While the reputation of lobbyists as sleazy influence merchants seems immutable, the practices and tactics of advocates are not. Lobbying began as a practice of representing individuals (nineteenth century), evolved into advocating for groups (first half of twentieth century), and then morphed again into more specialized and fragmented interests, exercising what some have called "the rise of direct participation by interest groups."[24] Not only were peak associations such as the American Medical Association joined by individual company involvement in Washington (such as pharmaceutical companies and medical diagnostic companies forming their own Washington offices); but the peak associations were also joined by even more specialized associations like the Federation of American Hospitals, an association representing for-profit hospitals, and the American Community Bankers, a subset of the financial community representing savings and loans.[25] The lobbying world continues to morph and change into a more fragmented, balkanized system, both in *whom* they represent and *how* they do so.

The lobbying industry has institutionalized tactically, forming a number of subspecialties such as fund-raising, grass roots, and strategic communications. Some aspects of the changing advocacy industry grew rapidly during the 1970s and 1980s—such as the number of PACs and corporate Washington DC government relations offices. The growth in these areas has now stabilized or slowed due to mergers, acquisitions, and industry consolidation. Others—such as the growth of online advertising or use of the Internet as an organizing and information dissemination tool—are just now experiencing an initial period of rapid change, acceptance, and utilization. This pattern of adaptation and transformation will continue.

As E. Pendleton Herring observed nearly 80 years ago, "Politics are dynamic. And as popular feeling veers and changes, as the commercial and social life of the people evolves and develops, so the institutions of government are transformed."[26] But that is only half the story. As we've seen throughout this book, the advocacy industry has a reciprocal relationship with its external environment. And just as changes in popular feeling transform government, changes in Congress, other institutions (such as the media), business competitors, technology, and campaign finance and ethics rules alter the lobbying world.

This dynamic aspect of the advocacy business is not well understood. One expert summarized 30 years of research and writing on interest groups and lobbying with these thoughts about change:

> . . . interest group politics is dynamic and protean over time, and there are processes of learning and adaptation quite continuously at work among all the active players in the policy-making system. There are many stable components to be sure. Indeed, we were surprised to discover how much of the lobbying system was staffed by veterans of the policy wars. Still, there is much that

changes, not always discernible each week or month, but moving enough to require the scholar to keep coming back to mark successive modifications."[27]

Examples of this kind of learning and adaptation among those in the advocacy industry repeat throughout this book. Business leaders saw the legal opportunity and the political need to institutionalize their campaign finance operations, so they began to form PACs. Once one major firm in an industry created one, others quickly followed suit. The same pattern holds true for the creation of corporate Washington offices, as the lobbying world adapted from relying exclusively on peak associations and became more specialized. We have witnessed a similar adaptation trend when it comes to using new media as part of the lobbying tool kit. New techniques begin on Madison Avenue, migrate to political campaigns, and then get adopted by K Street lobbyists—a now familiar sequence in the ever-changing lobbying world.

Another example of the lobbying world's dynamic nature concerns changes following the terrorist attacks on New York and the Pentagon on September 11, 2001. Shortly after these attacks, another threat rocked Washington: anthrax. The combination of these new threats was another reminder of how changes in the external world reshape lobbying. One trade association executive who used to work on Capitol Hill says this:

> The changes September 11 wrought in terms of how we lobby are among the biggest changes I've seen in the last 20 years. It's harder to get into the congressional offices to see people. It's harder to go to hearings and harder to visit staff in person. Thank goodness for the Internet because now many of the things lobbyists had to do in person—pick up memos on the Hill, go to hearings, sit down for face-to-face meetings with staff—are all done online.

It has also changed the way staff and members deal with e-mail. I remember when e-mail was discouraged on the Hill because we thought we'd get too much of it, or it would be dominated by fake groups. Now, it's welcomed and encouraged. Between e-mail and the Internet, it's almost like you don't have to be in Washington anymore to be a lobbyist.

Welcome to advocacy in the twenty-first century!

CAMPAIGN-INFUSED ADVOCACY

Grasping the heavy impact of electoral campaigns on the lobbying process is another key to understanding modern advocacy practices. The growth of partisanship impacts the lobbying world at many levels. This reality means blurring lines between the politics of campaigns and the politics of public policy, according to some political scientists.[28] The best lobbying efforts indeed emulate political campaigns in many ways. Research-based message development, monitoring movements in public opinion, utilizing expert "validators," mounting paid media campaigns, and mobilizing grassroots support are just some of the ways lobbying efforts mirror political campaigns. Underscoring these points, one journalist writes, "Modern advocacy resembles political campaigns more than an old boys club."[29]

This mind-set creates a host of new opportunities for campaign operatives who want to transition into the lobbying world. For example, many current and former political workers now offer their services to clients as media consultants or grassroots/grasstops organizers for large advocacy campaigns. "We left our campaign shoes behind, but we brought the campaign mentality with us," one veteran Republican political operative, who now works in the lobbying business, explains.

UNINTENDED CONSEQUENCES OF REFORM

Conventional wisdom often overlooks the unintended consequences of political reform on lobbying. Campaign finance changes were supposed to root the big money interests out of politics. Limiting contributions from large donors—the centerpiece of the Federal Election Campaign Act and its amendments during the 1970s—caused members of Congress to spend more time fund-raising. This also meant more regular interactions with lobbyists as the-agents to help raise these funds. Most long-time lobbyists would agree that their interactions with lawmakers on fund-raising have expanded exponentially over the past 30 years. Most of the reformers of the 1970s probably did not believe their efforts to curb money in the system would increase the closeness between lobbyists and lawmakers. But they clearly did.

Other "lobbying reforms" instituted in 2007 by the new Democratic majority that impose "gift and travel bans" on members of Congress also created unintended consequences. More interactions between lawmakers and lobbyists now occur in a fund-raising context—an outcome reformers probably did not envision or desire. Under the new rules lobbyists can only join lawmakers for meals if they do it while combining that interaction with a campaign check. Moreover, an increasing amount of "lobbying" resources are being deployed on the activities outlined in Chapter 7, such as advertising and grass roots, that are completely immune from lobby disclosure requirements. Both of these outcomes demonstrate how trying to "regulate" lobbying usually leads to unintended results.

Reforming the committee process also had an unintended effect on the advocacy world. For example, "markup sessions" used to be more closed before the mid-1970s. Lawmakers spent more time together in these sessions—interactions that kept lobbyists out of the process and boosted the amount of information possessed by lawmakers and staff. They got to know each other in these sessions. They would know the vote counts, the policies, and how to cut deals. Yet the changes advocated by "reformers" ended all that, and these reforms also empowered lobbyists. "Congressmen had information and talked to each other. The Members stopped doing that when we went to open markups," a prominent Democratic lobbyist said.

The so-call "sunshine laws" passed during the 1970s and other efforts to "open up the process" also had the unintended effect of spurring growth in the lobbying world. A former Democratic Senate aide makes this point:

> A much smaller group of people used to run Washington. As the system opened up due to "sunshine laws," like open markups, recorded votes and television, you had to lobby a bigger universe of people. And as you had to lobbying more people, that required more lobbyists.

The same can be said about the proliferation of subcommittees. "This reform created too many experts," a veteran Democratic lobbyist recalls. "It used to be that the congressmen were the best 'lobbyists' for their constituents. They could hear from the folks back home and then take these concerns to their colleagues. With the proliferation of subcommittees, everyone became an expert and was too busy or not knowledgeable enough to help. They had to rely on lobbyists, who knew the issues and the process."

When Congress attempted to create a more open, decentralized, transparent, and accountable process, it had the unintended effect of stimulating the growth of lobbying. More people involved in the decision-making process meant demand for more lobbyists. Ironically, opening the process, and other changes such as campaign finance reform, while intended to rid the system of influence peddlers and make it more transparent, actually strengthened the link between lobbyists and lawmakers.

And as lobbyist Bruce Gates points out, government rule changes can also have unintended consequences:

> I remember when I was first interviewing to join a tax lobbying firm. Tax policy was supposed to be an area where there were no conflicts (representing multiple corporations on an issue). But during the 1990s especially, as the need for government revenue increased and the PAYGO rules were implemented, we started to have one company fighting another trying to get the tax burden moved.

Once again we see how new *demands* due to government policy changes, such as pay-as-you-go rules, create a new *supply* of lobbying activity—in this case the unintended consequence of business fighting business about who gets taxed or whose benefits get cut.

Another paradox of lobbying concerns why lawmakers take these advocates so seriously, given the advocacy industry's sullied reputation. Moreover, why has an industry apparently so reviled continued to grow, prosper, and expand? In other words, why do policymakers even listen to lobbyists? True, they help in the money chase. But there must be other factors. "It's because they are easily and reliably punishable. This system has become so complex and fraught with risks, how can you have these interactions with someone you don't know?" according to a Democratic lobbyist at a law firm. Most lobbyists, he says, will always have the "next ask." That makes it difficult not to be a straight shooter. Lawmakers know that and it helps build trust. Very few lobbyists lie to congressmen. Or they do not stay in the lobbying business very long.

Reformers probably never considered these implications of their suggested changes. Opening up the system created a new form of fragmentation and the number of players in the process who could impact decisions burgeoned. And more actors participating on the *demand* side of the government equation facilitated a bigger *supply* of lobbyists. Not the kind of outcome Ralph Nader or Common Cause would have wanted or predicted, but a definite unintended consequence of reform.

These are all critical lessons for students of politics and interest groups. Change never occurs in a vacuum, and most reforms aimed at reigning in money or influence usually have unintended consequences.

LOBBYING BOTH A CAUSE AND A CONSEQUENCE OF GOVERNMENTAL ACTION

It's also important to note that "influence" flows in both directions. Interest groups try to influence public policy, but policymakers impact the lobby too. As described in earlier chapters, changes in the structure and behavior of Congress led to transformations in the structure and style of lobbying. Sometimes lawmakers will ask the lobby to make investments that help pass legislation or defeat policy proposals. Or, as we have often seen, government officials will lobby interest groups to stand down and not get involved in particular issues or escalate their activities. These "reverse lobbying" actions represent public officials trying to "influence" the lobbyists, another side of the advocacy game.

The vice president of government affairs for a major health care company reinforces this point: "We were approached by the Democratic leadership and asked to endorse a piece of legislation in which we only had a minor interest. We sent a letter supporting the bill because they asked and we thought it would build goodwill on some other issues we cared about down the road." In this case, the "lobbyists" were lobbied. Governmental actors were the *cause* of change in the lobbying world. Lobbying activity was a consequence of governmental action, rather than lobbyists causing governmental action.

And sometimes lobbyists negotiate with each other. When lawmakers can't act, due to political or policy constraints, they often ask the lobbyists to arbitrate themselves. In the 108th and 109th Congresses (2003–2006), Congress tried unsuccessfully to reach some kind of compromise on comprehensive asbestos reform legislation. Manufacturing companies (defendants in many asbestos liability lawsuits), insurance companies (responsible for paying claims), and unions and trial lawyers (representing workers and plaintiffs) wrangled for years trying to get Congress to pass legislation to cap damages and end a litigation backlog. In the end, Congress decided legislation could only pass if the competing interests reached some kind of accommodation outside the legislative process. The message senators sent to the interest groups: find a compromise and we'll enact it. Don't bring us your differences; we cannot deal with that; bring us a deal. In the end, despite prodding from senators—lobbying the lobbyists—the various stakeholders could not compromise and Congress remained stalemated.

This *reverse lobbying* also takes on another form—lawmakers encouraging lobbyists to raise the visibility and pressure on an issue in order to help the legislative process move forward. Chapter 5 outlines several examples where congressmen and senators asked lobbyists to help pass partisan-backed legislation through investments in advertising, grass roots, and hiring partisan lobbyists and other advocacy resources. In these cases, it is the politicians doing the "asking," trying to persuade the advocates to invest money, time, and resources in helping political actors, as opposed to the other way around. Reverse lobbying is an important part of what happens in the real world, yet it is neither exchange (vote buying) nor persuasion. It is really best understood as a "legislative subsidy," a theme developed in more detail in Chapter 5.[30]

Governmental action sometimes induces increased lobbying activity. Earmarking is an example of such an inducement. As this practice of congressional directed spending grew, the more it stimulated growth in the lobbying world. One veteran lobbyist with a bipartisan firm knowledgeable about the earmarking process says this: "Earmarks seemed to stimulate their own demand," he said. "The more the Congress did it, the more colleges and universities said, 'We want part of that money too. We want our own earmark just like that other university.' " The more the supply for earmarks grew, the greater the demand. And the more demand, the greater the supply. These factors working together led to the explosion of earmarking and lobbying activity aimed at securing this directed spending.

Finally, another little-understood nuance related to the growth of the advocacy industry concerns the extent to which policymakers take actions they otherwise would not have taken simply because of the burgeoning size and presence of the lobbying world. In other words, is government bigger just because lobbyists make requests to justify their existence? You bet.

"In the old days we used to call them 'fetcher' bills," a retired member of the House remarks. "Lobbyists would ask us to introduce a bill just to convince their clients something was happening on an issue—good or bad. Their clients would have to then ask the lobbyist to chase down these issues—hence the name 'fetch.' " That may be an extreme case, but in everything from getting questions asked at hearings that would have never been asked, to requests of agencies that would have never been made, or legislation introduced that would have never been offered—the greater the supply of lobbyists, the more activity and action in the policy process they will produce—needed or not.

Getting under the influence means understanding that more lobbyists probably generate unnecessary government action, just as much as more government action produces a bigger lobbying industry.

So government causes lobbying growth, and more lobbyists cause government to expand as well. Those who want to reduce the number of lobbyists and special interest groups should consider an indirect approach—reduce the size and scope of the federal government. Probably the only way to get fewer lobbyists in the system is to significantly cut back on the size of government—a difficult and unlikely prescription.

LOBBYING GROWTH AND REFORM—THE ONE-WAY DOOR

This book outlines many factors that contribute to lobbying growth. Changes in the size and activism of the federal government, technology, the media, and competition/deregulation among interest groups themselves have all contributed to the growing advocacy industry. One other factor that deserves note, however, is what I call "the door only swings one way" phenomenon. The principle is simple; new forms of advocacy usually *supplement* rather than *supplant* existing lobbying arrangements, meaning the trajectory of advocacy is usually in the upward direction. In other words, lobbyists are rarely replaced, only reinforced.

Consider the example from Chapter 3 involving the move from peak associations to more individualized participation by interest groups—the transition from banks being represented by the American Bankers Association to individual financial institutions, such as Citigroup, J.P. Morgan and Wachovia, creating their own government affairs units. At the end of the day, the individual institutions never replace the trade association, they only add to their advocacy efforts. The same phenomenon has occurred in health care, telecommunications, energy, and insurance, to name a few. Peak associations normally remained active, but their members supplemented their efforts. The supplement versus supplant phenomenon contributes to the overall growth in the size of the lobbying world—a universe unlikely to contract anytime soon.

As I argued earlier, a smaller, less complicated, more stable government environment is the only way to reduce the size of the lobbying industry. And few are projecting that kind of change on the government side of the equation. And even if that were to occur, for the reasons outlined above, contraction in the advocacy world would not occur quickly.

Changes in partisan or institutional control of Congress and the executive branch also lead interest groups to hire lobbyists that *supplement* rather than *supplant* their advocacy teams. For example, after Democrats took majority control in Congress in 2007, there was a major push on the part of business interests to hire more "Democratic help." Yet in most cases, these new Democratic consultants and lobbyists were added to an existing team. Most corporations and trade associations simply increased their roster size rather than replace Republicans with Democrats.

"We decided to stick with our existing team and make some additions on the margins," the head of the Washington office of a major corporation observes. "We know our team, they know us and our issues. We know how to work together, and we just decided that was how we wanted to organize things for now." This company added to their ranks of Democratic consultants but kept their Republicans in place. Bottom line is that their net expenditures on lobbyists probably increased. The circumstances could have been different had there not been a Republican president in the White House, but it is not unusual for lobbyists, particularly those with long-term ties to a client, to weather institutional and partisan shifts due to corporations and trade associations adding to their stable of consultants rather than replacing them. Obviously, exceptions to this rule exist, but it is not unusual—in fact it is normal—for the advocacy industry to grow by interest groups adding to their teams as circumstances change. In other words, old lobbyists rarely die in Washington; they just get more help!

SUMMARY

This book tells a story that I hope changes minds and challenges conventional wisdom. Much of what we think we know about lobbying in America, and how we think about it, deserves reconsideration. Public perceptions about the practice of influence are exaggerated, replete with intoxicating myths and drunken anecdotes. Developing a more sober understanding requires stepping back and taking a fresh look at this important dimension of the American public policy process.

Many journalists and academics subscribe to a far too narrow paradigm of *what* lobbyists do and *how*—and even *why* —they do it. As in the examples of "reverse lobbying," advocacy is sometimes best understood as a legislative subsidy, providing the resources to move the legislative process forward.[31] And when it comes to "influence," studying agenda setting, helping friends and allies, or how advocates use tools to break through the "poverty of attention" is usually more important than just focusing on who wins or loses roll call votes. Focusing on the ongoing, broader questions of lobbying, such as how advocates define issues and shape the debate, is critical to developing a more realistic view of the power of interest groups.

A thorough reconsideration of lobbying also requires expanding the dependent variable. Most journalistic and academic literature on advocacy focuses only on the impact interest groups have on the process—their external environment. This book has turned that question on its head.

Instead of only investigating how lobbyists influence the process, this book takes an in-depth look at how factors such as change in government, partisanship, technology, and media all impact the advocacy world. Looking through the prism a little differently helps reveal new insights about the way the lobbying business really works.

Our final stop in this story outlines three major ways to frame our reconsideration of lobbying. First, we need to examine its impact and goals. Money does talk in politics. And as some have pointed out, more financial resources help amplify those voices. Political scientists Darrell M. West and Burdett A. Loomis remind us of the famous observation of E.E. Schattschneider, "The flaw in the pluralist heaven is that the heavenly chorus sings with a strong upper-class accent."[32] This observation is true, but also requires some real world nuances. Lobbying power is more conditioned than a literal interpretation of that quote would suggest. Moneyed interests may spend a lot of resources. But that doesn't guarantee success. Resources promise certain interests a voice in the process or a way to gather information and reduce uncertainty, but not always the policy outcome they desire. A more accurate picture of lobbying may be closer to a paraphrase of the words of Red Auerbach: "It's not what you say that is important, but what people hear." Lobbyists and interest groups say a lot of things, but not all are heard, and advocacy *activity* is not always the same as public policy *accomplishment*. At a micro-level, interest groups often try to build what John Kenneth Galbraith called "countervailing power."[33] But it's also true that this is done under conditions of great uncertainty. No one can accurately measure the full impact of advocacy. And this leads to a tendency to spend resources, try new tactics, and build new institutional structures despite often losing in the public policy environment.

Second, we also need to realize lobbying is structurally and tactically diverse, and that it's constantly changing. And that the tools, tactics, and strategies of lobbying vary based on some predictable conditions (see Chapter 8). I also argue that lobbyists are both a cause and a consequence of government growth and have been heavily impacted by partisan polarization as well as changing technology in the past several years. The unlikely prospect of reducing the size of government is the indirect antidote for fewer lobbyists.

Finally, many congressional and campaign finance reforms aimed at curbing the power of money and special interests have ironically enhanced them. One common denominator of many well-intentioned changes aimed at limiting the power of lobbyists is that the "reforms" actually empowered interest groups and their agents. As we've seen in this book, a more transparent, open, decentralized, and specialized public policymaking process has its advantages, but it also has facilitated lobbying industry growth in a variety of ways.

Lobbying scandals like the Jack Abramoff affair indeed give the advocacy industry a black eye. But they do a lot more. They also deepen and reinforce a host of misconceptions about lobbying and mask many of the important questions and insights raised in this book. Lobbying is larger, more structurally complex, tactically varied, and dynamic than suggested by conventional wisdom. Lobbyists are not outside the process but an integral part of it.

Organized advocacy also has some often unrecognized upsides, such as its mobilizing and educational functions (see Chapter 2). Moreover, as the Washington Establishment grew, the advocacy business became even more necessary, according to some experts. And paradoxically, despite the lobbying industry's historically sullied reputation, many lawmakers routinely turn to these advocates as trusted advisors and confidants, because lobbyists are "easily and reliably punishable," as one veteran Democratic lobbyist says. Lawmakers seem to know instinctively that most lobbyists do not lie because they will have to come back and ask for something down the road. For those very pragmatic reasons, advocates rarely burn bridges of trust, and the political class knows it. It is my hope readers will grasp these important nuances and reshape their thinking about the nature and role of advocates and interest groups in the policymaking process.

Even if we adopt this broader and more accurate view, an aura of mystery still shrouds the advocacy world. The system of lobbying by private interests in the United States is far from perfect. Asymmetries in resources raise important questions about inequality in political power, access to the system, and the ability to shape agendas.

As it is imperfect, interest-group advocacy is also far from predictable—and maybe that is another reason why so much confusion and misunderstanding surrounds it. Sometimes interest groups spend large sums of money and don't get what they want. Other times advocates "invest" very little and still prevail. Many lobbyists—as we have seen—actually spend very little time in direct "lobbying." These issues all add to the mystery.

But by getting under the influence, we have raised the curtain obscuring the real world of lobbying. We see that advocacy is more nuanced and conditional than suggested by conventional wisdom, giving us a better view of how changes in government, partisanship, technology, and the media impact this permanent and critical part of public policymaking in the new Washington Establishment. And for those still interested in reducing the number of lobbyists, the formula is clear – start by shrinking the government Leviathan that spawns them.

NOTES

1. Paul Taylor, "One Stop Shopping," *Washington Post*, August 1, 1983, A1.
2. Pendleton Herring, *Group Representation Before Congress* (Baltimore, MD: Johns Hopkins University Press, 1929), 253.
3. Ibid. 31.
4. McIver J. Weatherford, *Tribes on the Hill: The U.S. Congress Rituals and Realities*, Revised Edition (Massachusetts, MA: Bergin and Garvey Publishers, 1985), 124.
5. Darrell M. West and Burdett A. Loomis, *The Sound of Money: How Political Interests Get What They Want* (New York, NY: Norton, 1999), 227.
6. Theodore Lowi, *The End of Liberalism* (New York: Norton, 1969); Grant McConnell, *Private Power and American Democracy* (New York: Alfred Knopf, 1966).
7. Harold Lasswell, *Politics: Who Gets What When and How* (New York: McGraw-Hill, 1936).
8. Jeffrey M. Berry and Clyde Wilcox, *The Interest Group Society*, 4th ed. (New York, NY: Pearson Longman, 2007), 161.
9. Ibid.
10. West and Loomis, *The Sound of Money*, 19.
11. Connor McGrath, *Lobbying in Washington, London, and Brussels: The Persuasive Communication of Political Communication* (Lewiston, NY: Edwin Mellen Press, 2005), 98, Quoting Matthews, 1960, 182.
12. Robert H. Salisbury, "The Paradox of Interest Groups in Washington," In *Interests and Institutions: Substance and Structure in American Politics* (Pittsburgh, PA: University of Pittsburgh Press, 1992), 359.
13. Paul Taylor, "Lobbyists Lose the Game, Not the Guccis," *Washington Post*, July 31, 1983, A12.
14. West and Loomis, *The Sound of Money*, 225–226.
15. Ibid.
16. Aoife McCarthy, "Students, Lenders Clash Over Loan Subsidies," *Politico*, March 20, 2007.
17. For example, Timmons and Company represents The American Petroleum Institute and Daimler-Chrysler, while The Duberstein Group does work for British Petroleum and General Motors. The oil interests "won" their lobbying battle while the autos "lost." Both deployed similar resources and lobbying tactics, but realized different outcomes.
18. Edmund L. Andrews, "Senate Adopts an Energy Bill Raising Mileage for Cars," *New York Times*, June 21, 2007, A14.
19. Ibid.
20. Salisbury, "The Paradox of Interest Groups in Washington."
21. Hall, Richard L. and Deardorff, "Lobbying as Legislative Subsidy," American Political Science Review 100(1) (February 2006).
22. See James A. Thurber, "Political Power and Policy Subsystems in American Politics" in Peters, Guy B. and Bert A. Rockman. *An Agenda for Excellence 2: Administering the State* (New Jersey: Chatham House, 1996), 76–104.
23. Patrick O'Connor, "Downtown Firm Acquires Down Home Shop," *Politico*, June 28, 2007. Accessed online (www.politico.com).
24. See John P. Heinz, Edward O. Laumann, Robert L. Nelson, and Robert H. Salisbury, *The Hollow Core: Private Interests in National Policy Making* (Cambridge: Harvard University Press,1993), 375.
25. Ibid. 376.
26. Herring, *Group Representation before Congress*, 1.
27. Robert H. Salisbury, *Interests and Institutions: Substance and Structure in American Politics* (Pittsburgh, PA: The University of Pittsburgh Press, 1992), xvii.

28. Ibid. 382.
29. O'Connor, "Downtown Firm Acquires Down-Home Shop."
30. See Richard L. Hall and Deardorff, "Lobbying as Legislative Subsidy."
31. Ibid.
32. Darrell M. West and Burdett A. Loomis, *The Sound of Money: How Political Interests Get What They Want* (New York, NY: Norton, 1999), 225.
33. John Kenneth Galbraith, *American Capitalism* (Boston: Houghton-Mifflin 1952).

INDEX